LUKÁCS TODAY

SOVIETICA

PUBLICATIONS AND MONOGRAPHS
OF THE INSTITUTE OF EAST-EUROPEAN STUDIES AT THE
UNIVERSITY OF FRIBOURG / SWITZERLAND AND
THE CENTER FOR EAST EUROPE, RUSSIA AND ASIA
AT BOSTON COLLEGE AND THE SEMINAR
FOR POLITICAL THEORY AND PHILOSOPHY
AT THE UNIVERSITY OF MUNICH

Founded by J. M. BOCHEŃSKI (Fribourg)

Edited by T. J. BLAKELEY (Boston), GUIDO KÜNG (Fribourg) *and*
NIKOLAUS LOBKOWICZ (Munich)

VOLUME 51

LUKÁCS TODAY

Essays in Marxist Philosophy

Edited by

TOM ROCKMORE

*Department of Philosophy,
Duquesne University, U.S.A.*

D. REIDEL PUBLISHING COMPANY

A MEMBER OF THE KLUWER ACADEMIC PUBLISHERS GROUP

DORDRECHT / BOSTON / LANCASTER / TOKYO

Library of Congress Cataloging in Publication Data

CIP

Lukács today.

(Sovietica; 51)
Includes index.
1. Lukács, György, 1885–1971. I. Rockmore, Tom, 1942– .
II. Series: Sovietica (Université de Fribourg. Ost-Europa Institut); v. 51.
B4815.L84L885 1987   199'.439   87–32339
ISBN 90–277–2661–2

Published by D. Reidel Publishing Company,
P.O. Box 17, 3300 AA Dordrecht, Holland.

Sold and distributed in the U.S.A. and Canada
by Kluwer Academic Publishers,
101 Philip Drive, Norwell, MA 02061, U.S.A.

In all other countries, sold and distributed
by Kluwer Academic Publishers Group,
P.O. Box 322, 3300 AH Dordrecht, Holland.

CONTENTS

INTRODUCTION

As this century nears an end, it has become increasingly clear that Georg Lukács is one of the most talented intellectuals of our time, not only in the Marxist tradition, but in general. Lukács' name is well-known, and his views are increasingly attracting attention; but it cannot be said that his thought has so far been widely studied, or that it has been studied to the degree its place in the Marxist tradition warrants or its intrinsic interest demands.

In the relatively short period since Lukács' death, there have been a number of books and many articles devoted to his work. But, despite some efforts in that direction, there is still no adequate treatment of his work as a whole, surely a formidable task.[1] If, as I believe, Lukács is the most important Marxist philosopher since Marx, and one of the most influential intellectual figures of this century, then surely his ideas are worth scrutinizing frequently and in detail.

This is not the place to provide a general description either of Lukács' life or of his work. Descriptions of his life, especially his early career, are widely available. For present purposes, it will suffice to provide only the barest mention of some biographical facts, together with a brief account of some items in his bibliography.

Lukács' early career has been extensively studied; but I do not believe that it has often been well-understood.[2] He was born in Budapest on April 13, 1885 and he died there on June 4, 1971. After a period in which Lukács studied widely and wrote on such topics as literary criticism, aesthetics, drama, *etc.*, he joined the just established Hungarian Communist Party in December 1918. From this moment until the end of his long life, he remained faithful to institutionalized Marxism, and he made numerous contributions to Marxist theory. Although his interpretation of Marxism evolved greatly during this lengthy period, there is no reason to believe that he ever doubted the wisdom of his decision to adhere to the Communist Party.

Lukács' bibliography is imposing by any standard. The complete list of his writings, including their translation into various languages, runs to more than seventy pages.[3] It is not possible here to describe even the major writings in his entire corpus. Since our interest at present is focussed on his contribution to Marxist philosophy, it will be useful to mention in passing several of the main texts from his Marxist period (1918-1971).

Any account of Lukács' Marxist thought must begin with *History and Class Consciousness*, which appeared in 1923. This work, which is widely thought of as his masterpiece, has continued to influence generations of Marxists, including most recently Jürgen Habermas, the German social theorist. It is certainly difficult, indeed perilous, to

1

T. Rockmore (ed.), Lukács Today, 1–12.
© *1988 by D. Reidel Publishing Company.*

evaluate the importance and influence of any book, especially one as controversial as this text. But I do not hesitate to say that *History and Class Consciousness* is one of the most significant theoretical texts in the Marxist tradition. And from the strictly philosophical perspective, I believe that this is the single most important contribution to Marxist philosophy since Marx.

Like any book of seminal importance, *History and Class Consciousness* is a difficult book to describe, especially so in brief compass. Suffice it to say that Lukács here takes up a series of problems from an angle of vision located somewhere between the disparate perspectives of Lenin and Rosa Luxemburg. The interest in Luxemburg, symbolic of the politically unorthodox nature of the work, is one of the reasons for which it was strongly and immediately attacked, even before Lenin's *Materialism and Empirio-Criticism*, originally published in 1908, became available in German translation in 1927. In order to maintain and strengthen his ties to Marxist orthodoxy, Lukács criticized and renounced his book. He realigned himself on Leninist orthodoxy, as it was known to him, as early as 1924, in a slim volume, entitled *Lenin*.

History and Class Consciousness is a series of essays touching on many themes, some of which (*e.g.* alienation, totality, Hegel interpretation, *etc.*) continue to recur in Lukács' later writings. Lukács here shows the importance of the concept of class consciousness for Marx' thought. He calls attention, prior to the publication of the *Paris Manuscripts* (in 1932), to the Marxian view of alienation, which he discusses in brilliant fashion under the heading of "reification". He also stresses the approach to Marx in terms of the Hegelian background. Lukács' emphasis on the significance of Hegel for the interpretation of Marx was closely followed by Karl Korsch in his book *Marxism and Philosophy*, which also appeared in 1923. Lukács and Korsch were the prime architects of the still widespread tendency to understand the philosophical dimension of Marx' thought mainly, or even solely, in relation to Hegel.

Lukács was certainly not the first writer to call attention to Hegel's importance for the comprehension of Marx. Even before Engels' famous remark about Marx' debt to German philosophy[4], Marx had indicated the importance of this relation in the well-known comment in the Second Afterword to *Capital*.[5] Here, in a celebrated passage, Marx unclearly suggested that his own position is to be grasped as the materialistic inversion of Hegelian idealism. It has always been recognized that this passage is important for the interpretation of Marx' position, although it is difficult to specify the meaning of Marx' suggestion. In part for this reason, this passage has given rise to an extensive discussion, which need not detain us here. For present purposes, it will be sufficient to observe that although many participants, especially Marxist writers, were not well grounded in

Hegel's thought, this was not the case for Lukács. When he wrote *History and Class Consciousness*, he already possessed a firm grasp, from a Marxist perspective, of Hegel's thought, which he continued to explore in ever greater depth and detail in his later writings.

Lukács' interest in Hegel later led to a major monograph on his thought, *The Young Hegel. Studies in the Relations between Dialectics and Economics*, which appeared in 1948. This book was conceived as a contribution to the history of classical German philosophy from the Marxist perspective. Although Lukács explicitly acknowledges the importance of Hegel's approach, he constantly stresses that it is an "idealist distortion" which requires a "materialist transformation" in order to be adequate as an interpretation of social reality.

According to Lukács, the renaissance of Hegel studies in what Marxists call the "imperialistic" period represents an attempt to utilize Hegel for what he regards as the "imperialistic, reactionary development" of neo-Kantianism. Dilthey, in particular, has supposedly provided an influential contribution in the service of what from a Marxist angle of vision appears as reactionary imperialistic tendencies through his interpretation of Hegel in close relation to philosophical romanticism. From the Marxist perspective, Lukács regards it as important to refute the legend of Hegel's romanticism in order better to understand his role as the predecessor of Marx.

Lukács' study is limited only to the social and historical components of the historical problem of the development of the dialectic. From the historical perspective, he was principally concerned with the French Revolution and its consequences for Germany. According to Lukács, Hegel's importance is not limited to his profound insight into the French Revolution and the Napoleonic period; Lukács stresses that Hegel is above all interested in the problems of the industrial revolution in England and the problems of philosophy, upon which dialectic depends. Although his thought is "idealistic", and not "materialistic", Hegel was arguably the predecessor of Marx. Like Marx, Hegel strove to comprehend the veritable internal structure, and the veritable driving forces of capitalism, in order to ground the dialectic of its movement.

This is the wider framework of Lukács' Hegel study; it should not be confused with the study itself. In general terms, the book is an attempt to read the development of Hegel's concept of dialectic as the result of an effort to come to grips with political economy and the economic relations prevailing in England. As concerns Hegel, Lukács' aim is not only to bring out the importance of the history of philosophy for philosophy; it is further to show in a concrete fashion, through reference to the social context and the historical background, the inner connection between economics and dialectic.

Like virtually all of Lukács' Marxist writings, the Hegel book is polemical; but it is also in every sense a major scholarly monograph - closely argued, solidly documented, highly original. It is no accident that Lukács' Hegel monograph has had considerable influence on the subsequent Hegel discussion. It was followed in the same year (1948) by a much slighter, even scurrilous work, *Existentialism or Marxism?* Unlike the Hegel study, this book is not intended as a scholarly contribution; it is rather intended as an occasional *Streitschrift* in a manner well-represented in the Marxist tradition, where political broadsides abound.

The occasion is the rancorous debate that broke out after the end of the Second World War among partisans of existentialism and Marxism. This debate, which was especially fierce in French circles[6], played a major role in Sartre's concern, in his later thought, to come to the aid of Marxism from an existentialist perspective; it was equally important in Althusser's politically orthodox, Marxist effort, from a structuralist angle of vision, to distinguish between philosophical and scientific periods in Marx' thought. According to Lukács, this type of debate is peculiar to the imperialistic stage of capitalism and represents the clash of two opposing forms of thought: that running from Hegel to Marx, and that which links Schelling to Kierkegaard, the latest form of which is existentialism.

Like Lenin, Lukács believes that philosophy cannot remain neutral; it must address practical concerns. From the Marxist perspective, the present philosophical combat consists in the confrontation between existentialism, which misleadingly presents itself as a "third way" between idealism and materialism, and historical materialism. This debate concerns three groups of problems, including: the search for objectivity, the effort to safeguard freedom, and the fight against nihilism. Some existentialists, for instance Sartre, like to draw a distinction between their perspective and bourgeois thought. But Lukács believes that existentialism in all its forms carries the imprint of the same spontaneous nihilism which infects all of what Marxists call modern bourgeois ideology.

In all his writings beginning with *History and Class Consciousness*, Lukács constantly relies on a Marxist approach to the history of philosophy. In the book on existentialism, he opposes a view which he regards as socially pernicious because of its intrinsic relation to "imperialism". He continues his attack on forms of what he labels as "bourgeois ideology" in a detailed study of the relation of non-Marxist philosophy and the rise of fascism, entitled *The Destruction of Reason* (1954).

According to Lukács, what he describes as irrationalism is the dominant tendency in so-called bourgeois philosophy in all its forms. He rejects what he regards as the idealist view that philosophical problems can be studied immanently, or wholly on the philosophical plane, in favor of the view that such problems are "located" in the context circumscribed by the forces of production and historical development. He further justifies his evidently anti-bourgeois, Marxist ap-

proach on the grounds that there is no "innocent" angle of vision
("*unschuldige*" *Weltanschauung*), or neutral standpoint.

Lukács particularly stresses the unity of different forms of
irrationalism which, from the Marxist angle of vision, he regards as the
reactionary answer to the various problems arising out of class
struggle. He believes that the first important period of modern irrationalism arose in the progression from Schelling to Kierkegaard, in the
fight against the dialectical and historical concept of progress found in
German Idealism. Just as Marx studied the *locus classicus* of capitalism in England, so Lukács thinks he can show that nineteenth- and
twentieth-century Germany is the "classical" land of fascism. He is
aware that the transformation of "philosophical irrationalism" into
political fascism occurs on a non-philosophical terrain. Hence, his aim
is not to equate "philosophical irrationalism" with fascism; his aim is
rather to show that the possibility of a so-called fascist, aggressive-
reactionary ideology is contained in every philosophical form of
"irrationalism".

The last work I will mention is the unfinished study of *The
Ontology of Social Being* which properly belongs to his *Nachlass*.
This immense work, more than two thousand pages long, is not
well-known, even to Lukács specialists, because of its length and an
unfortunate publication delay. It was originally conceived as a kind of
giant prolegomenon to a work on ethics, which Lukács did not live to
write. The main topic is, as the name implies, an ontology of social
being, as distinguished from natural being which had been the concern
of metaphysicians since Aristotle. Lukács' task in this book is to
develop a Marxist theory of social ontology by building upon insights
drawn from the Marxist and non-Marxist sides of the philosophical
tradition.

The study is divided into two main parts: 'The Present State of the
Problem' (*Die gegenwärtige Problemlage*) and 'The most Important
Problem Complexes' (*Die wichtigsten Problemkomplexe*). In the first
part, after a discussion of neopositivism and existentialism, Lukács
turns to the ontological approach favored by Nicolai Hartmann, who,
with Heidegger, is one of the two main representatives of ontological
thought in Germany in this century. Lukács turns to Hartmann because
of his importance for ontology, but also since, as was noted in *The
Destruction of Reason*, Lukács believes him to be the only non-Marxist
thinker with a positive attitude towards dialectic.[7] He ends the first
volume with a detailed account of the intrinsic contradictions of
Hegelian "idealism" and Marx' allegedly decisive advance beyond
idealism through the "materialist" concept of work.

In the second volume, Lukács develops this concept further. He
works out in detail a teleological concept of work, with obvious roots in
Aristotle. In this connection, we are reminded of Lukács' belief that
Marxism is a form of left-wing Aristotelianism. He also discusses in

detail problems of social reproduction, ideology, and alienation. In a word, we can say that in this work, in the final phase of his career, he returned after some fifty years of thought and discussion to themes which already occupied his attention at the beginning of his Marxist period.

This ends my brief survey of some of Lukács' major Marxist writings. For anyone even casually acquainted with Lukács' massive bibliography, it will be apparent that this survey is highly incomplete. It does not include his numerous contributions to literary criticism and sociology. It is not even complete as a list of the philosophical *oeuvre*, since I have omitted both pre-Marxist texts, such as the recently discovered *Heidelberger Ästhetik*, as well as the important, recent work on *The Specific Nature of the Aesthetic* (*Die Eigenart des Ästhetischen*, 1963). And if we recall that Lukács' philosophical productivity is approximately equalled by his contributions to literary criticism and sociology, we will at least have a general idea of the corpus of this many-sided intellectual, perhaps most comparable in this century to such other philosophical giants as Sartre, Russell, and Croce.

The huge size of Lukács' corpus is only one of the difficulties to be encountered in any effort to come to grips with his thought. I will now mention some other obstacles which might arise for many Western and, I suspect, numerous Eastern European scholars. From the political perspective, there is an obvious problem. The proscription of his brilliant early Marxist writings on grounds of political unorthodoxy, combined with his decision to embrace Marxist-Leninist orthodoxy, helped to turn attention away from much that was of genuine worth in his writings.

There is a specific difficulty in securing access to Lukács' work. This difficulty took different forms, of which several can be mentioned here. Two forms of this difficulty arise from Lukács' dual dependency on Hungarian culture and German philosophy, especially neo-Kantianism. It is evident that, mainly for linguistic reasons, most scholars, East and West, have long been hindered in any attempt to evaluate, or even to become familiar with, Lukács' writings in Hungarian, his specific interaction with Hungarian intellectual figures, and more generally in an understanding of his debt to Hungarian culture.

Another, non-linguistic form of this difficulty derives from Lukács' dependence on German neo-Kantianism. His association with the Weber-Circle in Heidelberg before the First World War, and his deep knowledge of neo-Kantianism and personal acquaintance with many of its leading representatives left permanent traces on his later thought. These traces have become ever more difficult to decipher or even to discern with the passage of time since neo-Kantianism has become a kind of *terra incognita* increasingly unknown to contemporary writers, especially to those interested in Lukács' writings.

A further obstacle is provided by the physical inaccessibility of

Lukács' major Marxist text. *History and Class Consciousness* appeared in 1923 and immediately attracted a large audience. But it was not reprinted in the original German, other than in a pirated (*Raubdruck*) form for some 45 years. During this period, the book was difficult to acquire. As early as 1955 Merleau-Ponty called attention to this study in a chapter of *The Adventures of the Dialectic*, misleadingly entitled '"Western" Marxism'. But even at that late date Lukács' study was still not available in other major Western languages. To the best of my knowledge, it is still not available in the main Eastern-European languages, including Russian, although some of his other writings have been translated.

A further problem is due to the constant attempt of institutional Marxism to censure Lukács' writings. We have already mentioned the outcry in orthodox Marxist circles which caused him publicly to renounce *History and Class Consciousness*, his major Marxist publication, shortly after its appearance. Similar pressures further obliged him to practice that peculiar Marxist sport known as public self-criticism on more than one occasion. We can also point out that the institutional desire to impede the spread of the occasionally unorthodox views disseminated in Lukács' writings under the cover of orthodoxy continued even after his death. It is worth noting that an item from his *Nachlass*, in which he discussed the problem of democracy in socialism, was published in 1985 and almost immediately withdrawn from publication.[8]

We can also mention Lukács' style in this and other works. *History and Class Consciousness* was composed in a difficult, highly complex style, which Lukács himself later characterized as an attempt to "out-Hegel" Hegel. It is not true, as has been suggested, that at the time he wrote this book he had not yet mastered the German language.[9] Even if he spoke German in the home, his early style may fairly be said to leave something to be desired. A somewhat different stylistic problem is characteristic of his mature work. The dimensions of this linguistic obstacle, even for a knowledgeable reader, can be inferred from a comment by George Steiner, the literary critic and a native German speaker, about Lukács' later writing. He writes: "German is Lukács' principal language, but his use of it has grown brittle and forbidding. His style is that of exile; it has lost the habit of living speech."[10]

The present volume is limited to studies of various aspects of Lukács' contribution to Marxist philosophy. I believe that the time is ripe to address this side of Lukács' thought for a variety of reasons. First, Lukács has passed from the scene. It is always difficult to evaluate the work of any important figure, and even more difficult for a figure as controversial as Lukács. This task becomes even more difficult if that person is still alive and able to influence the discussion. Second, attention was drawn to Lukács in 1985, the centenary of his birth, through a number of conferences, which need not be enumerated here. Third, there is the on-going publication of his collected writings by Luchterhand Verlag. Fourth, we can note the recent, helpful appearance of a bibliography of the secondary literature on Lukács.[11] Finally, there is a point specific to Western philosophy: the fact that interest in Marxism now seems to be waning may paradoxically facilitate dispassionate discussion of Lukács' thought.

To end this Introduction I will say only a few words about the essays presented here since, in an obvious sense, each essay must be able to justify its own inclusion in this volume. Any effort to provide this justification in external fashion would not only be superfluous; it would also be misleading.

All of the papers were either written for the occasion, or largely modified. In general, the authors are deeply familiar with German philosophy, with Marxism in particular, and above all with Lukács' thought. But no effort has been made to impose a particular point of view or to stress one approach more than another. The aim is to cast light on Lukács' contribution to Marxist philosophy, not to cast a particular kind of light.

It might be desirable to attempt to tackle all facets of Lukács' Marxist thought, but that is not our present goal. It will be satisfactory if this volume awakens interest in various themes in Lukács' thought. To that end, the selection of the material has been guided by criteria of quality and diversity. A particular effort has been made to gather contributions from authors representing different points of view - East and West, Marxist and non-Marxist. It may be hoped that those who write from highly contrasting perspectives can engage in useful dialogue, since that is one of the goals of this volume.

The contributions to this volume divide naturally into four sections, including: a general introduction, themes in *History and Class Consciousness*, Lukács' interpretation of Hegel, and Lukács' later thought. In the first section, three papers by Marković, Buhr, and Hevesi provide an interesting introduction to Lukács' Marxist thought. Marković offers a description of Lukács' career ; a comparison between the views of Lukács and Ernst Bloch, his peer, opponent, and sometime ally; and a critical discussion of some main themes of Lukács' Marxist thought. He raises the question of Lukács' intellectual honesty, comments on Lukács' tendency to isolate knowledge from the social context, and criticizes Lukács' failure to observe in his own conduct the standards appropriate to rigorous thought.

Buhr's paper, which also raises the question of intellectual honesty, contrasts nicely with Marković' effort. Unlike Marković, Buhr stresses Lukács' moral integrity, which he connects to Lukács' unswerving attachment to reason. He attributes a dual role to Lukács within late bourgeois thought and as a critic of it. He touches in passing on various problems concerning Lukács' relations to Heidegger, to the Frankfurt School in general, and especially to Adorno.

Buhr raises the problem of Lukács' relation to bourgeois thought. Hevesi pursues aspects of this complex theme. She begins by noting that we can now perceive with increasing clarity the nature of Lukács' contribution to the development of European philosophy and esthetics. She discusses different phases of the interest in Lukács in bourgeois philosophy, with special attention to the reception over time of *History and Class Consciousness*. She is less concerned with attention to Lukács' influence on bourgeois philosophy than to his position as seen by it, and she insists on the need to study Lukács' Marxist thought.

The second and longest section contains detailed discussions of some aspects of *History and Class Consciousness*, Lukács' most widely known and most influential book. Larrain situates Lukács' understanding of the concept of ideology within the wider Marxist context. As concerns ideology, he suggests that Marx' and Lenin's views of this concept are incompatible. He argues both that Lukács follows Lenin's view of ideology throughout his writings, and that this point is routinely overlooked in the discussion of Lukács. He further identifies essential ambiguities in Lukács' concept of ideology and in its link to Lenin's view of the supremacy of the Party.

In *History and Class Consciousness*, in order to interpret Marx' thought, Lukács elaborates the influential concept of reification. In this section three papers address the concept of reification respectively in relation to Marx, to post-Lukácsian Marxism, and as such. Dupré borrows Lukács' concept to explore Marx' position, especially the economic writings. He shows how Lukács generalizes Marx' critique of economic objectivism to bourgeois culture in general; and, from this perspective, he points out how Marx' position differs from previous thought.

Grondin discusses the later career of the concept of reification in the Frankfurt School, with special reference to Habermas. After a careful reading of the relevant portions of *History and Class Consciousness*, he studies the influence of Lukács' view of reification on the views of Horkheimer, to a lesser degree of Adorno, and especially of Habermas. He argues that Habermas' effort to restate the concept of reification is vitiated by a subtle misinterpretation.

Whereas Dupré and Grondin are concerned with applications of reification, McBride raises the question of the viability of this notion. He begins by noting that some of Lukács' own students have objected to Lukács' use of the idea of reification in his later writings. McBride then examines this concept and related difficulties, in order to indicate the problematic nature of Lukács' idea. After some remarks about the relation of reification to the views of Sartre and of feminism, he suggests that the view of reification is no longer as relevant as it once was.

Feenberg discusses Lukács' often overlooked contribution, in this early work, to organizational questions linked to the possibility of revolution. He shows that, as concerns this particular problem, Lukács' position evolved during the writing of his book, from a dual allegiance to both Luxemburg and Lenin, to a more Leninist attitude, with a Luxemburgian residue. Feenberg suggests that in his early Marxist phase, Lukács attempts to synthesíze ideas drawn from both Luxemburg and Lenin. He argues that Luxemburg is closer than Lenin to Marx, and that Lukács' task was to reconcile Lenin to Marx.

In *History and Class Consciousness*, Lukács opposed the traditional philosophical concern with epistemological neutrality in favor of a proletarian class standpoint, intended to overcome the antinomies of "bourgeois" thought. Ignatow criticizes this concept, with special attention to the concept of totality. He argues for the existence of a tension between the "bourgeois status" of Marx and Engels, and the insistence on the correctness of proletarian thought. He further refutes claims by Lukács and other Marxists for the class-conditioned nature of thought in general.

Ignatow examines the result of Lukács' effort to surpass bourgeois philosophy. In a related paper, Bernstein studies Lukács' aim. He argues that in *History and Class Consciousness*, Lukács' intent is to surpass Western metaphysics through a philosophy of praxis. Bernstein addresses this theme from the angle, unusual in any discussion of Marxism, of the views of Heidegger and Derrida. He maintains that for Lukács, the possibility of socialism is related to the overcoming of bourgeois philosophy, especially to the concept of class consciousness. After specific discussion of the views of Heidegger and Derrida, in order to raise the question of presence, he ends his study with the assertion that Derrida's attack on presence is subject to the same criticisms it raises against other positions.

The third section contains two divergent assessments of Lukács' contribution to our knowledge of Hegel's thought. Ojzerman studies Lukács' interpretation of Hegel in the context of the interpretation of the history of philosophy, with constant reference to the views of Marx, Engels, and Lenin. He focusses on *The Young Hegel* (and the emergence of Hegel's thought as a reflection of the rise of bourgeois revolution in Western Europe) in relation to Marx' *Paris Manuscripts* and Lenin's *Philosophical Notebooks*. His discussion consists mainly in following carefully and in evaluating the different phases of Lukács' reading of Hegel's position in this work. He concludes that Lukács' interpretation of Hegel's thought represents an important contribution to our knowledge of the latter's position from a Marxist perspective.

Rockmore studies the related question of Lukács' reading of modern philosophy in general and Hegel's thought in particular. After noting the relation of Lukács' effort to refute what Marxists call bourgeois thought in general to a neo-Kantian interpretation of the German philosophical tradition, he follows the evolution of Lukács' approach to Hegel's position through various phases. The point of the examination is to show that none of the various formulations of Lukács' argument will suffice to establish that, as Lukács believes, "bourgeois" thought in general and Hegel in particular cannot know (social) reality. He concludes that Lukács' apriori, quasi-Kantian approach to the history of philosophy is methodologically flawed.

The fourth section contains a single paper, by Tertulian, on Lukács' unfinished, major study, *On the Ontology of Social Being*. Tertulian examines Lukács' effort to develop a Marxist theory of social ontology against the background of Lukács' earlier writings and his interest in the thought of Nicolai Hartmann. He contrasts Lukács' views on ontology favorably with Heidegger's, and he examines Goldman's well-known suggestion that *Being and Time* is in part a reaction to *History and Class Consciousness*. He ends with the assertion that in time Lukács will be regarded as one of the main ontological thinkers of this century.

It is appropriate to end this Introduction with a comment on the need for this particular volume. In a sense, the only adequate justification is the result; but it is easy to demonstrate a need for the present discussion. If, at this late date, philosophy is still to seek the truth, it must actively seek dialogue. The alternative is for philosophy to be reduced to a series of mere assertions or declarations of belief, which must not be confused with statements of knowledge. As Marxism is one of the major intellectual tendencies of our time, at this late date there is no better way to seek the truth than through the dialogue which emerges in close discussion, from contrasting perspectives, of the writings of Georg Lukács, the outstanding Marxist philosopher.

NOTES

1.   The best, but incomplete attempt of which I am aware is G.H.R. Parkinson, *Georg Lukács*, London, Routledge and Kegan Paul, 1977.

2.   For an excellent recent study, see Lee Congdon, *The Young Lukács*, Chapel Hill and London, The University of North Carolina Press, 1983.

3.   See the bibliography compiled by Jürgen Hartmann, in F. Benseler (ed.), *Festschrift zum achtzigsten Geburtstag von Georg Lukács*, Neuwied, Luchterhand, 1965, pp. 625-696.

4.   See F. Engels, *Die Entwicklung des Sozialismus von der Utopie zu Wissenschaft*, in *Marx-Engels Werke*, Berlin, Dietz Verlag, (1956-1968), Vol. 19, p. 188: "...that German socialists are proud to be descended not only from Saint-Simon, Fourier, and Owen, but from Kant, Fichte, and Hegel as well" (my translation, *T.R.*).

5.   See K. Marx, *Das Kapital. Kritik der politischen Ökonomie I*, *Marx-Engels Werke*, vol. 23, p. 27: "Basically my dialectical method is not only different from Hegel's; it is its direct opposite." (my translation, *T.R.*).

6.   For a discussion, see Mark Poster, *Existential Marxism in Postwar France. From Sartre to Althusser*, Princeton, Princeton University Press, 1975.

7.   See *Die Zerstörung der Vernunft*, in *Lukács Werke*, Neuwied, Luchterhand, 1962, vol. 9, p. 498.

8.   See Georg Lukács and László Sziklai (ed.), *Demokratisierung heute und morgen,* Budapest, Akad. Kiadó, 1985.

9.   For this criticism, see K. Axelos, 'Préface de la présente édition', in *Histoire et conscience de classe*, K. Axelos and J. Bois, trans., Paris, Éditions de Minuit, 1960, p. 8: "The task of translation was extremely difficult. Lukács wrote these essays in Marxist dialectic directly in German at a time when the language of Hegel and Marx, of Goethe and Nietzsche still had many secrets for him. Since then, he has made all kinds of progress." (my translation, *T.R.*).

10.   George Steiner, *Language and Silence*, London, 1969, p. 295, quoted in F. Jameson, *Marxism and Form*, Princeton, Princeton University Press, 1975, p. 160.

11.   See François H. Lapointe, *George Lukács and his Critics. An International Bibliography with Annotations*, 1910-1982, London and Westport, CT, Greenwood Press, 1983.

PART I

LUKÁCS' MARXIST THOUGHT

MIHAILO MARKOVIĆ

The Critical Thought of Georg Lukács

Georg Lukács belongs among the most authentic, original and creative Marxist thinkers in the twentieth century. To be authentic in the Marxist tradition means to be praxis-oriented; and engaged in changing the world, which, to be sure, involves a rich network of theoretical mediations - from discussion of the most abstract methodological and anthropological grounds to elaborating most specific projects of radical restructuring individual societies and communities. However, for thought to be praxis-oriented means that it must, in the first place, be critical. Social structures, political institutions, patterns of social behavior, the world of culture will not be regarded as a given object of detached contemplation, of mere impartial description, of value-free analysis and explanation, of mere understanding. The entire social world, including that part of nature that has been transformed into our immediate environment, will be seen as a human product, therefore as a phase of history, as an incomplete work that both fulfills and frustrates human aspirations, in which, alongside of forms of life that are indispensable for any meaningful human future, there are also glaring limitations that cripple the best human efforts, that cause continuing human suffering, and which therefore wait to be more or less urgently overcome. In that sense of a dialectical *Aufhebung*, Lukács is a first-rate critical thinker.

I. THE HISTORICAL CONDITIONS SURROUNDING LUKÁCS' WORK

However, it must be immediately emphasized that the epoch in which Lukács reached maturity and produced his life-work is essentially different from the one which ended in 1917.

For Marx and Engels, for Labriola, Kautsky, and Plekhanov, even for Luxemburg and Lenin, it was still possible to believe that critique was only one of the mediating links between a negative reality and the ideal project of a radically emancipated humankind. There was the unilinear dialectic of history that in the long run allowed only progressive resolution of contradictions (only *Aufhebung*). There were economic laws which "relentlessly" led to the breakdown of capitalism and the emergence of a classless society. Under the pressure of increasing exploitation and oppression, the proletariat had to acquire

14

revolutionary consciousness and to make the decisive step from the class-in-itself to the class-for-itself. The party of the working class, the most articulated expression of its revolutionary consciousness and will, guaranteed not only that the class rule of the bourgeoisie would effectively be overthrown but also that the transitional form of the dictatorship of the proletariat would as quickly as possible give way to a new self-governing democracy - to a federation of associations of immediate producers. "A relentless criticism of all existing reality", as Marx put it, had to bring to consciousness what existed in itself as a real possibility of the movement of history. This criticism had to raise consciousness to a necessary high level of understanding of the historical process in its totality and it had to provide the necessary theoretical guidance. Philosophy had to be the "head of the revolution"; without the realization of philosophy the transcendence of the proletariat as a propertyless, oppressed, alienated class was not possible.   In contrast to his positivistic followers and his own occasional attacks on moralism, Marx emphasized the role of ethical principles and very early formulated the categorical imperative of his entire emancipatory project: "abolition of all those social relations in which human beings are oppressed, abandoned, despised beings".   Such an ethical imperative provided the basic standard of critical evaluation. It was supposed to be an abstract ought for human energies that spontaneously strive in completely different directions.

When Bloch, Korsch and Lukács appeared as critical thinkers on the world-historical scene, bourgeois society was still ugly, reified, fragmented, dominated by a tremendous amount of alienated economic and political power; Communism as projected by Marx was still a most attractive ideal - but mediating forces hardly existed. The *Weltgeist* had fallen asleep or forgotten its emancipatory end. Revolutions failed in Germany, Finland, Hungary, and Bulgaria. Right-wing social democrats undertook to stabilize capitalist society.

In the United States the October revolution sounded the signal for the beginning of a wholesale destruction of all socialist forces.   Most disturbing of all, the Russian revolution underwent its own Thermidorian reaction, involving the massacre of almost the entire revolutionary leadership. It eventually ended up as an authoritarian bureaucratic society, which indeed destroyed private property and socially promoted large segments of the working class but, from the point of view of human emancipation, bore hardly any resemblance to the Marxian project.

In the West capitalism managed to survive the crisis of the 30's, and entered an age of consumerism and welfare which effectively blocked any rise of revolutionary consciousness.

With the collapse of all mediating forces, Marxist critical thought found itself in a rarified atmosphere. With Communist parties aspiring and clinging to power and hostile to "confused intellectuals" who pathetically tried to remind them of their great emancipatory tasks, with trade unions struggling for small improvements within the capitalist framework, with workers increasingly co-opted into the consumer society, with third-world radical movements struggling for basic preconditions of industrialization and urbanization, it might have seemed that appeals to a normative, moral consciousness remained the only mediating link between reality and the ideal.

Both Bloch and Lukács were well aware of the weaknesses of a purely moralistic position, of merely preaching what ought to be done in the situation when people, for all kinds of reasons, were not motivated to do it. Bloch came up with a radical solution in this new situation. Great emancipatory values were to be kept alive as part of a spirit of utopia which cannot die simply because it does not prescribe anything for here and now, but sustains a hope that historical conditions might be created under which those values could be implemented.

Lukács, a more contradictory and, to some extent, even a split personality adopted a dualistic position. On the one hand, there are in his works dramatic, passionate appeals to ought - which to some extent could be attributed to the influence of his friends, the great Hungarian writers Endry Ady and Bela Balacz. For Ady,"Either this faith of ours turns into reality or, bereft of reason, we are doomed to the last." The way Lukács writes about Balacz is most characteristic. He sees in Balacz's work "the triumph of dramatic decisions over opportunistic accomodation, the triumph of living in the spirit of 'either-or' over the philosophy of 'one could have it both ways'".[1] But the truth is that while he passionately longed to live in the spirit of "either-or", and he ventured to live that way a couple of times (which almost cost him his life), most of the rest of the time he lived the life of "both ways". "Ought" was ideologically construed as if, at least to some extent, it already is; ideals were translated into end-products of already existing trends; organizations, institutions, and daily struggles were rationalized and idealized in order to make personal participation in them meaningful.

II. THE PHASES IN LUKÁCS' CRITICAL ACTIVITY

As every truly radical intellectual in our age, Lukács was a tragic personality. The hiatus between an optimal historical possibility of human emancipation, to which he committed himself and a retarded reality, which refused to become reasonable and emancipated - was so huge. One had either to perish in incessant clashes with the establishment of one kind or the other (like Gramsci and many old Bolsheviks), or one had to despair and withdraw (like Karl Korsch), or one had to adapt, to be cunning and cautious, and try to outlast the power. Lukács combined the first and the third possibilities. He took all the risks in two revolutionary situations, in which he found himself (in 1918 and 1956), and both times he barely survived. The rest of the time, in situations which clearly were not revolutionary, he tended to conform in order to stay inside the working class movement.

And yet, no matter how different various phases of his life were, there was an invariant structure of his thought: It could be characterized as a radical critique of the bourgeois reality and culture of his time, and more specifically a radical critique of German philosophy and literature. He responded to many significant intellectual influences: George Simmel, Wilhelm Dilthey, Emil Lask, Erwin Szabo, George Sorel, Heinrich Rickert, Max Weber. But the decisive influence was that of Hegel and Marx. That is why he treated the society of his time as a totality, saw cultural phenomena in the context of history, focussed on the antinomies of bourgeois thought, and searched for the possibilities of a radical transcendence (*Aufhebung*).

Although Lukács came from a rich Jewish family (his father was the director of the Hungarian General Credit Bank in Budapest), from his early youth he was critical of the conservatism and bureaucratic inertia of Hungarian society. In this early stage of his intellectual development Lukács concentrated on literary criticism. In 1906-7 he wrote his first large work, *History of the Development of Modern Drama*[2]; in 1908 he completed *The Soul and its Forms*[3], in 1911-14 he produced works on esthetics (which he did not finish or publish); and one year later wrote his *Theory of the Novel*.[4] The main problem with which Lukács wrestled in this early period of his development is fragmentation, subjectivity, and partiality, which he sought unsuccessfully to overcome. He says for example in *The Soul and its Forms*: "Human knowledge is a psychological nihilism. We see a thousand relations, yet never grasp a genuine connection. The landscapes of our soul exist nowhere, yet in them every tree and every flower is concrete."[5] The way he writes about Kassner's style is characteristic. He says: "Kassner sees synthesis only as it were with his eyes closed - in the realm of values. But honesty immediately compels him to look at them again and once more they are separated, isolated, without air. The oscillation between these two poles determines Kassner's style."[6]

Lukács dealt in those essays with partial problems and set out to find concrete solutions to them. He wrote therefore in an essayistic form without any general theme, but he ended up in frustration. The concreteness of the "trees and flowers devoid of landscape" is meaningless and synthesis is not possible in the realm of values. For this reason he longed for an objective totality and that longing remained his basic philosophic concern for the rest of his intellectual life.

Again he tried a synthesis in *The Theory of the Novel* but did not find it. The analyzed works are only "pillars of an intellectual construction", without real structure. Lukács himself referred to that work as a "six-legged monster".[7] The objective totality has not yet been found and he passed through a deep personal crisis.

But then the October Revolution seemed to offer that objective totality to which he aspired: The unified Party - the expression of the unified will of the unified proletariat - practical objectification of the *logos* of history.

The Hungarian revolution in 1918 was the crucial event which began the second phase of his critical thought. He anticipated the destruction of the great empires in Central and Eastern Europe: Austrian, German, and Russian. But he was skeptical about the superficial empiricism and liberalism of the West, and desperately asked the question "Who will save us from Western Civilization?". Back from Heidelberg in Budapest, he founded a discussion circle (the Sunday Circle, with Bela Balacs, Bela Fogarasi, Karl Mannheim and others), and in 1917 they gave a series of public lectures within the framework of what they called the "Free School of the Sciences of the Spirit". Lukács greeted the October Revolution with enthusiasm, joined the Hungarian Communist Party in 1918, and played a leading role in the Hungarian revolution. He was a member of the Central Committee, the Minister of Education and the Political Commissar of the 5th Division of the Hungarian Red Army. After the collapse of the Hungarian revolution, Lukács lived in emigration in Vienna. There he wrote his most important philosophical work, *History and Class Consciousness*. All the rest of his time was taken up by his political activity as a member of the more liberal Landler fraction of the Hungarian Communist Party in exile. The years 1918 to 1928 constitute the period of Lukács' most intensive and coherent critical activity. Direct participation in revolution as a form of practical criticism of a stagnant, conservative, anachronistic society gave way to deeper and more general critical inquiry into the crisis of bourgeois society and into the antinomies of its thought.[8] This again led in the period 1923-28 to a concrete political critique of dogmatism in the Hungarian workers' movement in order politically to prepare another revolutionary attempt.

Lukács' philosophical critique of capitalism was humanistically founded. The basic limitation of bourgeois society is reification.[9] In a society of extremely rationalized, mechanized, calculated, specialized production and exchange of commodities, both the object and the subject become fragmented. Human beings are reduced to mechanical parts incorporated into a mechanical system. All human activity -

whether in the field of economy, or politics and law, or culture and everyday life - becomes contemplative, subordinated to fixed heteronomous rules, measured by purely quantitative criteria. A brilliant example of a philosophical critique of culture is his examination of the basic contradictions implicit in bourgeois thought, those between form and content, object and subject, fact and value, individual and community. At the same time Lukács fought an already existing and increasingly influential anti-humanist tendency within Marxism. In 1925 he published a severe critique of mechanistic determinism in Bukharin's book on historical materialism[10] - a courageous move considering that Bukharin at that time was the leading theoretician of the Russian Bolshevik Party and of the Third International.

The main target of his political criticism in the Hungarian Party was the dogmatism and sectarianism of Bela Kun, the leader of the unsuccessful Hungarian revolution. In the *Blum Theses*, a programmatic text prepared by Lukács for the 1928 Congress of the Hungarian Party[11], Lukács offered the prospect of an alliance with all anti-totalitarian forces struggling for a democratic republic in Hungary. Those theses anticipated the later popular front strategy, but were defeated, mainly owing to the intervention of the Executive of the Communist International. They were labeled "a replacement of Lenin's theory of proletarian revolution by a half-social-democratic liquidationist theory". This event was another turning point in Lukács' critical activity. Condemned for his philosophical humanism (which was labeled "idealism") and for his political commitment to the struggle for democratization, which was characterized' as betrayal of true revolutionary goals, he turned to pure philosophy that would be more materialistic, more in line with Lenin.

In 1929 he moved to Moscow, to the Marx-Engels-Lenin Institute. With the exception of the two years that he spent in Berlin (1931-33), he stayed in Moscow continuously until the end of World War II. He did not publish much - mostly articles and mostly conforming to the very harsh ideological conditions of growing Stalinization. But he completed a major work, *The Young Hegel*, published only ten years later in 1948.[12] Through the critique of Hegel he there settled accounts with his own philosophical youth. The will to adapt turned into a will to believe that his previous writings were much less valuable than they really were. However, a bright spot in his critical activity during this period was his struggle - together with Mikhail Lifshitz, against the literary sectarianism of the Proletkul't and against a Zdanovist version of "socialist realism".

A new period began in 1945 when Lukács returned to Budapest. He became a member of the Hungarian parliament, head of the chair in Aesthetics of Culture at the Budapest University and a member of the

Presidium of the Hungarian Academy of Science. He could publish what he wanted and he published a lot. He fought now on two fronts. On the one hand, as a Marxist philosopher in a "people's democracy" with very limited socialist cultural forces, he launched an attack on bourgeois philosophy, on existentialism[13], on degenerate "irrationalist" nineteenth-century German Idealism[14], on modernistic art.[15] On the other hand, especially before 1949, he raised the issue of democracy in culture (in the writings *Hungarian Intellectuals and Democracy* 1945, *Cultural Problems of the Hungarian Democracy, The Crisis of Democracy and of its Right-Wing Critique, Democracy and Culture*, all published in 1946). He was savagely attacked in 1949, in connection with Rajk's trial, but emerged on the move again after Stalin's death. In 1956 he was very active in the Petofy Circle and presided over the philosophy debate in the Circle on June 15. On October 24, 1956 he became a member of the enlarged Central Committee of the Party and Minister of Culture in Imré Nagy's government. After the Soviet military intervention, Lukács took refuge, together with Nagy, in the Yugoslav embassy. As soon as he left the embassy, he was arrested and deported to Romania (while Nagy was shot.)

The last period of Lukács' work began with his return from deportation to Budapest on April 10th, 1957. Now he wrote his two monumental works: on *Aesthetics* in two volumes on which he worked from 1957 to 1962[16], and on *The Ontology of Social Being* that he was not able to complete.[17] These are not polemical or explicitly critical works, although in a sense that we will not consider here, all theory is implicitly critical with respect to other theories. However, it is to Lukács' credit that even after the major political showdown with Stalinism, which nearly cost him his life, he continued occasionally to take a sharply critical position toward Stalinism. Two examples are a 'Postscript' that he wrote already in 1957 for an Italian edition of *My Road to Marxism*[18], and an open letter to Alberto Carocci, editor of *Nuovi Argomenti*.[19] He also strongly protested against the Soviet occupation of Czechoslovakia in 1968. After that, he expressed his critique of political bureaucracy and suggested its destabilization in a series of interviews and articles.[20] But he also rejoined the Party in his 84th year, two years before his death.

So until the end of his life, George Lukács avoided "either-or" as much as he could. He had it both ways. He is now celebrated both by truly independent, radical, critical thinkers and by the official establishment of his home country. The former admire his originality, creativity, enormous erudition, complete dedication to his great intellectual projects, his occasional extraordinary boldness which brought him outside the borders of the possible or what was permitted by the powers that be. They deplore his occasional falls and take him as one of the drastic examples of what primitive despotism and the *Unter-tan*-mentality can do to one of the greatest minds of our century.

On the other hand, the official establishment does everything to co-opt him. A Lukács monument was erected in Budapest recently, an exhibition opened, a conference was organized to celebrate him, in which exclusively loyal scholars and Party functionaries were scheduled to give long papers on him, and in which no discussion whatsoever was allowed. The story presented was of a long journey through the mists of idealistic petty-bourgeois confusion until eventually, owing to his coming to Moscow, he saw the light and became a real Leninist, who despite occasional deviations stayed the course to the end.

The truth is that Lukács deserves both treatments.

III. SOME CHARACTERISTIC LIMITATIONS OF LUKÁCS' CRITICAL THOUGHT

In the following critical analysis of Lukács' critical thought I shall compare him with Ernst Bloch, his peer, opponent and ally, whose hundredth anniversary was also celebrated this year.

First, despite all his continuing concern about "ought", about ethical grounds of critique, Lukács searched always for a deterministic view of history, for a dialectical necessity of the totality of the historical process, which would involve a transcendence of capitalism. When this necessity is brought to consciousness and understood, a decisive step is taken by the historical process "toward its proper end". This is how Lukács wrote in *History and Class Consciousness*:

> The facts no longer appear strange when they are comprehended in their coherent reality, in the relation of all partial aspects to their inherent but hitherto unelucidated roots in the whole: we then perceive the tendencies which strive towards the centre of reality, to what we will call the ultimate goal. This ultimate goal is not an abstract ideal opposed to the process, but an aspect of truth and reality. It is the concrete meaning of each stage reached and an integral fact of the concrete moment. Because of this, to comprehend it is to recognize the direction taken (unconsciously) by events and tendencies towards the totality ... The total process is the emancipation of the proletariat.[21]

The basic thesis here is obviously that reality itself tends toward this emancipation of the proletariat. The facts can be properly understood only against this inherent trend of the objective historical process.

More than four decades later, in his *Ontology of Social Being* Lukács elaborated the view that despite all that happens at the phenomenal level to individual men, there is an objective dialectic of economic process, that has an "ontologically immanent intention towards the humanization of men in the broadest sense". Economic laws that "run beyond the will of any individual men", "produce and reproduce social men at an even higher level". Lukács says that "this contention is in itself completely value-free" and "it only emphasizes the simple fact of existence".[22]

The form of a value-free ontology only makes even worse a certain tendency toward historical determinism, which stems from Marx himself, and which is one of the most vulnerable elements of Marx' theory. In this respect Bloch's treatment of possibility as the basic modal category of a philosophy of history serves much better the needs of a contemporary Marxist critical theory. Once we stop reifying society, the proletariat, and the Party, as collective subject-object entities, above and beyond individuals that constitute them, once we stop projecting individual preferences into ontological laws, history must be seen as a process in which nothing in the future is inevitable and guaranteed, a process in which at every juncture there are open alternatives, whose realization depends on free, creative, and therefore unpredictable, human practice.

Second, a favorite target of Lukács' critique is utopian consciousness. He searches for objective knowledge, for truth. That is understandable. A critical theory that intends to contribute to real social change must be seriously concerned about all available knowledge. There is, however, a tendency in Lukács to reduce theory to knowledge, and revolutionary consciousness to self-knowledge. Again in a deterministic sense, the faith is expressed that truth must eventually win. Lukács liked to paraphrase Zola: "La vérité est lentement en marche et à la fin des fins rien ne l'arrêtera." (Truth is slowly on the way and in the end nothing will stop it").[23] But, of course, if there is no social inevitability there is no certainty. Bloch's principle of hope expressed well this non-cognitive, passionate dimension of revolutionary consciousness. Commitment to humanization, autonomy, genuine community, creativity - short of any guarantees of their realization - cannot but have a utopian character. In that sense and precisely to the extent to which he acted as a revolutionary, Lukács himself was a utopian.

Third, Lukács believed that true, critical-practical activity was possible only within an organization, or at least that one could not successfully participate in a struggle for worker's liberation, for democracy or against fascism, outside of an organized political movement. The element of truth in this attitude is, of course, that in organizations ideas have a chance of becoming material forces and that only organizations and movements have the energy necessary practically to restructure social institutions.

However, the question is, first, what kind of organization is in question, and, second, is it a true dilemma that either one has to cling to an organization at any cost or else one is condemned to a solitary, passive existence.

As to the first, Lukács must have gradually learnt that the Stalinist parties to which he belonged were in practice distorting beyond recognition great revolutionary goals to which he was committed. He was rudely attacked, insulted, humiliated, compelled to renounce his best convictions, arrested in 1941 in Moscow, deported in 1956 from Budapest to Romania - he barely escaped death at thé hands of his comrades. Nothing affected his almost religious loyalty.

This leads us to the second question concerning the possible alternatives to acting as an 'organization' man. Lukács' explanation of his strange attitude was that staying in the Party was "the entry ticket" for continuing political activity and for the participation in the struggle against fascism. It is, of course, true that joining the Hungarian Communist Party in December 1918 gave him the opportunity to participate and be a leader in a genuine socialist revolution. After the failure of the revolution and the escape to Vienna, until 1929 he was still actively engaged politically Once he was defeated and forced to recant publicly he was finished as a political personality in the organization. It is not at all clear that staying in the Party all those subsequent decades gave him a chance of practically contributing to the cause of socialism more than by educating young people, writing in the mass media, and of course publishing important books, which is what was done by Bloch, Goldmann, Marcuse, Fromm, Lefebvre, E.P. Thompson, Miliband and other independent critical thinkers.

Fourth and the final point of difference between Bloch and Lukács. More than any other contemporary critical thinker, Bloch conveyed a sense of enormous human dignity which was theoretically articulated in his idea of "staying upright". And indeed dignity is as important to a critical thinker as his reason, the passion of his convictions, and his civil courage. All relevant and especially radical criticism, criticism that challenges the entire human condition in a society, is regarded as subversive by governing powers. There is hardly a single Marxist critical thinker, whether in the East or in the West, who was not at least once insulted and expelled from his own Party and who did not lose friends, family, job, motherland, and in some cases life itself. (For example, most Soviet philosophers criticized by Mitin on Stalin's orders in 1931 perished in the purges 1936-38.)

Lukács found himself under devastating onslaught three times. In the year of Lenin's death, 1924, soon after the appearance of *History and Class Consciousness*, the book was attacked first by his former supporter, Laszlo Rudas, then by Bukharin and Zinoviev. Zinoviev, at that time the general secretary of the Komintern, finished with Korsch and Lukács - the two most brilliant Marxist minds of that time - in the following simple way: "If a few more of those professors come and dish out their Marxist theories, our cause will be in bad shape. We cannot in our Communist International allow theoretical revisionism of this kind to go unpunished."[24]

In 1929 the political platform for the Second Congress of the Hungarian Communist Party, that was prepared by Lukács in the name of the more flexible and democratically minded Landler faction, was viciously attacked by the sectarian group of Bela Kun (who enjoyed the support of Zinoviev). Lukács was labelled as an "opportunist" and "liquidator" who should be expelled from the Party. This was the end of Lukács' political career.

The third attack came after a few years of feverish activity by Lukács upon his return to Hungary in 1945. The year was 1949, the year of Cominform pressures on Yugoslavia, of the preparation for Rajk's trial, and of a most militant Stalinist offensive on the cultural front in all countries of the "people's democracies". Two volumes of essays published by Lukács (*Literature and Democracy* and *For a new Hungarian Culture*) were, first, viciously attacked by his old friend Rudas, who accused him of "revisionism", "right-wing deviationism", "cosmopolitanism", of "having insulted Lenin", of objectively being a "servant of imperialism". Then came Fadeev's attack in *Pravda*, threatening severe punishment.

These are all well-known facts and the reason I mention them is to ask the following two questions:

First: Did the critical thought of Lukács, or of Bloch, Kosík, Kołakowski, the Yugoslav journal *Praxis*, Lukács' younger followers from the Budapest school, really effectively damage the cause of socialism and did it thus provoke some understandable and justifiable self-defense measures of the ideological establishment in all those countries?

Second: What is the proper response of critical intellectuals to such a repression?

The answer to the first question is simple and brief. As a rule, the victims of ideological repression are precisely those critical intellectuals that have given the most creative contributions to contemporary Marxist socialist theory. Their crime is that they keep the spirit alive, that they remind the former revolutionary activists of the meaning of their original project, that they serve as the bad conscience of the order which emerges rigid and ossified out of a promising revolutionary movement.

The usurpers of power, who are invariably extremely successful in producing "bad consciousness" among the intellectuals and in ideologically manipulating the rest of the population, look at those few critical intellectuals with a growing apprehension that at least these surely understand what is going on in the society. Spreading that understanding would undermine the system, since it rests on false pretenses. That is why a critical thinker must sooner or later face the following options: either continue to walk upright no matter what, or else choose one of the following three variants: 1) to pretend that one does not see what one sees; 2) to escape into abstractions which a man from the street will not be able to understand; 3) to engage in self-criticism from time to time.

This leads us to the discussion of the second question. Lukács survived by combining all three mentioned variants of the second strategy.

He pretended not to see what he must have seen, maybe better than anybody else. As late as 1967 he still says that "he agreed with Stalin about the necessity for socialism in one country".[25] How could he still believe that what emerged in USSR was socialism?

He withdrew after 1929 and again after 1957 into a world of abstract philosophy: *The Young Hegel, Aesthetics, The Ontology of Social Being*. This is clearly the most reasonable alternative to continuing one's work boldly no matter what. Unfortunately, Lukács also continued to engage in humiliating self-criticism.

The first time was after the failure of the *Blum Theses*. Four decades later, he says: "I was indeed firmly convinced that I was in the right but I knew also - *e.g.* from the fate that had befallen Karl Korsch - that to be expelled from the Party meant that it would no longer be possible to participate actively in the struggle against fascism."[26]

The second self-criticism was published in 1949.

The third and in a way the worst of all appeared in 1968: it was a preface to the new edition of *History and Class Consciousness*. This time it was a self-criticism in advance, before the book was even republished, after the long interval of forty-five years. Lukács obviously felt that it was a price that had to be paid for the reappearance of his greatest work.

It is a sad task to have to defend this extraordinary book, one of the most original philosophical works in this century, from its own author. It is simply not true that the work "lacks any genuine economic foundations", that "conception of praxis in the book is idealistic", that "the category of totality is a source of confusion", that "the concept of alienation is treated in purely Hegelian terms", that the entire book is "based on mistaken assumptions".[27] To the many compliments that this work has received since it first appeared, let me add only one: the analysis of political reification in the modern bureacratic state not only fills a gap in Marxist theory, but constitutes one of the major contributions to twentieth-century political philosophy in general. It was depressing to read Lukács' words in 1968: "I sincerely did believe that *History and Class Consciousness* was mistaken and I think that to this day".[28]

We can no longer help Georg Lukács either by passing harsh moral judgments on him or by defending him.

Maybe it would also be irrelevant to discuss to what extent his self-critical statements are purely tactical devices to reduce hostility toward him, and to what extent they are rationalizations, expressions of a will to believe what was in his interest.

The more one knows about the personality of Lukács, the more one begins to understand the nature of this basic duality in his thought. It seems (especially on the basis of the revelations by Agnes Heller written for the occasion of the hundredth anniversary of her teacher) that in Lukács - many a very fundamental characteristic of all of modern culture was reflected. This is the tendency to isolate knowledge from morality. In interpersonal relations, Lukács seemed to be a cold, cerebral man interested exclusively in the intellectual capacities and achievements of his colleagues and students. Their emotional, moral and other existential problems did not interest him at all, and he avoided any emotional contact even with the people closest to him. Friends were ideological allies; pupils were knights selected to spread the true ideas of the master. Lukács behaved as if he were the objectification of the absolute spirit. But this spirit was pure reason, *logos*, without emotions, without moral passion. It is very revealing that while he assumed that many young people were intellectually gifted, he never assumed that people had a capacity of being moral. Disloyalty, even betrayal, by friends and his closest pupils did not really bother him. But when someone passed a moral test well he would consider that an extraordinary event, a miracle, a true gift.

His entire life was extremely limited, ascetic, poor in needs, entirely dedicated to intellectual work. It is clear that if one, in the name of rationality and objectivity, disregards morality and isolates it from knowledge (which is very characteristic of the entire epoch of modernity), if one believes that knowledge itself will eventually emancipate people and secure progress and that therefore the most important spiritual work is "spreading truth" (conceived in a purely rational way), then one is less sensitive to morality and more ready to play all kinds of tricks with the establishment in order to survive and make it possible for the truth to continue its march. It would also be interesting to establish, although I cannot enter into this question here, to what extent Lukács was under the influence of his friend (and opponent on the issue of expressionism), Bertolt Brecht. Brecht defended the view that those individuals who were the carriers of knowledge had a special task and responsibility to themselves - to survive. This view was spelled out in the play, *Galileo*, and in the stories about Herr Keuner.

It is of course not at all clear whether a heroic, upright Lukács would at all have survived the Thirties, once he made the dangerous decision to go and live under Stalin. Then all those books - from *The Young Hegel* to *Aesthetics* and *Social Ontology of Labor* - would not have been written and the Budapest school, composed of his students from the Fifties, would probably not have been what it is. However, I should like to emphasize another dimension of this problem. Galileo could renounce his teachings about the movement of celestial bodies - without affecting either the meaning or the truth of his theories.

It is different with statements of a critical humanist theory. An essential part of the meaning of those statements is that they project a standard for potential human behavior in an ideal human community. What characterizes this potential human behavior is, among other things, sincerity, integrity, reliability, courage, dignity. The point here is that a critical thinker does not persuade his audience by producing syllogisms or by deriving his statements from ever higher and more general principles. He must demonstrate in his own praxis that the projected possibility really exists. The unity of theory and praxis does not consist in the fact that what one person says, the other will practically bring to life. It consists, on the contrary, in the fact that one lives one's philosophy, that one's own practical behavior demonstrates the existence of the possibility one speaks about.

This is where Georg Lukács fails. His socialist project could be realized only if millions of people would risk whatever established existence they have (and usually nowadays this existence involves having more than just chains). In order to decide to take such a risk, these people must believe not only that there is in principle a better, more human alternative in comparison with the situation in which they find themselves, but also that the kind of people that the new, more human, world requires do really exist.

That is why the failure of a critical humanist thinker to live according to ethical demands which are implicit in his theoretical projects - is utterly self-destructive. His ideas may exert great intellectual influence; his works may remain as a lasting contribution to human knowledge. But they will not be able to spark noble motives, to inspire people to make bold ethical choices. And in that case the true name of the brave new world will at best be "goulash socialism".

NOTES

1.   Istvan Mészáros, *Lukács' Concept of Dialectics*, London, Merlin Press, 1972, p. 125-6.

2.   *A modern drama fejlodesenek tortenete* (History of the Development of Modern Drama), 2 vols., Budapest, Franklin 1911.

3.   Lukács, *Die Seele und die Formen*, Berlin, Egon Fleischel & Co., 1911. (*A lelek es a formak*, Budapest, Franklin, 1910).

4.   *Die Theorie des Romans. Ein geschichtsphilosophischer Versuch über die Formen der grossen Epik*. Berlin, Paul Cassirer, 1920.

5.   *Die Seele und die Formen*, London, Merlin Press, 1971. p. 189.

6.   *Op.cit.* p. 54.

7.   I. Mészáros, p. 50.

8.   *History and Class Consciousness*, London, The Merlin Press, 1971 (*Geschichte und Klassenbewusstsein*, Berlin, Malik-Verlag, 1923).

9.   *Op.cit.* 'Reification and the Consciousness of the Proletariat', pp. 83-223.

10.   'N. Bucharin: Theorie des historischen Materialismus', *Archiv für die Geschichte des Sozialismus und der Arbeiterbewegung*, 1925.

11.   'Blum: Declaration' (Oj Marcius), 1929.

12.   *Der junge Hegel. Über die Beziehungen von Dialektik und Ökonomie*, Zürich & Wien, Europa Verlag, 1948.

13.   *Existentialisme ou marxisme?*, Paris, Nagel, 1948.

14.   *Die Zerstörung der Vernunft,* Berlin, Aufbau-Verlag, 1954.

15.   *Essays über Realismus*, Berlin, Aufbau-Verlag, 1948; *Deutsche Realisten der 19 Jahrhunderts*, Berlin: Aufbau-Verlag, 1948; *Balzac und der französische Realismus*, Berlin, Aufbau-Verlag, 1952; *Der russische Realismus in der Weltliteratur*, Berlin, Aufbau-Verlag, 1952; *Probleme des Realismus*, Berlin, Aufbau-Verlag, 1955.

16.   *Die Eigenart des Ästhetischen*, Werke Bd. 11 & 12, Neuwied, Luchterhand, 1963.

17.   *Zur Ontologie des gesellschaftlichen Seins. Hegels falsche und echte Ontologie*, Neuwied, Luchterhand, 1971.

18.   'La mia via al marxismo: Postscriptum 1957', *Nuovi Argomenti*, 1958.

19.   'Lettera a Alberto Carocci', *Nuovi Argomenti*, 1962.

20.   *Gespräche mit Georg Lukács, Hans Heinz Holz, Leo Kofler, Wolfgang Abendroth*, ed. by Theo Pinkus, Reinback: Rowohlt, 1967; 'An Interview with G. Lukács: On his life and work', *New Left Review*, London, 1971.

21.   'What is Orthodox Marxism?', *History and Class Consciousness*, p. 23.

22.   *The Ontology of Social Being, 3. Labour*, London, Merlin Press, 1980, pp. 85-88.

23.   'Postscriptum 1957 zu Mein Weg zu Marx' (Georg Lukács, *Schriften zur Ideologie und Politik*, Neuwied und Berlin, Luchterhand, 1967, p. 657).

24.   *Ibid.* p. 720-721.

25.   'Preface to the new edition', *History and Class Consciousness*, p. XXVIII.

26.   *Ibid.* p. XXX.

27.   *Ibid.* p. XXXVII.

28.   *Ibid.* p. XXXVIII.

MANFRED BUHR

Georg Lukács and the Bourgeois Mind
in the Twentieth Century

I

Georg Lukács was one of the most significant and most influential thinkers of the twentieth century. His moral integrity cannot be doubted, nor can his intellectual honesty. Lukács' intellectual development was contradictory - it could not have been otherwise since the reality towards which his thought strove was (and is) itself contradictory. It must be taken in its entire historical dimension, that is as the epoch of the world-wide transition from capitalism to socialism.

Lukács' work and its influence, or better his works and their influences, were and are praised and criticized, ignored, not commented upon, brought into the foreground, not infrequently misused, however rarely really studied and considered in a critical-constructive manner. This is the reason why - without consideration of the numerous richly rewarding and worthwhile studies available - Lukács' intellectual biography is still to be written.

An encounter with Georg Lukács must not pass over in silence the contradictions, or hide the agreement, or even dehistoricize the historically limited. It is not easy to respond to such a requirement. It presupposes a constructive-critical attitude which remains free of prejudices as well as of exaggeration. This requires avoiding all labels as well as overly hasty capitulation before the difficulties of historical and ideological-critical research.

Accordingly, the encounter with Georg Lukács requires the use of subtle dialectic and presupposes the art of historical relativization. Lukács' developmental process should not be approached either for itself or in isolation. His writings and their effects must be considered in the ideological and political dynamic of our century. They turn on the questions concerning: the conditions of the maintenance of freedom, the demand for justice and for social progress, and the production of actual humanism in our time.

In this sense, Lukács' writings - and he himself understood them in this way - offer energetic forays (*Eingriffe*), whose form is truly philosophical, esthetic, literary-theoretical (or whatever one wants to name them), but whose content goes further, indeed intentionally enters into the political sphere. This is also the case for those of Lukács' writings

T. Rockmore (ed.), Lukács Today, 30–41.
© *1988 by D. Reidel Publishing Company.*

which he himself desired to understand as more or less "pure" theoretical works. His *Ontology of Social Being*, for instance, despite its theoretical character, is also a political work; for, in it - to consider only a single aspect - he again takes up the problems of *History and Class Consciousness*.

In Lukács' case, we are not confronted with a purely intellectual development, if this is ever the case. It is important for us to keep this in mind in order to judge the greatness and limits of Lukács' thought and influence correctly, that is with respect to the historical process. Whoever does not know how to make this distinction does not think in theoretical, but in theological, categories and misses the contradiction whose breadth must be accepted in order to remain within it.

II

After 1917-1918, after the Socialist October Revolution in Russia (for Lukács the event of the age), after his entry into the Hungarian Communist Party, Lukács' intellectual development is not to be considered solely as a phenomenon of the history of ideology, but rather as embedded in the development of the international Communist movement. Lukács sought to bring his thought into agreement with this movement. However, his theoretical thought not infrequently diverges from it, presents it in exaggerated or distorted fashion, remains behind it, stimulates it, anticipates it, or takes up a position to one side of it, if we may employ one of his own expressions. On this basis, an encounter with Lukács takes place under the heading of "profit" and "loss": "profit" because it is worthwhile to preserve, to defend, to render fruitful and to develop his thought further; "loss" in that the necessary criticism of Lukács must not be accompanied by a mere rejection (*Verdammung*).

The roses on Lukács' cross must be the metamorphoses of his thought, whose *caesurae* - and this is the difficulty - are not really such. If his pages, from the *Soul and its Forms* until the *Ontology of Social Being*, are inspected in order to grasp Lukács' intellectual development in its entirety, then basic themes appear which clarify this situation. Ought one either to affirm or to deny the unitary development of Lukács' thought? On the contrary, one must assert the continued presence in it of basic themes.

One, if not the, key for this assertion is in a statement from the *Soul and its Forms*: "Until now Novalis has only seldom been mentioned here although the discussion always concerned him. No one has ever more directly affirmed the exclusive value of final goals than this youth destined to death."[1]

We are simplifying somewhat if we insist: in his different creative periods Lukács certainly utilized this theme more than once, although never - in our opinion - did he leave it behind.

This ought to be taken neither as a criticism, nor as a denunciation, but rather as a sober, simple observation. For this, there are in Lukács' work - or so it seems to us - numerous indications. For instance, there is the fluid, but continually reappearing, concept of totality, which is of classical-romantic 'origin, and which brings into play a classical standard of evaluation. A further indication lies in Lukács' continued search, again renewed in the *Ontology of Social Being*, for "what being is": above all his search was for human being.

The dynamic of Lukács' thought consists in a mixture of the Enlightenment-classical-romantic tradition, insistence on bourgeois culture and an opposition to it, Marxism as the ideology of freedom, the struggle for freedom, the educative process and its Marxist analysis, continuity and discontinuity, revolutionary impatience and romantic desiring. With Lukács, all this is bound up with morality as the social condition, sensitivity towards the crisis of consciousness, a missionary urge to save culture from barbarism, heroic illusions and historical optimism.

Because of this context, Lukács' work and influence can only be approached through precise thought and through knowledge of the classical and romantic traditions. Lukács' thought resists slogans and labels and, above all, any type-casting. In fact, Lukács' thought requires a deep examination.

Georg Lukács and contemporary bourgeois ideology - this implies two situations to which we would like to refer: 1. Lukács as a part of the late bourgeois development of ideas; 2. Lukács as a critic of late bourgeois ideology.

Ad 1. It is often (actually more and more) overlooked that Lukács was the godfather of an influential and durable, late bourgeois, ideological creation - in fact its secret, but normally unmentioned, founder. To be historically accurate, this should not go unmentioned. In fact, even more so, since the usual formula, which has it that Lukács developed out of a bourgeois mentality and ended as a Marxist, hides this situation. We do not mean that this formula is false. Rather, it is too simple and too linear, and accordingly fitting only to separate Lukács from his developmental course, and, in consequence, to impoverish the latter. This formula, hence, masks important developments in the dynamics of late bourgeois, ideological development that are characterized, among other things, by the production of forms of thought that are in opposition to the bourgeois forms, are transitional forms toward Marxism, or are frankly Marxist.

In Lukács' developmental course, all these moments are contained and - what ought not to be overlooked - become thereby available. The assertion that Lukács is to be regarded as the initiator of an influential, late bourgeois form of ideology does not, however, signify the negation of his Marxism. Rather, it refers to a weakness in the development of late bourgeois ideology. Without retreating from this, or even desiring (or even being able) to be complete, the following should be noted. Lukács' great Kierkegaard essay (1909) with the significant title, 'The Fragmentation of the Form in Life. Soren Kierkegaard and Regina Olson', can be regarded as the onset of the development of existentialist philosophy, whose beginning it is. As concerns the force or depth of expression, it leaves all later philosophy of the existentialist school behind. In the Kierkegaard essay, we read the sentence, which we would like to advance as a litmus test: "The gesture is the great paradox of life, since it is only in its rigid eternity that each disappearing instant of life has a place and through it becomes true actuality."[2]

Lukács' 'Metaphysics of Tragedy' (1910) is in closest relation to the Kierkegaard essay and offers the "philosophy of life" (*Lebensphilosophie*) in perfected form. We cite: "Life is an anarchy of chiaroscuro; nothing in life fulfills itself entirely or attains the end ... life: that is, to be able to outlive something."[3] If we add to the 'Metaphysics of Tragedy' the Novalis study with the title 'On Romantic Philosophy of Life' (1909), we can further supplement it with the Stefan George study (1908), which has the following observation as its central statement: "Art is suggestion with the help of form."[4] In this way we have the basic categories of late bourgeois *Lebensphilosophie* for the period between the two world wars. This is the very trend of which Lukács will become a consistent and brilliant Marxist critic twenty years later.

We have attentively considered this aspect of Lukács' thought in order to refer to the tangle of his conceptual road, to interpret it in isolation from its influence, and to stress the denunciatory intent (*Gehabe*) of certain parts of late bourgeois mentality. The latter is recognizable in such terms as "secret counsel", "writer's savant", "great mufti of Marxist literary criticism", "official party critic", "forced reconciliation", and others. Such terms are not dictated by controversy with a great mind, but rather by the bad conscience of the sources of ideas on the other side and by mindless anti-Communist partiality.

The possible relations between *History and Class Consciousness* and Heidegger's *Being and Time* have often been noted.[5] Karl Mannheim's sociology of knowledge - especially *Ideology and Utopia* - cannot be thought of without *History and Class Consciousness*. The influence deriving from Lukács' *Theory of the Novel* (as examples we name only Herbert Marcuse and Theodor W. Adorno) is considerable. One can raise a question that is not just rhetorical: what would the Frankfurt School really be without its often criticized, condemned, and advertised Lukács? What would this most critical of critical theories be without the *Theory of the Novel* and without *History and Class Consciousness*?

In this respect, a small marginal comment is worth making. In Adorno's Hegel writings there is no reference to Lukács' book, *The Young Hegel,* although for long stretches Adorno takes up the same set of problems as Lukács: the role of work and of alienation for the development of Hegel's dialectic. One must, hence, assume that Adorno did not know Lukács' Hegel book. But in the Archives of the Institute for Social Research one can find a two-page summary of Lukács' book which - one is astonished - stems from Adorno. It bears the title: 'Re: economy and society in the young Hegel' and underlines in general that Adorno had benefited from reading Lukács' book. Also he seems to have been impressed, since no less than twice in two pages Adorno inscribes the, for him, uncommon words: "important passage". At the conclusion of this entirely positive summary, Adorno notes, however, that Lukács, "out of anxiety in respect to the guns" did not dare to bring out Hegel's "materialistic element" in Hegel himself, but only from the perspective of Marx.[6]

This state of affairs speaks for itself and requires no commentary. It refers to the more than strained relationship of Adorno to Lukács, and to Marxism. Adorno was unable to free himself from Lukács' hypnotic spell, which became his neurosis, and for which he compensated through refutation and denunciation.

Let us be content with these references to Lukács' influence on the late bourgeois way of thought. It seems to us sufficient to justify speaking of Lukács as the founder of a basic form of late bourgeois ideology and of German *Lebensphilosophie*. We have sought to make this aspect of Lukács' influence visible because it is too undervalued, indeed often overlooked, and because it might be submerged in the controversy over Lukács' closeness to Marx. On the other hand, there is another, important, and seldom clarified reason for considering this controversy. Neglect of this aspect carries the danger of cutting Lukács' thought in half; and this is not peculiar to Lukács' thought. In regard to other figures such as Walter Benjamin or Ernst Bloch, we find an analogous set of problems, which in the first place is not a matter of subjectivity, but of the historical process and of its ideal articulation. The historical process is inconceivable without the category of "transition" in order to avoid applying to Lukács Ernst Bloch's image of the "world in between".

Ad 2. If we consider what has already been noted, then it can, indeed must, be said of Lukács as a critic of contemporary bourgeois ideology that his intellectual and political development, like almost no other, brings with it the presuppositions necessary to criticize late bourgeois ideology in its essential forms. Lukács' criticism of late bourgeois ideology exhibited a break with parts of his own thought. This break manifests intellectual and moral trustworthiness.

Lukács not only knew late bourgeois German *Lebensphilosophie* thoroughly; he had also contributed to its development and suffered with it. Lukács' coming to terms with German *Lebensphilosophie* was, hence, also a coming to terms with his own thought. At the latest, at the end of the Twenties, Lukács became aware of the political and ideological fate implied by such thought.

The criticism which Lukács then raised is bound up with a renewed involvement with Marx, with the introduction of Leninism into the latter's thought, above all through *Materialism and Empirio-Criticism*, and with the return to classical German philosophy, above all to Hegel. For Lukács, this was, as he himself in retrospect admitted, a kind of "mental enthusiasm associated with the new beginning".

In this process of coming to terms and of entering into controversy, Lukács discovered the revolutionary and mobilizing potential of classical bourgeois rationality, as it had developed in classical German philosophy and literature. His critique of ideology is now oriented towards three goals which must be seen as related: (a) the enrichment of Marxism in the light of the classical bourgeois tradition, (b) the working up of the heritage of classical German philosophy and literature in order to render it fruitful for the struggle against imperialist-fascist ideology, and (c) the rejection of the falsifications and misinterpretations of the classical bourgeois German tradition by imperialist and fascist ideology.

The program of the *Destruction of Reason* remains as an over-arching summary of this orientation in the years during and after the Second World War.

Lukács' ideological-critical orientation is not only directed towards the theoretical profit resulting from such a study; but, in a return to an interest in Lenin, it also takes on a concern with "the reality of revolution". This means that Lukács understands his ideological-critical activity as a world-intuiting, intervention-desiring thought, which ought to make a contribution to the problems of the epoch. Its content was, even at a very early stage, described by him thusly: "... to make use, for the rescue of mankind, of the entry into the last phase of capitalism and the possibilities (offered by) the here unavoidable struggle concerning a decision between the bourgeoisie and the proletariat in favor of the proletariat".[7]

Let us not consider the extent to which Lukács in this context is subject to heroic illusions. For us, as we have said, their presence is clear. It seems to us, that on this point the questioning recognition by Walter Benjamin should be noted, that is of the "secret agreement between the preceding generation and our own" in respect to Lukács: "Ours, like every preceding generation before it, has been given a weak messianic power, which has a claim on the past."[8]

However, without regard to this, we can say that the major thrust of Lukács' ideological-critical activity after the beginning of the thirties (and continuing until the fifties) was directed against the ideology of German fascism, its preparatory ideologies, its effects, and its restoration in the imperialistic system of the Federal German Republic in the years after the Second World War. In virtue of the direction of his major thrust, Lukács is, despite whatever one can and must criticize separately, in general up to date - up to date in respect to the constant tendency of forms of thought associated with irrationalist *Lebensphilosophie* to push themselves into the foreground of the late bourgeois mind.

III

Lukács sees, as a generalized phenomenon of the worldview of fascist ideology, as a particularly reactionary form of late bourgeois thought, its general eclecticism (Engels had already spoken of "eclectic beggar's soup"), where there are perverted forms of criticism (in which resentment predominates) together with human biological and social attitudes (in which racist ideologies predominate), interwoven with a quasi-religious mysticism. According to Lukács, the source for this already formally grotesque worldview of the fascist ideology was above all the development of *Lebensphilosophie* in Germany after Schopenhauer and Nietzsche.

The theoretical helplessness of German *Lebensphilosophie* expresses itself in the desire and capacity still to perfect knowledge of the essence (if at all) with discursive means and methods. The conceptual effort and the daring for knowledge which is paradigmatically displayed in classical bourgeois thought until Hegel and Goethe is increasingly criticized as a work of Sisyphus and then rejected. Soon this need is transmuted into a virtue, and then a clarification of unknowability begins: a total rejection with respect to the knowability of the world, of its rationality, of meaningful activity within it, and altogether a fetishization of the enigmatic character of history.

Lukács is not only concerned by the public, theoretical and conceptual deficiency of this train of thought. He is also concerned above all with the danger of a practical-conceptual vacuum, deriving from different forms of using the then current, popular borrowed parts in a more or less bizarre eclecticism.

According to Lukács, the practical-ethical, problematic result of the decline of late bourgeois ideology resides in the destruction of humanism in respect to its programmatic worth for the progressive bourgeoisie.

The psychic description of the German bourgeoisie which Lukács advances in his ideological-critical writings between the Thirties and the Fifties - clearly with different accents and accounts of its origin - counts as a complaint and a warning in respect to "self-acknowledged immaturity" (Kant) as well as an appeal to consciousness of reason and the value of humanism. If we may describe the situation with the terminology of someone opposite to him, but on the same side of the barricade, that is Bertolt Brecht, Lukács is aware that reason prevails only as far as the rational prevails. Lukács is (and always was) an important fighter for reason. He is always immediately concrete if one confronts the even sketchily indicated results of Lukács' ideological critical work with the elements of the late bourgeois ideological development of the present day - for instance, in such key terms as conservative and irrational modes of thought, "concrete thought of order" (*Ordnungsdenken*), the Nietzsche renaissance, biologism, revanchism, the rediscovery of Carl Schmitt, Preyer, Gehlen, Baumler or Krieck, the case of André Glücksman - a list which can be extended at will.

In Lukács' program of the destruction of reason there are many - above all historically limited - distortions of object and method. But this is not an adequate basis on which to question the program of the destruction of reason in general, or to replace it in an inconsequential manner by trivialities. The presuppositions of this program are to be known and recognized - historical optimism, unlimited insistence on reason, the demand for the binding together of the rational, the calling into consciousness of the dangers for humanity, that appear with every turn away from reason.

We must also emphasize the statements: "...the taking up of a position for or against reason is at the same time decisive for the essence of philosophy as philosophy, for its role in social development" and "there is no 'guiltless' philosophical attitude".[9] Whoever declines to stress this proposition is like the savage on whom Lichtenberg reports: "A Canadian savage, who was exhibited to all the Parisian gentry, was finally asked what he best appreciated. The knife stores, he answered."[10]

IV

Lukács is often criticized for having subordinated himself to his own abstract schemata. Most often Schelling and Nietzsche are named as examples. Clearly, as we have already indicated, there are distortions in Lukács' work, even on occasion important ones. But is this enough to refute our statement on the significance and contemporary relevance of Lukács? We answer in the negative. In the first place, distortions in the writing of the history of ideology are on the agenda and hence nothing special. In general, the history of philosophy, the history of literature and the history of ideology are written by finite beings. But that is not the point. The point is that if we regard the means-ends relation in the controversy, then we cannot renounce it, even at the price of an "esthetisization", which means the uncoupling of ideological development from politics and history.

Those who are born later have the duty to consider the social-historical limitations under which a struggling ideologue has brought forth his results - and then, as necessary, to make corrections. The standard for the history of ideology cannot be advanced from a later, contemporaneous perspective, which considers an earlier perspective. This is valid for Lukács and in regard to Lukács, in a double sense.

Werner Krauss, in many ways opposed to Lukács, rightly stated in this context: "It is historically incorrect (and one must have the courage not to do so) to measure the significance of a prior ideology in terms of its effect on the succeeding period."[11]

V

In the afterword to the *Destruction of Reason* (January 1953), Lukács refers to William Faulkner, who stated in his Nobel Prize address in 1950: "The tragedy of our time is a general, overall anxiety. We bear this in us only so long as we can. There are no longer any spiritual problems. There is only the question: when will I be blown up?"[12] Lukács does not reject this observation by Faulkner with respect to the imperialistic politics of the Cold War. He, however, does not remain idle with respect to this surely realistic, however somber, prognosis for humanity. This is forbidden to him by his optimism, rooted in Marxism-Leninism. Against this, Lukács demands "the protection of reason as a mass movement". [13] He sees this mass movement in the growing, world-wide peace movement. "The ... new moment in the

active, mass defense of reason is the peace movement."[14] Several lines
earlier, Lukács had noted what should not be overlooked, and which
was not, either by Lukács or in general in the activity of the social
movements of our epoch: "Around 1848 the great, really decisive
opponent of the destruction of reason first appeared: Marxism. After
1917, it not only developed as the world view of a sixth of the earth,
but also appeared on a conceptually higher plane, as Marxism-
Leninism, as the further development of Marxism ..."[15]

Lukács' points of orientation were real socialism, the Communist
world movement, Marxism-Leninism, and the struggle for the preservation of freedom. These guarantee the up-to-date character of his
theoretical thought and his social activity.

At the World Congress for Cultural Creativity in 1948 in Wroclaw,
Lukács strongly warned: "At present it is an important concern of the
bourgeoisie to destroy the social-historical capacity for orientation of the
intelligentsia. If an important part of the intelligentsia cannot be transformed into unconditional adherents of imperialistic reaction, at least it
can wander around without the capacity to orient itself in an uncom-
prehended world." And Lukács continued:

> Many intellectuals already feel today from where freedom and
> culture are really threatened. Many oppose - even with strong
> moral pathos - imperialism and the preparation for war. But our
> worth as representatives of the intelligentsia demands from us to
> make of this feeling knowledge... The intelligentsia is at the
> crossroads. Ought we to become, like the French intelligentsia in
> the eighteenth century, and the Russian intelligentsia in the
> nineteenth century, forerunners and vanguard fighters for a
> progressive world-turning (*Weltenwende*) - or, like the German
> intelligentsia of the first half of the twentieth century, helpless
> victims, will-less helpers of the agents of a barbarian reaction?
> There is no question which attitude with respect to the essence, the
> knowledge, and the culture of the intelligentsia is worthy and which
> is not worthy.[16]

Lukács was clear that at the completion of such an attitude divergences
must and should remain. He, so to speak, clarified his Wroclaw
warning five years later when he added:

> As little as the freedom movement knows 'conformism', its mere
> existence, its growth, its concrete development contains a pro-
> posing and a responding to the great question of world view: for or
> against reason. Naturally within the new unity of the freedom

movement the questions and answers for both the individual and the group are different and often fully opposed. The great principle of such divergences, however, is: the defense of human reason and truly not only of its existence in general, but rather of its reality, its capacity to be effective in history, for which we are all more or less active participants.[17]

Georg Lukács was an unflinching representative of reason, and because of this, he was also an important fighter for freedom and concrete humanism.

Georg Lukács thought and acted according to Rabelais' commandment: knowledge without awareness is the decline of the soul. Let us accept this as the legacy of Georg Lukács.

NOTES

1. G. von Lukács, *Die Seele und die Formen, Essays,* Berlin 1911, S. 111.

2. *Ibid.* S. 65.

3. *Ibid.* S. 328.

4. *Ibid.* S. 175.

5. Most recently by W.-D. Gudopp, *Der junge Heidegger. Realität und Wahrheit in der Vorgeschichte von "Sein und Zeit",* Berlin und Frankfurt am Main 1983, S. 128ff.; see also W.-D. Gudopp, V. Behm, '"Zum Fallen geneigt"-Anmerkungen zu Heideggers Politik', in: M. Buhr/H.J. Sandkühler (Hg.), *Philosophie in weltbürgerlicher Absicht und wissenschaftlicher Sozialismus,* Köln 1985, S. 106ff.

6. See the instructive essay by N. Tertulian, 'Lukács, Adorno et la philosophie classique allemand', in: *Archives de Philosophie,* 47/1984, S. 177ff.

7. G. Lukács, *Lenin. Studie über den Zusammenhang seiner Gedanken* [1924], Neuwied und Berlin(West) 1969, S. 8.

8. W. Benjamin, *Allegorien kultureller Erfahrung,* Leipzig 1984, S. 157.

9. G. Lukács, *Die Zerstörung der Vernunft,* Berlin 1954, S. 6, 28f.

10. G.C. Lichtenberg, *Sudelbucher,* hg. von F.H. Mautner, Frankfurt am Main 1983, S. 365.

11. W. Krauss, *Gracians Lebenslehre,* Frankfurt am Main 1947, S. 160.

12. G. Lukács, *op. cit.* p. 671.

13. *Ibid.* S. 673.

14. *Ibid.* S. 670.

15. *Ibid.* S. 669.

16. G. Lukács, *Schicksalswende,* Berlin 1956, S. 244f.

17. G. Lukács, *Die Zerstörung der Vernunft,* S. 672.

MARIA HEVESI

Lukács in the Eyes of
Western Philosophy Today

When Georg Lukács died in 1971, Academician L. Matrai wrote in his memory that one of the brightest stars in contemporary European culture had disappeared from the firmament, and that only the future could tell what would be lasting in Lukács' thought. Matrai wrote that we lacked historical perspective for a judgement as to which of Lukács' works are classics - which belong to the summit of his creativity and which belong to the base of this summit. It was too early to define his role in the international workers movement and in the history of European philosophy. There are too many myths surrounding him - both from friends and enemies - as is the case with most important personalities. (*Kortars*, 1971, 8, 1179-880).

It has been more than fifteen years since then, and Lukács' contribution to the development of European philosophy and esthetics, as well as his influence on contemporary philosophy, are becoming clearer and clearer. When we enquire as to the sources of this influence, we have to cite his powerful intellect and his vigorous search for a world view that would enable twentieth-century man not only to orient himself among the complex and contradictory phenomena that mark the twentieth century, but also to act on these phenomena and to change the profile of the age.

It is well known that Georg Lukács began his creative path as an idealist philosopher. All of Hungarian cultural life at the turn of the century was pervaded by a sense of profound crisis, of instability, and of the fall of the monarchy. The pre-war period and the early years of World War I brought disappointment and doubt about all - about God, about man, and about the perspectives and goals standing before humanity. All this facilitated the generation of a peculiar, mystically unreal relationship to reality. Lukács, too, undertook a search for moral absolutes that would anchor man amid these terrible threats. From the beginning, Lukács found unacceptable the old feudal-clerical traditions of feudal Hungary, and those of capitalism with its enslavement of man, culture and spirituality. The world of capital was, for him, a world of alienation and of the destruction of culture. He sought to anchor a totalizing worldview that would withstand the chaos and formlessness pervading the world.

In these circumstances, the young Lukács condemned bourgeois society. Characteristic of bourgeois philosophy of the turn of the

42

T. Rockmore (ed.), Lukács Today, 42–50.
© *1988 by D. Reidel Publishing Company.*

century was a sense of the crisis of capitalism and of its culture. Romantic anti-capitalism was widespread in those years among Western European intellectuals. Since he received his philosophic training in Germany, Lukács was very familiar with most philosophic trends - from neo-Kantianism to *Lebensphilosophie* and the sociology of Max Weber. Most of Lukács' works of this period are clearly influenced by these trends. It was the fall of the Austro-Hungarian Empire that brought him to an extreme non-acceptance of this world. Coming to a final and uncompromising rejection of bourgeois society and not seeing any real forces for the accomplishment of this rejection, Lukács treats the existing world as "absolute sinfulness", toward which one cannot be obligated, even purely theoretically.

Such an attitude was described adequately by Antonio Gramsci in 1916, when he reported that they had said 'All or nothing'. And they saw the war proving them correct. Their program for tomorrow had to be 'all or nothing'; the blow of the hammer and not patient, methodical undermining; the impact of irresistible phalanxes, rather than the tunneling of moles working in the fetid underground.

Then came the October Revolution! Lukács experienced it enthusiastically as the incarnation of the "vigorous judgment" against capitalism and against its alienation of man and culture. The ethical problem came to the fore of Lukács' attention, but his solution was purely idealist. In his declining years, Lukács himself said of his views in that period that they were an "amalgam" of the most contradictory views.

> Was even Faust permitted to have two souls in his breast so that in the presence of contradictory tendencies appearing simultaneously, he could take first one and then another position in the midst of world crisis. Characteristic of my views of that period was, on the one hand, mastery of Marxism for political activism and, on the other, ever more intensive work on ethical questions from a purely idealistic perspective. (G. Lukács, *Geschichte und Klassenbewusstsein*, Neuwied, 1968. S.12-13)

It was while on this tortuous path of transition from one class position to another, while mastering Marxism, that Lukács wrote *History and Class Consciousness* (1923), his work that is best known in the West and which has had the greatest influence on bourgeois philosophy. It is clear that this book is one of the first efforts philosophically to rethink the theoretical and organizational problems of the revolutionary movement - especially of the October Revolution. Just treating Marxism as a philosophy was of tremendous significance. Lukács' book was the first to analyze German classical philosophy and to view the workers' movement as its spiritual heir. Of special importance here was the study of the Marx-Hegel relationship and attention to the problem of alienation. It is generally agreed that the problems spotlighted in *History and Class Consciousness* came to occupy a central position in such philosophic doctrines as existentialism and the social philosophy of the Frankfurt School. Raymond Aron quite pertinently wrote in 1983 that "not one of Horkheimer's books or of his colleagues had the resonance of Lukács' *History and Class Consciousness*" (R. Aron, *Mémoires*, Gallimard, Paris, 1983. p.87).

The influence of Lukács is due mainly to the fact that in *History and Class Consciousness* he poses the problem of the existence of man in capitalist society - the problem of his alienation and of overcoming it. At the same time, the book is pointed in its attacks on a positivistic, scientistic approach to social phenomena. It opposes the study of society and man through a set of disjointed disciplines, each of which looks at one or another part of a single, total social process.

The solution to these very important questions is provided from a position that is close to Marxism, but not yet Marxist. Many Marxist propositions are filled with a non-Marxist content. Lukács' idealist notions, drawn from the European philosophy of the time, are peculiarly associated with mechanistic-utopian conceptions of the historical role of the proletariat. The agglomeration of philosophy and practical-organizational problems of the workers movement was especially attractive among certain circles of the intellectuals in Western Europe, who were drawn to a form of philosophy of practice, where the active side of human nature was stressed in isolation from reality. It was a question, as I. Hermann correctly wrote about such a theory, that "it occurs in a mythical, not real, form at a stage of development whereas it should have occurred after a lengthy and contradictory development". (I. Hermann, *Lukács György gondolatvilaga*, Budapest, 1974. o. 143).

Interest in Lukács was very intense in the 1920s, the early 1930s and again in the 1950s and 1960s. The 1920s were the years of immediate reaction to the crisis of bourgeois consciousness, evoked by World War I and the October Revolution. The ever-increasing inclinations of left-leaning intellectuals toward a critique of capitalism increased their interest in Marxism. Especially attractive for such people was the version of Marxist philosophy to be found in Lukács' *History and Class Consciousness*.

The 1920s were also the years of the defeat of revolution in a series of European countries, and of the effort to explain the defeat. Here, too, Lukács' book with its treatment of the role of proletarian class consciousness and the problem of organization, proved very attractive.

Something similar can also be said of the 1950s and 1960s, after the defeat of fascism and the victory of the Soviet Union and other anti-fascist forces in World War II. These were years of unusually great interest in and influence of Marxism. This interest appeared both in the explanation of the basic essence of Marxism and in the effort of bourgeois ideology to react to Marxism, in particular by proposing its own distorted version of Marxism. This explains the great interest in the history of Marxism, in order to find the sources of such an interpretation.

Characteristic of the attitude of a part of this radical leftist intelligentsia was a yearning for revolutions that failed to come. It was a matter of the idea of basic social transformations in a series of European countries being 'unmarketable' at that time. Similar attitudes were still to be found among European intellectuals even twenty years after the defeat of revolution in Western Europe.

These were years of a clear polarization of bourgeois consciousness. The open crisis in bourgeois consciousness facilitated the spread of radical leftist attitudes, and occasionally of petty-bourgeois revolutionism, openly in opposition to official and unofficial conservatism. Refusing capitalism, such philosophic trends as existentialism and the social philosophy of the Frankfurt School criticized not only capitalist society but also the "bourgeois" in general, including its culture and civilization. In the context of such a critique, capitalism appeared not just as a stage in the development of mankind, or as a certain social-economic formation, but as a global evil, a "fiendish Hell". This explains the apocalyptic tone of such critiques of capitalism.

What is more, since the official ideology was often bound up with positivist, scientistic attitudes - with belief in science as the highest value - radical leftist ideology often appeared as espousing an anti-scientific orientation, which expressed alarm about the fate of man and humanistic ideals in an age of technocracy and the manipulation of human consciousness. If we take leftish existentialism or the social philosophy of the Frankfurt School, we see that they are against not just rationalism and calculatory reason in capitalism, but against the principle of rationality as such. Instead of a Marxian critique of the political economy of capitalism and of the social causes of alienation, there was a critique of culture and of the forms of consciousness. The problems of the depersonalization of man in existentialism and the great refusal of the Frankfurt School, with its negative dialectic, were characteristic reflections of the great cataclysms of the twentieth century; - with its two world wars, with its revelry of fascist barbarism in enlightened Europe, and with its menace to human destiny in an age of scientific-technological revolution.

All these central problems of our era are also in the center of Lukács' philosophy. He finds different answers at various stages in his development. In *History and Class Consciousness* many of them are solved in a Hegelian spirit that is not Marxist and which makes the book attractive. It was French existentialists who were most interested by this book in the 1950s. In 1952 Lucien Goldman cited this book in connection with the problem of social determinism. According to Goldman, already in *The Soul and its Form* Lukács had established the basic premisses of contemporary existentialism, and *History and Class Consciousness* represents the solution of all problems presented in the latest development of philosophy.

The interest in Lukács was in large part caused by emphasis on the problem of alienation which, as in Hegel, is treated as identical with objectivity as such. As of the publication in 1927 of Heidegger's *Being and Time*, the problem of alienation was central to existentialism. For Goldman, Heidegger's book is a polemic coming out of *History and Class Consciousness*. Heidegger retreats from the identification of being and consciousness in classical philosophy, and Goldman sees this as founding his opposition to Lukács.

Merleau-Ponty, too, in his *Adventures of the Dialectic* frequently cites this book by Lukács. Sartre's *Critique of Dialectical Reason* tries to rethink the Marxist conception of social-historical practice along the lines of *History and Class Consciousness*, in the sense that the material world stands over against man as something foreign and inimical to him, and in a Kierkegaardian critique of Hegel. The young Lukács' interpretation of Hegel is very attractive on this plane; his *History and Class Consciousness* is even cited as a Bible of French existentialism. The existentialist interpreters of Marx, who were not rare in the 1950s, followed Lukács in identifying alienation and objectification in Marx, claiming that Marx took *sans autre* the notion of alienation from Hegel and that he accepted the Hegelian account of objectification and alienation without substantial modifications.

A new wave of interest in Lukács' book could be observed in the 1960s in conjunction with the spread of the ideas of the Frankfurt School and the influence of the "New Left". The representatives of the Frankfurt School, of course, seldom if ever cite *History and Class Consciousness*; but the connection of their ideas with those of Lukács is generally accepted today. A series of propositions of the young Lukács appear in their critique of positivism, fetishism and especially of capitalist rationalization, where they both follow Weber. This last notion appears in *History and Class Consciousness* in conjunction with Marx' treatment of commodity fetishism. In the thinkers of the Frankfurt School, the critique of fetishism turns into a critical attitude toward technology, science and bureaucracy as such. Rationalism appears outside of all social conditioning, and is treated as a calculus, as the rule of reified consciousness, promoting an uncritical perception of the world. The basic opposition to the Frankfurt School thinkers comes from materiality. Through its "negative dialectic" the Frankfurt School tries to present itself as an extension of the Hegelian dialectic and of the Hegelian interpretation of the Marxian dialectic. Oskar Negt asserts that the vivacity of the Hegelian dialectic in Marxism is connected with the phases of the renewal and of the accumulation of experience, which undergoes ups and downs.

Lukács, the Frankfurt School thinkers, and Lenin, all try to renew Marxism and all begin with the critical content of the dialectic. Therefore, the opposition of the left intellectuals within Marxism - as represented by the young Lukács and, in a certain sense, by Adorno - proceeds from an actualization of the philosophy of Hegel.

It is known that the "New Left" that spread rapidly in the 1960s drew many of its ideas from the social philosophy of the Frankfurt School. The New Left's basic position involved a global refusal of capitalist society, and a total negation of all that is produced by capitalism. Proclaiming the need to revolutionize consciousness, it stressed the moral - abstractly considered - aspects of the fight against the old society. A voluntaristic cast was given to the problem of class consciousness by the assumption that any path can be taken to revolutionary victory and to the awakening of class consciousness. In fact, revolution itself is seen as the awakening of "new consciousness", *i.e.*, the full break with all structures of the past. All these ideas are similar to those of Lukács in the 1920s when he spoke of a total negation of capitalism and the transformation of the moral essence of man. This is why we can read in a review of a West German reprint of Lukács' early works: "The New Left can find a lot in the early works of Lukács. Capitalism is condemned with a Messianic intensity, some times approaching the demonic..." and, further, "...in the general character of the old and new efforts and aporiae is included a serious possibility that new radical left intellectuals find in *History and Class Consciousness* of Lukács their Holy Scripture... ". (T. Hanak, 'Georg Lukács *Geschichte und Klassenbewusstsein. Werke.* Bd.4', *Zeitschrift für philosophische Forschung,* München, Bd.28, Heft 1, Jan-Mar 1971. S.145)

Thus, the views of the young Lukács and his *History and Class Consciousness* were widely used by certain trends of bourgeois philosophy of those years. At the base of this influence, along with profound conceptual causes, one finds purely pragmatic aspects of a political character. There was a constant effort to turn Lukács and his work against Marxism-Leninism and to make of it a standard of so-called "Western Marxism". But, Lukács' ideas were often thereby distorted to make them conform to other doctrines. Most frequently, this happened along existentialist anthropological lines. As concerns the 1960s, one can say that *History and Class Consciousness* served not only as the

Bible of existentialism and Sacred Scripture for the New Left, but also
as the Bible of a revisionism that was trying to use the early Lukács to
re-examine a series of basic principles of Marxist philosophy and to see
this work as an "authentic" heir to Marx.

But, as of the middle of the 1970s, things changed relative to
Lukács - especially as regarded former members of the New Left. This
change was not accidental and is bound up with the reorientation of
bourgeois consciousness over the past decade. As this consciousness
turned neo-conservative, its relationship to Marxism also changed.
While, earlier, the New Left followed the Frankfurt School in seeking
and in finding in Lukács compatible elements in the form of a radical
critique of capitalism and a "victim for Communism", at the beginning
of the 1970s this began to change as several books appeared trying to
explain the collapse of the New Left. For example, in his *Lukács,
Bourgeois and Revolutionary. 1918-1928* (Cologne, 1978), Anton
Grünberg says that his title indicates just the paradox of Lukács, *i.e.*
that throughout his life he was unable to extricate his 'revolutionary
concern' from his idealistic philosophy. The book constitutes a critical
examination of Lukács' work and correctly assesses the influences on
him of Hegel, Weber and other bourgeois philosophers. This author
goes on to show that Lukács is mystical in his understanding of the
class consciousness of the proletariat, and that he was too bourgeois to
be a source for "leftists" and too dogmatic to be acceptable for
Marxism.

Such reassessments of Lukács continued into the later 1970s.
While Vranicki rather positively rated Lukács in his *History of
Marxism*, in Kołakowski's *Main Currents of Marxism* (Vol. III, Ch.
VII, pp. 253-307) Lukács fares rather badly for "...from the beginning
of his Marxist career and to the end of his life, Lukács proclaimed his
fidelity to Lenin and to Leninism...". Kołakowski goes on to say that
the category of totality comes to represent in Lukács a "typical
Communist defiance of facts and Lukács takes this defiance of the facts
to a high conceptual level in the name of systematic thought. One can
consider him to be an eminent interpreter of Marx but one who endows
Marxism with an irrational and anti-scientific character" who "despite
his inclinations, reveals the mythological, prophetic and utopian sense
of Marxism...".

Speaking about Lukács' account of the class consciousness of the
proletariat, Kołakowski asserts that he only appears at first glance to
adhere to the views of Rosa Luxemburg, while "throughout all of his
writings, beginning in 1919, there is no doubt that he held a Leninist
view of the Party and his whole theory of class consciousness served to
bolster this view".

Retreating from Marxism, Kołakowski does not find acceptable even Lukács' variant of Marxism. Assessing Lukács, he writes: "His dogmatism was absolute, and almost sublime in its perfection. ... Lukács is perhaps the most striking example in the twentieth century of what may be called the betrayal of reason by those whose profession is to use and defend it." (L. Kołakowski, *op. cit.*, Vol.III, p.307)

We have reported this extreme viewpoint in order to show the change in assessment of Lukács and *History and Class Consciousness*, due to the reorientation of bourgeois thought in the past decade. The spread of neo-conservatism - with its negative stance toward any revolutionary transformation and its rigid rejection of Marxism, and its rationalistic line in philosophy - could not fail to be reflected in changing assessments of Lukács in general and of *History and Class Consciousness* in particular.

The fact of the matter is that the Lukács of an earlier period did not attract much interest on the part of bourgeois philosophy. In the 1930s and later, Lukács was known as a Marxist philosopher; as such, he could not find a place within bourgeois philosophy. All of Lukács' more recent works were directed against twentieth-century bourgeois philosophy. From his *Young Hegel* with its opposition to neo-Hegelianism and its effort to show the young Hegel to be theological, to the *Destruction of Reason* (1954), with a critique of all irrationalist trends in bourgeois philosophy, or to even later works like the *Esthetics* or the *Ontology*, the solutions to basic philosophic problems are always presented in the form of a confrontation with bourgeois philosophy. This does not mean that bourgeois philosophy was not influenced by these works of Lukács - but this influence was not apparent and not admitted. There is no doubt that the *Young Hegel* constituted a sort of revolution in writing about Hegel. After the appearance of Lukács' book, a flood of works appeared in the West, looking at Hegel on such themes as "labor", "alienation", "bourgeois society", *etc.* At the same time, the bourgeois authors of these studies tried to remain aloof from Lukács, accusing him of bias and his Marxist analysis of Hegel of tendentiousness. They could not cope with the thought that Lukács does not interpret Hegel as an apologist of capitalist society, but as one with views closely allied to the revolutionary traditions of the French Revolution. The same sharp critique was applied to Lukács' own *Destruction of Reason*. This work is sometimes described as an illustration of the serious "collapse" of Lukács, where no account is taken of the fact that Lukács is analyzing the very class consciousness of the bourgeoisie that led to fascism.

The most vicious attacks are aimed at Lukács' defense of the Leninist theory of reflection. Lucien Goldman has disassociated himself from Lukács' works of 1930-1950. Adorno sharply criticizes Lukács' acceptance of the theory of reflection, and writes about the "neo-naïveté" of Lukács who insists, in his words, on an "outmoded" theory of reflection.

Lukács' works of 1960-1970 - his *Esthetics* and *Ontology* - are in fact not often studied in contemporary Western philosophy. The past decade has seen a spread of interest in Lukács that is more extensive than intensive; *i.e.*, he is being published in more and more countries, and being criticised in more parts of the world. Along with these works that have been recently appearing on Lukács, there is a sort of snobbish "prospecting" which inundates the reader with a flood of details that hides the true image of Lukács, the revolutionary thinker, as well as the essence of what he created.

One has to regret that on the contemporary philosophic scene the Marxist creativity of Georg Lukács is not being sufficiently investigated. As many of the circumstances that complicate an understanding of Lukács disappear and as Western philosophy changes its attitude toward him, there is an even greater need for a thorough analysis of the works of Lukács as a Marxist philosopher.

Translated from the Russian
  by Thomas J. Blakeley
    (Boston College)

PART II

THEMES IN *HISTORY AND CLASS CONSCIOUSNESS*

J. LARRAIN

Lukács' Concept of Ideology

I. INTRODUCTION

A discussion of Lukács' understanding and use of the concept of ideology cannot be properly attempted without situating it in the wider context of the evolution of this concept within Marxist theory. For although it may seem strange to those who believe that Marxism is a monolithic theory, the concept of ideology changed from the critical account Marx had conceived to the neutral version propounded by Lenin. Still, the most common error of many Marxist analyses of the concept of ideology is the failure to recognize this historical change - often coupled with a rather dogmatic attempt to prove that there is only one correct interpretation of ideology within Marxism - which leads either to dismissing one of the two versions as mistaken or to trying to reconcile and fuse them into one.[1] The main reason for the recurrence of this error is the tendency of Marxist official orthodoxy to avoid any important cleavage between Marx and Lenin. There is little doubt, though, that these two conceptions of ideology are historically successive and theoretically incompatible.[2]

In its inception, the concept of ideology was defined by Marx in a negative, or critical, fashion and meant a distorted kind of consciousness, which conceals contradictions in the interest of the ruling class. It is very important to realize that Marx, who did not equate ideology with false consciousness in general, or with a simple cognitive error, specified the kind of distortion he was referring to by relating it to certain social contradictions, whose reproduction guarantees the domination of the ruling class. In the case of the contradiction between capital and labor, Marx affirmed that "the private property-owner is ... the *conservative* side, the proletarian, the *destructive* side. From the former arises the action of preserving the antithesis, from the latter the action of annihilating it."[3] By masking this contradiction, ideology facilitates its reproduction, thus serving the interests of the ruling class. Marx provided a good example of the way in which ideology operates when he analysed the position of the French journal *La Réforme* in 1848. The journal tried to remind the proletariat and the bourgeoisie of their common struggle against feudalism and invoked their patriotic and national sentiments. Marx criticised this attempt to mask their antagonistic interests as ideological: "the *Réforme* knows no better way

52

T. Rockmore (ed.), Lukács Today, 52–69.
© *1988 by D. Reidel Publishing Company.*

of changing and abolishing these contradictions than to disregard their real basis, that is, these very material conditions, and to withdraw into the hazy blue heaven of republican ideology".[4]

The critical concept of ideology did not survive for long within the Marxist tradition after Marx' death. A number of factors contributed to the change in the meaning of the concept. On the one hand, through Engels' late struggle against economistic interpretations of the base-superstructure model[5], a tendency emerged to equate ideology with the 'forms of social consciousness' or simply with the so-called 'ideological superstructure'. Instead of a specific kind of false consciousness, ideology became an objective level of society, capable of some efficacy of its own, but ultimately determined by the economic structure. Its negative character assumed a secondary role and was progressively left aside after Engels' death. This change was facilitated, on the other hand, by the fact that *The German Ideology*, the most forceful exposition of a critical concept of ideology, was not published in its entirety until the mid-twenties, and hence the first generation of Marxist theoreticians did not have easy access to it.[6] It is not surprising, therefore, that their acquaintance with, and commitment to, Marx' critical concept of ideology was less than perfect.

In the writings of Mehring, Kautsky and Plekhanov one can see an increasing use of the concept of ideology to refer to ideas, moral ideals, mental processes and states of mind of an age without any necessary negative connotation. Plekhanov even distinguishes an ideology of the low kind from an ideology of the high sort, in which he includes science, philosophy and the arts.[7] Yet up until 1898 none of these authors openly refers to Marxism as an ideology. The first to do that is Bernstein. He too identified ideology with ideas and ideals but he went further and drew the obvious conclusion that, therefore, Marxism is also an ideology.[8] Although Bernstein was at this time under criticism for his revision of Marxism, no one of his critics, including Plekhanov and Lenin, took issue with him for calling Marxism an ideology. This clearly shows that the first generation of Marxists was not fully aware of the critical character that Marx had bestowed on the concept of ideology. For Marx would have never called, and in fact did not ever call, his own theory an ideology.

Still, the most crucial element in this process of change was Lenin's contribution. In so far as he needed theoretically to account for the mounting struggle between the political ideas of various classes in Russian society before the revolution, he found in the concept of ideology a useful tool to express the connection between certain class interests and the political ideas which purport to serve them. In describing the highly polarised political struggle, Lenin contended that "the *only* choice is - either bourgeois or socialist ideology. There is no middle course (for mankind has not created a 'third' ideology, and, moreover, in a society torn by class antagonisms there can never be a non-class or an above-class ideology)."[9] It was Lenin who finally gave intellectual currency to the new concept of ideology. With him the concept of ideology definitely lost its negative character and became neutral as a means to express the political doctrines and ideas of all classes in struggle. If a particular ideology is erroneous, this is not due to its being an ideology, but to the character of the class interests represented by it. The concept of ideology, of itself, no longer entails the passing of a negative epistemological judgement: socialist ideology is supposed to be true, while bourgeois ideology is deemed to be false; but both are equally ideological insofar as they represent the interests of the two major classes in struggle.

II. LUKÁCS AND LENIN

The vast influence of Lenin upon the subsequent Marxist movement determined that his concept of ideology played a crucial role in shaping practically all the new contributions to the debate on ideology. From Gramsci to Althusser, there is hardly any serious attempt to recuperate Marx' original critical concept of ideology. It is my contention that although Lukács' general contribution to Marxism is highly original, he did not go much further than Lenin in respect to the conceptual definition of ideology. What is new in Lukács' account is that the role of ideology in a revolutionary process acquires a much larger significance than it ever had for Lenin. This is partly the result of the influence of German historicism as developed in Heidelberg, particularly by Dilthey, which also had a profound impact upon Lukács' early writings. Yet whereas in several respects Lukács later overcame the historicist influence, the Leninist ascendancy grew stronger.

A case in point is Lukács' attitude *vis-à-vis* Engels' theory of reflection. In the 1920s Lukács was strongly critical of Engels' formulations because they "may easily give rise to misunderstandings" and "in the theory of 'reflection' we find the theoretical embodiment of the duality of thought and existence, consciousness and reality, that is so intractable to the reified consciousness".[10] In 1945, on the contrary, Lukács asserted that "it is a fundamental thesis of dialectical materialism that any apperception of the external world is nothing but the reflection of a reality existing independently of consciousness, in the thoughts, conceptions, perceptions, *etc.*, of men"[11], and, explicitly invoking Lenin, propounded a dialectical understanding of the theory of reflection. This is only one of the many instances in which Lukács altered his early views in order to conform to the official Marxist-Leninist orthodoxy. Nevertheless, it is hardly possible to overrate the extent of the Leninist influence upon Lukács' early writings.

It can be argued that in many respects *History and Class Consciousness* is a brilliant philosophical commentary on, and justification of, *What is to be done?* The similarities are easy to see. The most important similarity has to do with Lenin's distinction between the spontaneous consciousness of the working class which is limited and expresses itself in trade unionism, and the 'social-democratic' political consciousness, or a theoretical and scientific form of consciousness developed by intellectuals outside the working class. The latter is the socialist ideology whereas the former "leads to its becoming sub-ordinated to the bourgeois ideology".[12] According to Lenin "class political consciousness can be brought to the workers *only from without*", for "the history of all countries shows that the working class, exclusively by its own effort, is able to develop only trade-union consciousness".[13] Lukács proposed a similar distinction between the 'psychological class consciousness' and the 'ascribed class consciousness' of the proletariat. The former entails "the psychologically describable and explicable ideas which men form about their situation in life" and the latter refers to "the appropriate and rational reactions 'imputed' to a particular typical position in the process of production".[14] That in drawing this distinction he wanted to follow Lenin is explicitly confirmed by Lukács in his 1967 preface to *History and Class Consciousness*.[15]

Although the connection may seem plain enough from the point of view of a theory of class consciousness, different emphases are noticeable when one relates these distinctions to the concepts of ideology and science. Whereas Lenin tends to identify socialist ideology with theory or science, Lukács tends to identify theory and ideology with class consciousness. For Lenin socialist ideology is not a form of class consciousness although it is necessary to raise the level of consciousness of the working class. Lukács, on the contrary, indistinctly refers in the same context to the important role of class consciousness and to the 'power of a true or false theory' when the crisis of capitalism approaches[16], thus giving to understand that the ideology of the proletariat can be identified with its consciousness.

This has led many orthodox Marxists to underline the differences, rather than the similarities, between Lenin and Lukács. Stedman Jones, for instance, has argued that Lukács mistakenly collapses science into consciousness, whereas Lenin allows for their respective autonomy.[17] Schaff, in his turn, accuses Lukács of neglecting the psychological class consciousness of the proletariat and of equating class consciousness with class ideology, thus underrating the class' real state of consciousness.[18] Although it is true that some of Lukács' texts induce a confusion between ideology and class consciousness, and seem to neglect the empirical consciousness of the proletariat, it can also be argued that Lukács' frequent references to the Party as the true agent capable of disseminating consciousness through a dialectical interaction with the working class show his Leninist mettle clearly enough.[19]

Be this as it may, there is little doubt that Lukács' definition and use of the concept of ideology closely follow Lenin's understanding of it. This one can see throughout Lukács' intellectual development, from his early essays to his ontology. In order to show this consistent usage of the concept, I shall select writings from three separate periods: the early essays on history and class consciousness written in the 1920s, a preface to the aesthetic writings of Marx and Engels written in 1945, and a paper on the ontological foundations of human action prepared for the Congress of Philosophy held in Vienna in 1968.

III. THE TEXTUAL EVIDENCE

Even a cursory survey of Lukács' early essays immediately reveals a neutral use of the terms "ideology" and "ideological". They are equally applied to the bourgeoisie and to the proletariat without implying any necessary negative connotation. Thus Lukács can say that "*the fate of the revolution (and with it the fate of mankind) will depend on the ideological maturity of the proletariat*" and that "'ideology' for the proletariat is no banner to follow into battle, nor is it a cover for its true objectives: it is the objective and the weapon itself".[20] Even more, Marxism appears as "the ideological expression of the proletariat in its efforts to liberate itself"[21] and historical materialism is said to be "the ideology of the embattled proletariat".[22]

By contrast, bourgeois ideology has been progressively undermined and the faith in its mission to save the world has been destroyed[23], thus leading to bourgeois "ideological capitulation to historical materialism".[24] Whereas bourgeois ideology conceals the true situation, historical materialism unmasks capitalist society. Still, "the ideological defeat of capitalism" will not be easy to achieve "in view of the great distance that the proletariat has to travel ideologically"[25] and the existence of "an ideological crisis within the proletariat".[26] In addition to bourgeois and proletarian ideologies, there is also an "ideology of the broad masses, of the petty bourgeoisie"[27] which puts its faith in the general character of the state and in authority. In short, there is abundant evidence that in his early essays Lukács conceived of ideologies as the theoretical and political expressions of the interests of the various classes in struggle in capitalist society, just as Lenin did.

These ideas are confirmed by subsequent writings. Reflecting on Marxist aesthetics in 1945, Lukács refers equally to "the ideologies, including literature and art"[28] and to the "ideology of the proletariat" and maintains that "the working-class ideology and culture to be created, are the heir to all mankind has produced of value over the millenia".[29] Paraphrasing Lenin, he contends that the superiority of Marxism to bourgeois ideology lies in its ability critically to incorporate the cultural heritage of the past. Similarly, in his Vienna paper of 1968 Lukács points out that the foundation of what Marxism calls "ideology" is the series of teleological propositions with which human beings consciously anticipate the results of their work in class divided societies. Just as Gramsci frequently referred to Marx' 1859 Preface in order to justify his conception of ideology as the objective terrain on which human beings acquire consciousness of their position and struggles, so Lukács holds that "ideology provides the forms in which men become conscious of these conflicts and fight them out".[30] Furthermore, he seems to echo Plekhanov's distinction between high ideology and low ideology when he avers that "most ideologies have served ... the preservation ... of a *genus*-in-itself ...; only great philosophy and great art ... help to realize this (higher) kind of *genus*-for-itself".[31] In none of these writings which span over fifty years, is there an indication of Lukács' determination to confine the concept of ideology to the idea of false consciousness.

It is therefore surprising that most accounts of Lukács' concept of ideology seem to be unaware of this fact, and persistently present his conception as if it were firmly based on the notion of false consciousness.[32] This misunderstanding is so remarkably widespread that it affects equally structuralist and historicist, Marxist and non-Marxist, sympathetic and antipathetic interpretations of Lukács. Let us take for instance Goldman's historicist account. In analysing Lukács' early essays on class consciousness, he maintains that "the falsity or truth of consciousness, its ideological or non-ideological character, are determined by its relationship with production relations".[33] This proposition explicitly assumes that Lukács understands the relationship between ideological and non-ideological consciousness as a relationship between truth and error. Thus Goldman can assert that according to Lukács "the ideological element of these various types of consciousness con- sists in the misrecognition of the economic relation" and that "the political revolution of the proletariat could not happen ... without a

non-ideological consciousness, without a perfectly true consciousness".[34] Goldmann consistently presupposes that the early Lukács
uses a critical concept of ideology.

At the opposite extreme, Poulantzas' structuralist critique of Lukács
equally assumes that Lukács identifies ideology with false consciousness and alienation "and results in an inadequate theoretical
status being granted to ideologies: these are considered as the 'products'
of consciousness ... or of freedom ... alienated from the subject".[35]
Still, with typical Althusserian ambiguity, Poulantzas can claim further
on that because ideology fixes an imaginary relation it "is therefore
necessarily false; its social function is not to give agents a *true knowledge* of the social structure but simply to insert them as it were into
their practical activities supporting this structure".[36] So Poulantzas,
too, seems to hold a kind of negative concept of ideology; the
difference is that instead of being a product of consciousness, it is a
product of the structure which makes the social whole opaque to the
agents. However adequate the critique of 'false consciousness' may be,
Poulantzas fails to see that this is not the concept of ideology with
which Lukács works.

It is not surprising, therefore, that many other authors and commentaries should fall into the same mistake. Thus Adlam and col-
laborators maintain that "the central tenet of his [Lukács'] work is that
ideology is false consciousness, a distorting veil that hangs over the
eyes of men ... an illusion".[37] McDonough entitles her article
'Ideology as False Consciousness: Lukács'. Yet when dealing with
Lukács' notion of ideology, she asserts that "each class-subject possesses a conception of the world in which it lives and this dominates the
historical epoch in which it rules".[38] She never explains in which sense
the proletarian ideology is for Lukács a kind of false consciousness.

Seliger, in his turn, in a highly unsympathetic review of the Marxist
theory of ideology, maintains that "having used 'ideology' most of the
time in the pejorative sense established by the founders, Lukács was
inconsistent in taking it occasionally in a positive sense, as Bernstein
and particularly Lenin had been doing".[39] Despite his anti-Marxist
bias, Seliger proves to be more perceptive than many Marxists in that
he is at least able to find in Lukács a neutral use of the concept of
ideology. But he fails to see that this use is more than 'occasional'. His
problem is, as with many other commentators, that he mistakes the
critique of bourgeois ideology for the negative character of the concept
of ideology. Lukács is not inconsistent in this respect. He criticises
bourgeois ideology as false consciousness, not because it is an
ideology, but because of the inevitably limited character of bourgeois
interests. A neutral concept of ideology is perfectly compatible with the

critique of bourgeois ideology, as Lenin abundantly showed. Hence, the accusation of inconsistency is misplaced, and can only be sustained by misunderstanding the scope which Lukács confers on the notion of false consciousness.

Let us examine some passages, where Lukács refers to false consciousness with a degree of generality which may suggest that my analysis is flawed. In describing the "present acute crisis in capitalism" he argues that capitalism has become so weak that it could not survive "if the proletariat were to oppose it consciously and resolutely. Only ideology stands in the way of such opposition"[40], thus suggesting that important sections of the proletarian masses are still deceived by false consciousness, especially the belief in the unchangeability of the state and the law. Ideology in general seems to assume a negative character. In another passage Lukács holds that "in the class struggles of the past the most varied ideologies, religious, moral and the other forms of 'false consciousness' were decisive".[41] Again, ideology seems to be equated with false consciousness in general. Finally, in the best known passage Lukács claims that "men perform their historical deeds themselves and that they do so consciously. But, as Engels emphasises in a letter to Mehring, this consciousness is false."[42] The argument in favor of understanding ideology as false consciousness is provided by the fact that Engels' reference to false consciousness comes in the context of an attempt to define ideology in general.[43]

Despite a first impression, which seems to support a conception of ideology as false consciousness, a careful analysis of these passages clearly shows a different picture. Once the context is taken into account, it is possible to realize that Lukács is trying to contrast a specific form of consciousness, the genuine class consciousness of the proletariat, to other ideological forms of the past and of the bourgeoisie. When Lukács says in the first passage that "only ideology stands in the way" of a proletarian conscious opposition to capitalism, he refers to bourgeois ideology, not to ideology in general. What, if not bourgeois ideology, is the belief that the established state, the laws and the economy are the only possible environment for the working class to exist? This is why Lukács argues that the revolution requires people "who have become intellectually and emotionally emancipated from the existing system"; and in this precise context he speaks of Marxism not only as the "doctrine of revolution", but also as "the ideological expression of the proletariat in its efforts to liberate itself".[44]

The factor that determines whether an ideology is false consciousness, or true consciousness, is the structural position of the class whose interests that ideology serves. Lukács is quite explicit in explaining the cause of the falsity of bourgeois class consciousness: "the barrier which converts the class consciousness of the bourgeoisie into 'false' consciousness is objective: it is the class situation itself".[45] Conversely, the ascribed consciousness of the proletariat is true because, by virtue of its privileged historical position, the proletariat can understand the 'true driving forces' of history.

So it should be evident that the third passage mentioned above is not meant to be a general definition of ideology. On the contrary, in the same context Lukács argues that one should investigate false consciousness "concretely as an aspect of the historical totality and as a stage in the historical process".[46] It is certainly possible that this false consciousness can affect the empirically given consciousness of the proletariat, but it cannot affect its ascribed consciousness, the socialist ideology. The same idea underlies the second passage. Past ideologies are described as forms of false consciousness; but they are contrasted with the class struggle of the proletariat, which "obtains its sharpest weapon from the hand of true science, from its clear insight into reality".[47] It is therefore quite clear that Lukács uses a neutral concept of ideology and that his conception of false consciousness applies to particular class ideologies other than the proletarian ideology.

IV. THE CRITIQUE OF LUKÁCS

As I have already advanced, the continuity between Lenin and Lukács has been challenged by structuralist and orthodox Marxists. Apart from the widespread misunderstanding about the extension which Lukács concedes to the notion of false consciousness, and the confusion this induces in the concept of ideology, critics such as Stedman Jones, Poulantzas, McDonough and Schaff contend that Lukács' theory fails on three counts. First, it has the weakness of 'historicism', that is to say, it is supposed both to relativize the validity of general theoretical propositions to particular historical conditions and to reduce the complexity of the social whole to a simple, uniform essence. McDonough, closely paraphrasing Stedman Jones, contends that for Lukács "Marx's thesis that the dominant ideology in any society is the ideology of the ruling class is interpreted as the saturation of the social whole by the ideological essence of a pure class-subject, which in turn is depicted as a pure reflection of the conditions of life and world conceptions of that class."[48] The relationship between the class subject and its ideology is represented in genetic terms, and this is supposed to obscure the fact that the ruling ideology reflects a political relation between classes. As Poulantzas puts it, such a conception understands ideologies as if they were "number-plates carried on the backs of class subjects" and cannot "establish the existence within the dominant ideology of elements belonging to the ideologies of classes other than the politically dominant class".[49] This is contrasted to Lenin's more complex account of the relationship between ideologies and classes.

Second, Lukács would have disregarded the importance of the bourgeois institutional apparatus as the main support of bourgeois ideological domination. In Stedman Jones' view, "Lukács's whole account of bourgeois ideological domination is reduced to the invisible emanations of reification from commodities ... What is strikingly and completely missing in Lukács's account is, of course, the whole institutional superstructure of bourgeois class power: parties, reformist trade unions, newspapers, schools, churches, families are scarcely mentioned."[50] This is contrasted to Lenin's analysis of the massive superiority of cultural and material means enjoyed by the bourgeoisie.

Third, it is alleged that Lukács "diminished the role of working class consciousness such as it was empirically given within concrete and immediate conditions, to the point of almost totally ignoring it, thus displacing all the importance to the conscious expression of class interests".[51] Even more, as each ideology is genetically linked to a subject-class, "it is impossible to see the effects of ideological domination by the dominant ideology on working-class ideology".[52] Because Lukács has identified class consciousness with class ideology his theory would be unable to explain the ideological contamination of the spontaneous working-class class consciousness. The emphasis on the possession of a scientific ideology would have led to disregarding the question of its introjection in the consciousness of the masses, and consequently the spontaneous consciousness of the working class was assumed to have the key to Marxist science. This would be the source of voluntarist, spontaneist and sectarian trends within the working class movement, which Lenin combated in *What is to be done?*

The charge of historicism against Lukács' conception must be taken with caution, not because I want to deny historicist influences upon his theory, but because sometimes, as Arato and Breines have argued, Lukács' thought is reduced to one, or several, of its intellectual progenitors.[53] Poulantzas, for instance, finds a 'direct filiation' between Lukács and Weber's historicism. But, as McCarney points out, his critique moves "untroubled by any specific reference to Lukács's writings".[54] Nevertheless, it seems to me that there is an element of truth in the contention that Lukács relativizes the validity of general theoretical propositions. He treats historical materialism as a theory of bourgeois society in the first instance, and finds a 'weighty methodological difficulty' in bringing historical materialism to bear upon pre-capitalist periods. This difficulty lies in "the *structural* difference between the age of civilization and the epochs that preceded it" which arises from the fact, observed by Marx, that "in all forms of society where landed property predominates the natural relation is paramount. In those where capital is predominant the social, historically created element prevails."[55] What he does not seem to realize, though, is the fact that this structural difference is itself a general theoretical proposition of historical materialism.

However, the accusation that Lukács reduces the complexity of the social totality to a simple essence seems to me far more difficult to substantiate, and in fact neither Poulantzas nor Stedman Jones provides convincing evidence to support his case. The charge that ideology is for Lukács a pure reflection of the conditions of the life of a class, without reference to the wider social situation - as if a class existed in a social vacuum - is groundless. Both the ruling ideology and the proletarian ideology reflect a political relation between classes in Lukács' account. What is more, in the construction of their attack on Lukács, both Stedman Jones and McDonough make the basic mistake of referring to Marx' famous quotation in *The German Ideology* as if it said that the ruling ideology in any society is the ideology of the ruling class. In fact, the passage in question refers to the ruling ideas, and not to the ruling ideology. A distinction between ideology and ideas is obviously crucial for anyone who understands Marx' theory of ideology.

Moreover, it is a misunderstanding to argue that for Lukács ideologies are seen "as number-plates carried on the backs of class-subjects" - as Poulantzas contends - if by this characterization is implied that there is a genetic relationship between the class and its ideology. The critics seem to forget that Lukács introduces the distinction between class ideology, or ascribed consciousness, and class psychological consciousness. This means that for Lukács the form of consciousness a class has spontaneously developed is not its real ideology and can frequently be at variance with it. So the relationship between a class and its ideology is not conceived in genetic terms.

Consequently, one can hardly accuse Lukács of spontaneism, and of not considering ideological contamination. How could he speak of "the power wielded by such ideologies [non-proletarian] *within* the proletariat itself" and of nationalist ideologies which "still survive ... not only in the stratum of the petty bourgeoisie... but in the proletariat itself" and of the fact that "victory does not free the proletariat from contamination by capitalist and nationalist ideologies"[56], if he did not consider ideological contamination? What sense would there be in talking of the "ideological crisis" of the proletariat, if Lukács did not take into account the ideological impurities which contaminate its empirical consciousness? Lukács is fully aware that "the class consciousness of the proletariat does not develop uniformly throughout the whole proletariat", that "large sections of the proletariat remain intellectually under the tutelage of the bourgeoisie", and that "even in the very midst of the death throes of capitalism, broad sections of the proletarian masses still feel that the state, the laws and the economy of the bourgeoisie are the only possible environment for them to exist in".[57]

Lukács' analyses of opportunism and utopianism, as the main problems of proletarian consciousness, bear witness to the same central concern. Indeed, as McCarney has put it: "not only is Lukács able to acknowledge and theorise the phenomenon of ideological contamination, but it has in truth a central place in his view of the historical process".[58] Of course, Lukács would deny that the ascribed consciousness, the socialist ideology, is contaminated by bourgeois ideology; and so would Lenin.[59] But this does not apply to the empirical consciousness of the proletariat which is for both authors the battlefield of the ideological struggle. However, it is true to say that Lukács' account of bourgeois ideological domination over the working class differs from, although it is by no means inferior to, Lenin's account.

In Lenin's version, the ideological subordination of the spontaneous working-class consciousness to bourgeois ideology was explained in terms of bourgeois ideology being older, more resourceful and having more opportunities for being spread than socialist ideology.[60] Lukács, on the contrary, underlines the inhumanity and reification produced by the capitalist mode of production, which profoundly affects the proletariat's mode of existence and consequently its consciousness. The appearances fostered by market relations conceal the real relations and thus "the structure of reification progressively sinks more deeply ... into the consciousness of man".[61] So, whereas Lenin emphasizes the fact that the bourgeoisie possesses more powerful means of disseminating and transmitting ideas, Lukács stresses the idea that it is the very situation of the proletariat that induces its ideological subordination. In other terms, the proletariat does not need to be indoctrinated with bourgeois ideas through the educational system, media, *etc.*, but it itself, given its structural situation, spontaneously produces reified ideas.

Of course, Lukács' analysis does not deny the importance of bourgeois ideology being older and more fully developed than the socialist ideology; nor does it deny the fact that the bourgeoisie owns most of the means of intellectual production and dissemination of ideas. Perhaps, he could have paid more attention to these aspects of ideological domination. Yet his emphasis on reification and the situation of the proletariat within the capitalist system goes not only somewhat deeper than Lenin's explanation; it also has the merit of rediscovering the importance of Marx' *Capital* for the study of ideology. It is ironic that in this Lukács should anticipate the efforts of structuralist authors such as Althusser, Poulantzas, Godelier and Mepham[62], who, on the whole, have nothing but contempt for his conception.

However, Lukács' theory of ideology is not to be exempted from criticism. Lukács' emphasis on the structural situation of a class as the crucial factor which determines not only the objective possibility of its ascribed consciousness, but also the degree of ideological purity of its empirical consciousness, tends to neglect the determining role of the concrete class political practice. Lukács accentuates so much the role of the ascribed consciousness that it appears as a substitute for the political activities of the class. This means that Lukács consistently overrates the role of ideology and ideological struggle in the revolutionary process. In effect this is a charge of idealism which Lukács himself accepts in the 1967 preface to *History and Class Consciousness* : "what I failed to realise, however, was that in the absence of a basis in real praxis, in labour as its original form and model, the over-extension of the concept of praxis would lead to its opposite: a relapse into idealistic contemplation".[63]

The absence of a basis in real praxis is interpreted by Lukács as neglect of labor. It may be true that labor is the original form and model of praxis; but without further clarification, this formulation risks reducing praxis to labor and probably shows the impact of the official Marxist orthodoxy on the later Lukács.[64] Alternatively, the absence of a basis in real praxis can be interpreted in a wider sense as the unconscious neglect of the empirical political practice and consciousness of the proletariat, because it lags behind the political practice and official ideology of the Party. Although this second interpretation is not Lukács', it seems to me that it is a more adequate explanation of his overrating of ideology.

The consequences of this are abundantly shown in his early essays. It is not political practice that changes the world, but rather *"only the practical class consciousness of the proletariat* possesses this ability to transform things". This is why Lukács can say that proletarian thought gradually transforms itself "into a practical theory that overturns the real world"[65] and that *"the strength of every society is in the last resort a spiritual strength"* from which "we can only be liberated by knowledge".[66] If Marxism is revolutionary it is because "it understands" the process or "demonstrates" the line of future development. Consciousness seems to possess the ability to produce practical effects on its own. Thus "when the worker knows himself as a commodity his knowledge is practical. *That is to say, this knowledge brings about an objective structural change in the object of knowledge*".[67] It is no wonder, therefore, that Lukács should add that the "reform of consciousness is the revolutionary process itself".[68]

Thus the impression one gets is that consciousness and ideology for Lukács have gained an enormous degree of autonomy and a crucial role in the revolutionary process. This can be taken to be a result of his early reaction against the reductionist tendencies of a mechanistic form of Marxism. Yet the consequences of this effort are ambiguous. On the one hand, Lukács risks inverting the order of determination between practice and ideology. On the other, he seems to be propounding a new kind of determinism. In effect, the limitations and potentialities of consciousness are not explained by social practices but the limitations and potentialities of practice are explained by the objective possibility of consciousness, which is structurally determined by the class situation. The role of practice in the determination of ideology has almost disappeared. Lukács accepted and worked with the Leninist concept of ideology all his life, but in his early writings he tended to inflate its role to the point that ideology seems to determine the practical political activities of class and Party.

On the other hand, Lukács' emphasis on ideology as an ascribed consciousness which preordains the necessary and inevitable path of revolution results in a new determinism. Marx foreshadowed this aspect in the famous passage that Lukács quotes at the beginning of his essay on 'Class Consciousness': the question is not what the proletariat as a whole, or any of its members, envisages as the goal; the question is what the proletariat is and what it will be forced to accomplish in accordance to its nature. Lukács not only takes this idea as his motto but adds to it the Leninist touch: what the proletariat is and what it will necessarily achieve is expressed in its imputed consciousness and this in its turn is carried by the Party as its only bearer and true interpreter. The overrating of ideology is in the end transposed into the supremacy of the Party.

NOTES

1.   An example of the former is J. McCarney, *The Real World of Ideology*, Brighton, Harvester Press, 1980; an example of the latter is L. Althusser, 'Ideology and Ideological State Apparatuses', in *Lenin and Philosophy and other essays*, London, New Left Books, 1971 and 'Práctica téorica y lucha ideológica' in *La Filosofía como Arma de la Revolución*, Córdova, Cuadernos de Pasado y Presente, 1970.

2.   For a historical analysis of the evolution of the concept of ideology within Marxism, see J. Larrain, *Marxism and Ideology*, London, Macmillan, 1983.

3.   K. Marx and F. Engels, *The Holy Family*, Moscow, Progress, 1975, p. 43.

4.   K. Marx, 'The Paris *Réforme* on the Situation in France', in *Articles from the Neue Rheinische Zeitung*, Moscow, Progress, 1972, p. 142.

5.   See F. Engels' letters to C. Schmidt of 27 October 1890, to F. Mehring of 14 July 1893, to J. Bloch of 21-22 September 1890 and to Borgius of 25 January of 1894, in K. Marx and F. Engels, *Selected Correspondence*, Moscow, Progress, 1975.

6.   Although E. Bernstein published Part 3 of *The German Ideology* in 1903-1904, the most crucial section for a critical conception of ideology, Part 1, was first published separately in Russian in 1924, and in German and English in 1926. The whole book was first published in German in 1932. See K. Marx and F. Engels, *The German Ideology*, *Collected Works*, London, Lawrence & Wishart, 1976, note 7, p. 587.

7.   G. Plekhanov, *The Development of the Monist View of History*, in *Selected Philosophical Works*, London, Lawrence & Wishart, 1977, Vol. I, p. 625.

8.   E. Bernstein, 'Das realistische und das ideologische Moment im Sozialismus', in *Zur Geschichte und Theorie des Sozialismus*, Berlin, 1901, p. 282.

9.   V.I. Lenin, *What is to be done?*, Peking, Foreign Languages Press, 1975, p. 48.

10.   G. Lukács, *History and Class Consciousness*, London, Merlin Press, 1971, pp. 199-200.

11.   G. Lukács, *Writer and Critic*, London, Merlin Press, 1978, p. 73.

12.   V.I. Lenin, *op.cit.* p. 49.

13.   *Ibid.* pp. 98 and 37.

14. Lukács, *History and Class Consciousness, op.cit.* p. 51.

15. It is possible to argue that some of Lukács' reinterpretations of earlier writings were tactical ploys in order to appear more orthodox than he really was, especially during the Stalinist years. Even if this is true, I think that the Leninist filiation of *History and Class Consciousness* cannot be seriously doubted. L. Kołakowski has made the more general point that Lukács professed fidelity to Leninism throughout his Marxist career. (See *Main Currents of Marxism*, Oxford, Clarendon Press, 1978, Vol. III, pp. 253-4). Although this is probably the case, my argument here is restricted to showing a close relationship *vis-à-vis* the concept of ideology, an area of study in which Lenin and Lukács are frequently considered to be wide apart.

16. Lukács, *History and Class Consciousness, op.cit.* p. 69.

17. G. Stedman Jones, 'The Marxism of the Early Lukács, an Evaluation', *New Left Review*, No. 70, 1971, pp. 53-4.

18. A. Schaff, 'Conscience d'une classe et conscience de classe", *L'homme et la Société*, No. 26, Oct-Dec, 1972.

19. See on this A. Arato and P. Breines, *The Young Lukács and the Origins of Western Marxism,* London, Pluto Press, 1979, especially chapter 9.

20. Lukács, *History and Class Consciousness, op.cit.* p. 70.

21. *Ibid.* pp. 258-9.

22. *Ibid.* p. 228.

23. *Ibid.* p. 225.

24. *Ibid.* p. 227.

25. *Ibid.* p. 80.

26. *Ibid.* p. 228.

27. *Ibid.* pp. 266-7.

28. G. Lukács, *Writer and Critic, op.cit.* p. 63.

29. *Ibid.* p. 74.

30. G. Lukács, 'The Ontological Bases of Human Thought and Action', *The Philosophical Forum*, Vol. 7, 1975, p. 29.

31. *Ibid.* p. 36.

32. A notable exception can be found in J. McCarney, *op.cit.*

33. L. Goldmann, *Lukács et Heidegger*, Paris, Denoël/Gonthier, 1973, p. 125.

34. *Ibid.* p. 126.

35. N. Poulantzas, *Political Power and Social Classes*, London, New Left Books, 1976, p. 196.

36. *Ibid.* p. 207.

37. D. Adlam *et al.*, 'Psychology, Ideology and the Human Subject', *Ideology and Consciousness*, Nº 1, May, 1977, p. 15

38. R. McDonough, 'Ideology as False Consciousness:

Lukács', in *On Ideology*, Centre for Contemporary Cultural Studies, London, Hutchinson, 1978, p. 40.

39.   M. Seliger, *The Marxist Conception of Ideology*, Cambridge, Cambridge University Press, 1977, p. 67.

40.   Lukács, *History and Class Consciousness*, *op.cit.* p. 262.

41.   *Ibid.* p. 224.

42.   *Ibid.* p. 50.

43.   F. Engels, Letter to F. Mehring, 14 July 1893, in *Selected Correspondence, op.cit.* p. 434.

44.   Lukács, *History and Class Consciousness*, *op.cit.* pp. 257-8.

45.   *Ibid.* p. 54.

46.   *Ibid.* p. 50.

47.   *Ibid.* p. 224.

48.   G. Stedman Jones, *op.cit.* p. 40.

49.   N. Poulantzas, *op.cit.* p. 205.

50.   G. Stedman Jones, *op.cit.* p. 49.

51.   A. Schaff, *op.cit.* p. 7.

52.   N. Poulantzas, *op.cit.* p. 205.

53.   A. Arato & P. Breines, *op.cit.* p. 6.

54.   J. McCarney, *op.cit.* p. 46.

55.   Lukács, *History and Class Consciousness*, *op.cit.* pp. 229 & 232-3.

56.   *Ibid.* pp. 275-6.

57.   *Ibid.* pp. 304 & 262.

58.   J. McCarney, *op.cit.* p. 49.

59.   This does not preclude the existence of topics and elements which are common to various ideologies, but in this case one cannot speak of ideological contamination since these common elements are interpreted and rearticulated in very different contexts and with very different purposes.

60.   See V.I. Lenin, *op.cit.* p. 50.

61.   Lukács, *History and Class Consciousness*, *op.cit.* p. 93.

62.   See M. Godelier, 'Fétichisme, Religion et Théorie Générale de l'Idéologie chez Marx', *Annali*, Roma, Feltrinelli, 1970 and J. Mepham, 'The Theory of Ideology in *Capital* ', *Radical Philosophy*, Nº 2, Summer, 1972. Both articles draw heavily on *Capital* in order to reconstruct a Marxist theory of ideology.

63.   Lukács, *History and Class Consciousness*, *op.cit.* p. xviii

64.   The charge of reducing praxis to instrumental action has been levelled against Marx himself by J. Habermas, (*Knowledge and Human Interests*, London, Heinemann, 1972) and A. Wellmer, (*Critical Theory of Society*, New York, Herder & Herder, 1971), but it

seems to me that the charge is convincing only against Stalinist orthodoxy.

65. Lukács, *History and Class Consciousness, op.cit.* p. 205.
66. *Ibid.* p. 262.
67. *Ibid.* p. 169.
68. *Ibid.* p. 259.

LOUIS DUPRÉ

Objectivism and the Rise of Cultural Alienation

For a short period after the Second World War Marx' work was read as if he had delivered his entire message in the *Paris Manuscripts* of 1844. According to this existentialist interpretation, man, by means of a social-economic revolution, must close the breach in the process of his self-realization caused by an alienating attitude toward his own production and restore freedom to its pristine condition. If such a social adaptation of Feuerbach's theory of *Entfremdung* finds any textual support in the *Paris Manuscripts*, it is wholly absent from a work written only one year later. In *The German Ideology,* capitalism appears by no means as an unfortunate interlude in the progress of freedom. Nor does Marx advocate a return to a "natural" state of freedom. On the contrary, he credits capitalism with having surpassed this state altogether.

From the beginning, most explicitly in the *Manuscripts*, Marx insisted that man is able to realize his potential only by externalizing, or objectifying (*Entäusserung*) himself, as he does in industry, but also in art. The realm of culture for him includes economic, as well as aesthetic, production. Only when the object of his work turns into an independent power that escapes the control of its maker altogether can we speak of *Entfremdung* (alienation). In *The German Ideology* the symptom of such an objective enslavement is a division of labor determined by the most productive use of the instruments, regardless of its effect on the producing worker. In adopting it, the capitalist economy reverts, paradoxically, to some sort of "natural" division of labor, such as takes place in a primitive society, where "natural disposition, needs, accidents" alone determine the distribution of tasks. Yet the new system of production enslaves man more thoroughly in that it shifts from social need to objects of exchange.

In the following pages I shall not explore the issue of alienation in general, as it is stated in the early works, but only that particularly intensive aspect of it, reification, or objectivism, which Marx considers characteristic of the capitalist economy alone. It is well-known that Lukács, in his famous essay on 'Reification and the Consciousness of the Proletariat', does not use the term "alienation". He did not know the *Paris Manuscripts* when he wrote it. But there are good reasons to

T. Rockmore (ed.), Lukács Today, 70–85.
© *1988 by D. Reidel Publishing Company.*

keep the term "reification", according to which relations among things determine human relations, distinct from the more generic *Ent-fremdung*. Lukács - like the French Marxist Henri Lefebvre, who did know the early writings - reserved the name "reification" to the particular historical stage of industrial capitalism.[1] In speaking of "reification" or "fetishism", we indicate specifically that man no longer controls the conditions of his material production, nor, as a result, those of his cultural creativity. Alienation, more generally, refers to a lack of control of one's social relations.[2] In his later works, Marx mostly discusses what he considers the cause of the reifying attitude, namely, the conflict between the immanent goals of the economic process and the particular mode in which capitalism pursues them.

Thus, what began as a study of human alienation now turns into a critique of the internal contradictions of the capitalist economy. Yet Marx never loses sight of the wider issue: alienated freedom. As appears in the preparatory notes for the *magnum opus* on which he kept working all his life, and of which *Capital* constitutes a small fraction, the negation of the subject (*Entfremdung* in the original, Hegelian sense) continues to direct the scientific analysis. What has changed, however, is that the more humanistic and the economic views no longer appear as opposites of which one dictates its norms to the other. This kind of "moralistic" humanism, whereby the economic stands in a purely instrumental relation to the achievement of ultimate "human" goals, has yielded to a concept of praxis in which the individual himself is, rather than the cause, the outcome of social production. A conflict among existing economic forces, then, turns inevitably into a human conflict, that is, a conflict within man's social existence. Human nature has ceased to be an abstract, ideal a priori: it develops with the social-economic praxis. Thus, the notion of dialectical contradiction that had supported the earlier idea of alienation continues to operate as the driving force of the later theory. Only the immutable categories, independent of social-economic processes, have disappeared. The human has become historicized. No basically unchanging nature realizes itself through historical production: humanization coincides with the productive activity itself. Social-economic categories have likewise become historical. Thus, property is neither an eternal right (or the abuse of one), nor a universal social institution. On the contrary, according to the *Grundrisse*, it consists in the various forms of control a producer or producing class has over its productive activity. These conditions vary from one social system to another. Similarly, surplus value is far more than the value produced by the laborer, for which he has not been remunerated: it consists in the current system in objectified labor power, which in "an ever more colossal independence" confronts living labor as "an alien and dominant power" (*GR* 714; Nicolaus 831). Once again we see it defined in function of the actual labor process. Marx' terminology leaves no doubt about the constant presence of a subjective element in this process, to which the objective must correspond. He describes objectified labor as "the worker's non-objectivity, as the objectivity of a subjectivity antithetical to the worker, as property of a will alien to him" (*GR* 412; Nicolaus 512).

Thus enters the idea of reification to which I shall restrict my following discussion. Commodities in the process of exchange take on an existence independent of their function in the process of man's self-realization: instead they come to stand opposed to the original goals of the economic process itself and attain an abstract being of their own. Resuming a metaphor he had used in the *1844 Manuscripts*, Marx refers to their "heavenly existence" (*GR* 63; Nicolaus 145). We are reminded of Rousseau's *Social Contract*, where alienation acquires a negative sense only when a non-transferable right becomes estranged from a person or society. Marx' functional use of the concept here stands closer to the original idea than it ever came in the *Manuscripts*. Still the *Grundrisse* shows a continuity of thought with the *Manuscripts* which anti-humanist interpreters, such as Althusser, have not sufficiently recognized.

Remarkably like the existentialists against whom they reacted, the structuralists also unduly separate Marx' early theory from his later one. Progress in Marx' thought consists in an ever tighter integration of the subjective with the objective, not in a disjunctive shift from one to the other. To eliminate "alienation" from the later works seems unjustified both in fact and in principle. The recession of the language of alienation in the published works of Marx' mature age is not due to a reversal of position (Why else would he use the term so frequently in the notes in which he prepared these publications?), but to the practical, and perhaps also methodological, consideration that a critique of economy should be written in the language of economy. Ronald Meek has it right, I believe, when he writes in the 1975 preface to his *Studies in the Labor Theory of Value*: "*Capital*, in a very real and important sense, is in fact a book about alienation."[3] Certainly, Marx finds contradictions in the capitalist system and argues that eventually it will collapse under their weight. But beyond the technical economic discussion, he is attacking the more fundamental perversion of the subjective source of productive activity in a society that reifies labor power into a commodity. The issue concerns not merely the reduction of labor power to a commodity but the detachment of the entire economic process from the subject. In a wage labor economy all *Entäusserung* becomes *Entfremdung*, all objectification turns into reification. (Hence the two terms which were so clearly distinguished in the *Paris Manuscripts* now tend to merge again. (For an example, see, *Werke* 23, 124; *Capital* 1, 160). Typically for the interiorization of the economic problem, Marx' critique in *Capital* shifts from surplus labor (in *Grundrisse*) to what more directly perverts the subjective source of the production process, namely, its exclusive orientation toward the production of exchange value. The creation of surplus value, which is neither unique to a capitalist economy, nor by itself in conflict with the immanent goals of the production, becomes so only when the orientation toward exchange value reifies the producing subject into a market commodity. It is not the amount of surplus labor the subject yields which determines the degree of negation, but the requirement to objectify his productive activity for the subject as a condition for participating in the economic process at all.

Precisely here lies the ground for Marx' insistent critique of the capitalist theories' neglect of the distinction between labor and labor power. Beyond the immediate issue of wages merely providing a subsistence, which by no means equals the value of the produced labor, lies the more fundamental one that the equation turns the laboring subject into an object of exchange. In the manuscript of 1861-62, which continues the published part of the *Critique of Political Economy*, Marx refers to labor power as "the force of the living subject" (*MEGA* II3, 36) and shows how the subjective source of value cannot be measured by its natural needs. Yet the capitalist economy does precisely that; and it does it by means of the objective concept of labor time which homogenizes all work into quantified units of exchanged value. But the subjective source of labor does not allow such an equalization. Marx had to insist on it when his own fellow socialists, in the drafting of the Gotha program, proposed to grant each worker as much value as he had contributed in labor. "Here obviously the same principle prevails as that which regulates the exchange of commodities, as far as this exchange of equal value" (*Werke* 19:20; *Selected Works* 2:23). In the face of different endowments and social circumstances, to equalize the "value" of labor establishes a new inequality on the deeper, subjective level. Related to this elimination of the subjective is the separation of the sphere of economic activity from other social structures. Capitalism has severed economic production from any concern for the producing society as such. We may wonder, of course, whether in attributing a priority to the economic processes Marx has not followed it in the same direction. But the answer, whatever it may be, in no way prevents his critique from having been intended as a critique of the entire bourgeois social organization, not merely of its narrowly economic mode of production. Only in the light of this wider critique are we able to understand the famous passage on the fetishism of commodities in *Capital*. Marx' critique does not aim in the first place at the dehumanizing working conditions (child labor, prolonged working days, unhealthy shops) or the low wages; it aims at the final cause which affects all moments of the process, namely, the reduction of every stage to the level of exchangeable units of value - commodities. It is to this reification of the entire production process that Marx refers as the "fetishism of commodities".

> In the mist-enveloped regions of the religious world ... the productions of the human brain appear as independent beings endowed with life, and entering into relation both with one another and the human race. So it is in the world of commodities with the products of men's hands. This I call the fetishism which attaches itself to the products of labor. (*Werke* 23:86; *Cap*. I:72)

Marx had used the term "fetishism" in the *Paris Manuscripts* for the kind of economic reification that takes place when a society measures national wealth by the quantity of precious metals it possesses. Yet this characteristic of the mercantilist societies of the sixteenth and seventeenth centuries by no means affected all social activity. Nor did the Physiocratic principles of eighteenth-century France determine all structures of society. Once the creation of exchange value becomes the single goal of the economic process, however, the reification becomes universal and we can speak of a fetishism of commodities. Clearly, then, this expression applies only to an industrial capitalism, in which the commodity has become a universal determinant, not only of the economic process, but of all social relations. Since Marx wrote *Capital*, the term "fetishism" has extended its meaning to all ways of reifying human processes. Insofar as the link with the economic process is clearly established, such a usage is consistent with Marx' own thought. Thus the commercial quality of popular culture as well as the reaction of an elite that isolates culture in a different realm of being both follow from the all-determining reification of a commodity economy.

Lukács, then, justifiedly generalizes Marx' critique of economic objectivism to the entire bourgeois culture. "The problem of commodities must not be considered in isolation or even regarded as the central problem in economics, but as the central, structural problem of capitalist society in all its aspects".[4] The commodity attitude conveys to all relations in a bourgeois society what he calls "a phantom objectivity". He rightly insists, though, that fetishism cannot simply be regarded as a result of exchange.

> Commodity fetishism is a specific problem of our age, the age of modern capitalism. Commodity exchange and the corresponding subjective and objective commodity relations existed, as we know, when society was still very primitive. What is at issue here, however, is the question: How far is commodity exchange together with its structural consequences able to influence the total outer and inner life of society?[5]

Once reification has become a universal structuring principle, however, human subjectivity becomes estranged from itself and turns into a commodity "just like any convenience article".[6] Indeed, the very reality of things becomes hidden in their new appearance of commodities. Nor can the mind so affected simply step out of the circle that holds it captive.

It is hard to disagree with Marx' critique of the commodity mentality. Yet we wonder whether the roots, and even the early manifestations of a reification which culminates in the fetishism of commodities, do not lie far before modern capitalism. To grasp its full scope forces us to return to the very beginnings of methodic thought in our culture. When Greek thinkers first attempted to understand the cosmos as it is in itself, beyond its immediate appearance to the senses, they discovered what is surely the most distinctive trait of Western thought - objectivity. The discovery in no way jeopardized the exploration of the subjective dimension of the mind. On the contrary, it would, with Socrates, the Stoics, and the Christian Fathers (especially Augustine), result in a more conscious apperception of the self as a form of being in its own right. Nor did the Greeks consider objectivity to be the creation of an autonomous mental subject. Objectivity was grounded in the intrinsically rational structure of the cosmos itself. Far from being the only source of truth, the subject, in much of the Greek tradition, is held to be bound to the realm of appearance, the source of illusion. The only attitude that will secure the mind access to the true reality is one of active openness. Epistemological problems in the modern sense rarely emerge.

> One cannot ask, for example, about the correspondence of one's perceptions with the objects in the world. For with this version of consciousness understanding is not a question of correspondence,

but of being. Thus, there can be questions of appearance or
illusion, on the one hand, and reality, on the other, but there can
be no questions of correspondence of subject and object because,
from the modern point of view, there are no objects in ancient
thought: knowledge is a harmony, not correspondence. It is a
harmony of self with reality and the thing with reality.[7]

In the medieval Christian vision, likewise, a divine Logos, differently
interpreted, to be sure, inhered in the given nature of reality, rather than
emerging from a human mind that imposes its own categories upon it.
Reason existed in the cosmos before existing in the mind or in social
institutions.

Nominalist theology brought this view of an intrinsically meaningful
cosmos to an end. Since divine omnipotence was no longer considered
to be restricted by any intrinsic limits of its own creation, it henceforth
falls to the mind to find whatever structures of meaning enable it to
convey coherence to the world and to operate effectively in it. Here
then, begins the dominance of the subject; not Socrates' subject that
thinks in harmony with the cosmos, nor Augustine's that obeys an
order transcending both itself and the cosmos, but an autonomous
subject. Descartes legislated the principles of this new approach when
he set up his famous rules for breaking down the complex into its
simplest elements and then rebuilding it. Nature has ceased to "reveal"
itself as a reality that must be taken on its own terms. Instead, it has
become what we entrap and control as calculable, predictable force. In
being forced to answer only our questions and to respond to our
practical demands, it becomes a truncated reality. Its intrinsic
meaningfulness, previously articulated in the principle of final causality,
vanishes. Nature becomes mute, while its inner teleology is transposed
to that other, all-determining segment of the real, *res cogitans*.

Overall reason acquired a practical orientation, even in its theoretical
activity. Constituted objectivity and practical control ended the rule of
contemplation and introduced that of fabrication which, as Hannah
Arendt has argued, resulted in an unlimited instrumentalization of the
world: confidence in tools, supremacy of the principle of utility,
reduction of nature to a workshop for human tinkering.[8] Hans Jonas
illustrates the difference in the cognitive attitude, from purely theoretical
to practical, by contrasting Bacon to St. Thomas. The former writes:

> I would address one general admonition to all: that they consider
> what are the true ends of knowledge, and that they seek it not either
> for pleasure of the mind, or for contention, or for superiority to

others ... but for the benefit and use of life ... . For the matter in hand is no mere felicity of speculation, but the business and fortunes of the human race, and all power of operation.[9]

For Bacon, the end of knowledge is its practical use, that is to overcome the miseries of life. For Plato, Aristotle, and the Scholastics, knowledge is the end itself: the good life (which presupposes the satisfaction of basic needs) culminates in contemplation. Nor is the modern goal one in which we simply apply the conclusions of science. Theory itself becomes a practical, problem-solving concern that forces nature to respond to the "vexation of art".

In this apparent triumph of the subject, the subject becomes, in fact, reduced to the mere function of constituting objectivity. Thus, what began as a subjectivization of the real in the end deprives the subject of all content of its own.

> The more all nature is looked upon ... as mere objects in relation to human subjects, the more is the once supposedly autonomous subject emptied of any content, until it finally becomes a mere name with nothing to denominate. The total transformation of each and every realm of being into a field of means leads to the liquidation of the subject who is supposed to use them. This gives modern industrial society its nihilistic aspect. Subjectivization, which exalts the subject, also dooms him.[10]

Thus the problem of objectivism could not emerge until the subject had come to be regarded as the sole source of meaning and value. Once this position was established, however, the problem became inevitable. Thus the absolute dominance of the subject prepared in fact its demise, both in theory and in practice.

Marx appears at the end of this development and his position remains thoroughly ambiguous. Does the objectivist movement culminate in his Promethean theory of praxis? Or does he, critical of the subject-object split in modern thought, advocate a return to the more integrated view of nature of the Greeks? I think, both. Marx felt a deep empathy with the ancient concept of cosmic harmony and, at least in principle, rejected, from the beginning to the end, the objectivism of modern culture. Numerous passages in the *Paris Manuscripts* and the *Grundrisse* emphasize the need for a more wholesome relation to nature. Yet he never conceives of this relation as an immediate one (as many romantics did). Cultural activity must mediate all relations to nature. The *Paris Manuscripts* contains a dense passage on the humanization of nature and the naturalization of man. It discusses only industry, but its scope reaches much further.

> Industry is the actual, historical relationship of nature, and therefore of natural science, to man. If, therefore, industry is conceived as the exoteric revelation of man's essental powers, we also gain an understanding of the human essence of nature or the natural essence of man. In consequence, natural science will lose its abstractly material--or rather, its idealistic--tendency, and will become the basis of human science, as it has already become--albeit in estranged form--the basis of actual human life. To assume one basis for life and a different basis for science is as a matter of course a lie. The nature which develops in human history--the genesis of human society--is man's real nature; hence nature as it develops through industry, even though in an estranged form, is true anthropological nature. (*MEGA* I3, 122; *Works* 3, 303)

One may, of course, read this text as a justification of industrial activity, but, more importantly, it informs us about the specific quality of Marx' "naturalism" and the need to mediate all relations to nature. In the course of its cultural mediation, nature becomes human (even the science of nature turns into a branch of anthropology), while man becomes, once again, a natural being. Most revealing of the novelty of Marx' conception is the final statement: the nature "which develops in human history" is "man's real nature". This naturalism stands removed as far as possible from the "contemplative" attitude of both materialists and romantics. Still, it never degenerates into an "instrumentalist" theory. Henri Lefebvre interprets the term "exoteric" in the quoted passage as implying the presence of an "esoteric" relation as well - an ethical and an aesthetic. One promotes relations among individuals on a basis of full equality; the other prefigures an ideal unity with nature, such as is possible only in a socially liberated society.[11]

Marx' conception of the relation between man and nature is undoubtedly new, but it builds upon earlier neo-classical and romantic ideas. This continuity with the classical tradition contrasts sharply with the attitude of "modernist" writers, such as Baudelaire and the French symbolists. Lefebvre notes:

> [Baudelaire] has decided to repudiate nature, naturalism and the optimistic philosophy of the eighteenth century - the one which Marx prolongs and resumes. Baudelaire opts for the anti-nature, that is, for an art of total creation which imitates nothing that is

given or that comes from without, one that coincides with the purely factitious.[12]

Marx, on the contrary, aims at overcoming the opposition between man and nature. While modernism expresses the failure of the neo-classical ideal, Marx' theory of revolutionary praxis remains basically optimistic.

But here precisely emerges the other facet of Marx' vision. The union with nature is determined entirely by the quality of man's own activity. To be sure, he never yields to a romantically subjectivist theory of freedom, such as we find in Shelley, or in the young Schiller. For Marx, the subject does not pre-exist its own creative act. Through productive activity man creates both himself and his life-world. Yet if Marx opposes the romantic theory of subjective freedom as much as he opposes the contemplative attitude toward nature, he nevertheless fully accepts the underlying idealist principle, namely, that meaning and value are entirely constituted in the living deed. I doubt whether such a principle is in the end compatible with any genuinely naturalist worldview. We are no longer dealing with anything that remotely resembles what the Greeks would call "nature", but with a wholly new, essentially man-made "nature", with respect to which the old one fulfills a merely instrumental role. Marx' discussion of technology leaves little doubt about his conviction that "nature" should be fully subjugated and unromantically controlled. True, in the *Grundrisse* he holds the dominance of technology over human activity responsible for the anti-social quality of the division of labor, and charges the use of technology in the capitalist economy with transferring the reins of production from subjective action to the control of objective science. The machine no longer transmits the worker's activity to the object; rather, the worker transmits the machine's power to the materiel. Human intervention requires little skill: the real master is the machine. "Machinery appears as the adequate form of capital as such" (*GR* 586; Nicolaus 694). Yet while Marx severely criticized the role of technology within the capitalist economy, he appears to be largely unaware of the dangers inherent in the technological attitude itself. The *Grundrisse* even contains a profession of faith in the possibilities of technology which threatens to jeopardize his own theory of revolution.

To the degree that large industry develops, the creation of real wealth comes to depend less on labor time and on the amount of labor employed than on the power of the agencies set in motion during labor time, whose 'powerful effectiveness' is itself in turn out of all proportion to the direct labor time spent on their production, but depends rather on the general state of science and on the progress of technology, or the application of this science to production. (*GR* 492; Nicolaus 705)[13]

Related to this belief in technology is Marx' emphasis on the primary role of social-economic relations in the cultural process. Here man is presented as in the first place a production agent. Much as he disagreed with the narrowness of the social theories of the British classical economists, Marx continued to consider economic activity as the basis of cultural praxis - and hence never truly abandoned the perspective of the *homo oeconomicus*. To be sure, Marx never equated praxis with economically productive activity. His aim was precisely to liberate society from the dominance of the purely economic. Nevertheless he continued to assign to economic production a primary function in the socialization process. Indeed, he defends Ricardo's promotion at any cost against Sismondi's critique.

He [Ricardo] wants production for the sake of production and this with good reason. To forget that production for its own sake means to assert, as sentimental opponents of Ricardo did, that production is not the object, is to forget that production for its own sake means nothing but the development of human productive forces, in other words, the development of the richness of human nature as an end in itself. To oppose the welfare of the individual to this end, as Sismondi does, is to assert that the development of the species must be arrested in order to safeguard the welfare of the individual ... . (*Werke* 262, 111; *Theories of Surplus Value* (Moscow, 1963), Vol. 2, 117)

In evaluating this one-sided view of culture, one should take account of the social context of the nineteenth century, for which the economic question was, indeed, the primary social issue. Any consideration of social freedom would have remained abstract until it became based upon an economic foundation.

Yet, beyond this immediate ground for Marx' concern with the economic, we perceive a readiness to accept the more fundamental assumption implied in the technical as well as in the economist's worldview. That assumption consists in the primacy of praxis itself, the final stage of that development, which replaces the intrinsic rationality of the world order by a subjective one of man's own making. This attitude, as I have shown elsewhere, deviates substantially from the priority of *theoria* over action which Western culture has tended to favor since its Greek origins. Marx, a lifelong student and admirer of Greek thought, is not entirely unambiguous in his stress on the primacy of praxis, however strongly he asserts it. As Hannah Arendt once remarked, he continues to be fascinated by the ancient ideal of *theoria*[14] and sees, beyond the present economy, a saving of time "for higher activity" (*GR* 499; Nicolaus 711- 12), presumably of an aesthetic or purely theoretical nature. Yet, as long as the praxis ideal remains dominant, the absolute priority of the subject which gave rise to it will remain. This, however, is, I suggest, the real culprit for the problems of objectivism and ultimately of reification of which Marx wrote such a forceful critique.

Finally a word should be said about Lukács' theory of reification, because it presents at once a deepening and a corrective of Marx' position. Clearly, in his essay on reification the primacy of the economic, still so evident in orthodox Marxism, has moved to the background. For the Hungarian scholar, cultural productivity expresses itself in a number of forms. Artistic creation reflects the state of economic production, yet clearly surpasses it. Its harmonious synthesis of the theoretical and the practical, sensuous form and spiritual content, sets the model for all human productivity. In Lukács' emphasis on the aesthetic as the primary expression, we notice a shift in perspective from Marx' position. Yet Lukács remains faithful to what we have called the Promethean factor in Marx' thought: the primacy of the creative subject. Modern philosophy, he argues, in its "grandiose conception that thought can only grasp what it has itself created" (*History and Class Consciousness*, p. 122.) established the theoretical possibility of moving beyond the traditional attitude of passive contemplation. Yet, by restricting itself to pure speculation, it failed to come directly to grips with material reality itself. Kant anticipated the problem when he described the resistance of the thing-in-itself to purely theoretical knowledge. Yet, he concluded that what was closed to the theoretical approach would be accessible to the practical one. This crucial insight, Lukács claims, reduced the subject-object opposition to the original point of coincidence - praxis. Significantly, Kant himself never left the realm of pure theory and, as a result, was unable to provide this practical reason with any concrete content. To surpass his ethical formalism, the contemplative attitude has to be abandoned altogether.[15]

Thus far Lukács' argument has run parallel with Marx'. But then it takes a surprisingly new twist. With other twentieth-century critics, Lukács traces the predicament of modern culture to the rationalist opposition of the subject to an objective reality. Such a relation leads only to formal systematizations. The structures it creates in the practical order estrange modern man as much from this social nature as its purely conceptual ones alienate him from his life-reality.

> Man in capitalist society confronts a reality 'made' by himself (as a class) which appears to him to be a natural phenomenon alien to himself; he is wholly at the mercy of its 'laws,' his activity is confined to the exploitation of the inexorable fulfillment of certain individual laws for his own (egoistic) interests. But even while 'acting' he remains, in the nature of the case, the object and not the subject of events.[16]

Reflections of this nature by no means cause Lukács to question the subjective turn of modern consciousness (which posits the subject as the sole source of meaning). Instead Lukács attributes the alienation of modern life to the fact that the subject has become severed from its material substratum. Thus, man's economic, social, and technical activity has lost its dialectical relation to nature. The objective order it has established turns into a petrified construction that tolerates no further human interference. It presents itself to him as an unchangeable, given objectivity. Our practical attitude has not followed the path opened by idealist philosophy. It remains enclosed within the seventeenth-century pattern of objective laws ruling an immutable cosmic and social order. Nineteenth-century scientism only enforced this rigid conception of a wholly objective cosmos. Though placing the subject at the center of the objective order, it allows no genuine transformation of that order. Throughout its amazing technical achievements, it remains essentially "contemplative". It merely predicts necessary occurrences and prepares itself for their future coming.

> This activity consists in predicting, in calculating as far as possible the probable effects of those laws and the subject of the 'action' takes up a position in which these effects can be exploited to the best advantage of his own purposes.[17]

The subject's role decreases more and more to that of a purely "receptive organ". Overcoming the "contemplative" attitude, according to Lukács, requires far more than the availability of unprecedented technical powers. What precisely would it take? Lukács does not provide a clear answer. but, instead, points to the model of all human production - the aesthetic. Certainly the artist cannot remain within an abstractly established, purely formal schema of reality. Forced to conform his activity to the specific nature of the material on which he works, he remains to the end engaged in a concrete dialectical struggle between matter and form.

I wonder how much assistance such an aesthetic model will provide in solving the problems of modern culture. I also wonder whether the attitude of the modern scientist can be correctly described as one of contemplating scientific laws as if they were transcendent entities. Today, at least, they function as working models devised for solving particular problems that often arise in the process of attaining a particular mode of control over nature. I fail to see how one could call "contemplative" a procedure which adopts a practical orientation from the beginning. Technology may not be the goal of the individual scientist or science department, but neither is it a mere fringe benefit of scientific study, or a happy accident. In contrast to the inquisitive mentality of the Greeks, for whom the cosmos was, indeed, primarily an object of contemplation, for modern science control of nature has, from the start, been implicit in the enterprise. That this control remains subject to "laws" and, indeed, that the entire quest consists in an attempt to convey to the empirical field the regularity of law renders the scientific attitude neither passive nor contemplative. This qualification would apply only if the search were for a purely ideal reality which, so to speak, directs the empirical universe from above. Now, some such Platonic vision may have played a role in the formation of the scientific mind - in Galileo almost certainly, in Kepler and Newton possibly. Yet this attitude is far removed from the mind of contemporary scientists who, rather than claiming the existence of an ideal super-reality, freely assume the "subjective" quality of their scientific theories.

At times, Lukács appears to go even further and to consider the concept of objective law itself alienating.

> The freedom (of the subject) is neither able to overcome the sensuous necessity of the system of knowledge and the soul-lessness of the fatalistically conceived laws of nature, nor is it able to give them any meaning.[18]

But how could any freedom liberate itself of the "necessity of the system of knowledge"? I wonder whether two different issues have not become confused here: 1) the submission to a necessity not of one's own making; 2) setting up objective science (with its system of necessities) as a human ideal. Only in the latter case can one responsibly speak of the "soullessness of the fatalistically conceived laws of nature", not because of their own intrinsic essence, but because of the determining role they are allowed to play in the structuring of human behavior.

Nor is the primacy of praxis required to overcome "scientism". On the contrary, this primacy is greatly responsible for the objectivist attitude that led to it. When Marx converted the idealist philosophy of knowledge into a theory of action, he, in fact, absolutized its fundamental principle, that meaning and value are not given with the nature of things, but constituted by the living deed. Here the Promethean quality of his thought clearly gains the upper hand over this "naturalism". With this anti-contemplative vision, Marx radically transformed the tradition of Western thought, not only the Greek, but even the modern. In doing so he legitimated a cultural development that, without being recognized, had followed industrial capitalism and its concomitant technocracy. Work had turned into the very purpose of life and industriousness into the principal virtue. Marx' theory legitimated the practical conduct of his age by turning productive activity into the very essence of culture. This primacy of praxis appears most clearly in the basic role Marx conveys to economic production. Yet the primacy of praxis is not limited to this questionable axiom, and later Marxists (especially Marcuse and Lukács) have reinterpreted it in such a manner that it ceases to be a principle valid for all times. Yet all have retained the more fundamental primacy of praxis. To support their choice they refer to the aesthetic activity as to the prototype of all human activity. I have already expressed my doubt whether the aesthetic could really serve as a model for all other modes of acting. But even if it could, it would hardly present an anti-contemplative attitude. For, precisely in the aesthetic, the contemplative factor outweighs the active, although both are most intimately connected with one another. Leaving the aesthetic attitude out of consideration, we may still assert that human activity is never purely practical. Its universal scope transcends the immediacy of the task at hand. But a truly universal form of activity requires purely theoretical acts. Insofar as all work is a project it presupposes distance, observation, reflection - in short, contemplation.

NOTES

1.   Henri Lefebvre, *Critique de la vie quotidienne II*, Paris, 1969.

2.   Menachem Rosner, 'Entfremdung, Fetichismus, Anomie', in *Entfremdung*, ed. by Heinz-Horst Schrey, Darmstadt 1975, pp. 455-456.

3.   *Monthly Review Press* (1956), 1975, p. XII.

4.   *History and Class Consciousness,* Boston, M.I.T. Press, 1971, p. 83.

5.   *Ibid.* p. 84.

6.   *Ibid.* p. 87.

7.   James E. Faulconer, 'Subject, Object and Self', unpublished paper (1984). The author stresses that even the ethical attitude for the Greeks consists primarily in a responsiveness to a given, divinely instituted cosmic order. It culminates in a life of contemplation which Aristotle himself claimed no one can practice in virtue of being human, but only at God's instigation. *Nic. Eth.* X, 8, 8.

8.   Hannah Arendt, *The Human Condition*, Chicago, The University of Chicago Press, 1958, p. 305.

9.   *The Great Instauration,* Preface.

10.   M. Horkheimer, *The Eclipse of Reason*, New York (1947), 1974, p. 93; also pp. 107-108.

11.   Henri Lefebvre, *Introduction à la modernité*, Paris, 1962, pp. 144-148.

12.   *Ibid.* p. 173.

13.   For an intelligent discussion of the problem of technology in Marx, see Kostas Axelos, *Marx penseur de la technique*, Paris, 1961.

14.   Hannah Arendt, *Between Past and Future*, N.Y., Penguin Books, 1977, p. 24.

15.   Hegel, of course, would not have agreed with this conclusion. He at least thought he had found a theoretical solution to Kant's predicament.

16.   *Ibid.* p. 135

17.   *Ibid.* p. 130.

18.   *Ibid.* p. 134.

JEAN GRONDIN

Reification from Lukács to Habermas[*]

> "There is less a sense in
> history than an elimi-
> nation of nonsense."[1]

Is Georg Lukács one of the classical authors of the philosophical tradition? This question might appear somewhat odd in a collection of articles commemorating his centenary. It is just that, although the work of Lukács represents nothing less than a monument to all those who are interested in Marxism, as exemplified by a prodigious body of literature, it remains largely ignored in more traditional philosophy, which is often little disposed to consider even Marx himself as a genuine philosopher. Hermeneutics and analytic philosophy, two dominant currents at the present time, hardly ever concern themselves with the one who, since Merleau-Ponty, has been called the founding father of Western Marxism.[2]

The absence of Lukács is particularly glaring in some recent histories of contemporary philosophy. He has not found a place either in the *Classics of Philosophy* of O. Höffe[3] or even in the anthology of twentieth-century philosophy of R. Wiehl[4], who brings together no fewer than twenty texts of the eighteen greatest thinkers of our time, including Horkheimer, Bloch, and Adorno. This omission, which could easily be documented in a more exhaustive manner, can be blamed neither on the Hungarian roots of Lukács - because his great philosophical works were published in German - nor on the fact that Lukács, who gained a professorship only at the age of sixty, did not have the opportunity to build a very large following of students. Rather, it is the shadow of Stalinism that renders the thought of Lukács suspect for the majority of intellectuals in the West (and perhaps also, although other factors might be more relevant, in the East, where the heritage of his thought seems to be honored only in Hungary, however not without being considerably distorted, so that the true students of Lukács have been driven to silence or exile[5]). It is considered dangerous to draw on a brand of thought, which - though it were for tactical reasons (essentially, opposition to the fascist threat and the fear that the West might fall in behind Hitler against the Bolshevik revolution[6]) - has undertaken the defense of one of the most abominable tyrants in the history of humanity. Although he eventually recognized the perversity of Stalinism, Lukács did not deem it necessary to insert

86

T. Rockmore (ed.), Lukács Today, 86–107.
© *1988 by D. Reidel Publishing Company.*

Stalin into his three-volume history of *Destruction of Reason*, and he never disavowed the motives which had led him to his strategic apology for Stalinism - a singular phenomenon for a thinker so prompt at self-criticism. It is symptomatic in this regard that a disciple like Lucien Goldmann, who constantly emphasized the important philosophical value of the writings of the young Lukács, had a tendency to neglect the writings of the Stalinist period and of the last philosophical period of Lukács' life.[7]

The debate on the dogmatism of Lukács and his crypto-religious submission to the decrees of the Party will not be taken up again here. Rather we will try to show that, if Lukács does not seem to be at the center of philosophical debates today, it is because his presence is basically beneath the surface, that it works especially throughout critical theory, the third great current of our epoch, which has been on-going for some years, thanks to Habermas, in a fruitful dialogue with analytic philosophy and hermeneutics. By granting an especially privileged position to the theme of reification, we propose to delineate some of the aspects of Lukács' influence that lie at the heart of critical theory from Horkheimer to Habermas.

If one wishes to understand the way in which a number of problems concerning advanced capitalist society are posed in critical theory, it is necessary to start from Lukács' most acclaimed work, *History and Class Consciousness*. This book, published in 1923 during the period of Messianic fervor enkindled by the Revolution of 1917, seeks to illuminate the philosophical and historical significance of Marxism. At the time, it constituted an original reflection, since it remedied the mutual ignorance of philosophy and of Marxism.[8] Up until then, academic philosophy had little to do with Marxism, which it classified under the headings of "materialism" and "positivism", while orthodox Marxism thought that it had left behind the mists of philosophical speculation. Abstract reflection on the problems of consciousness no longer seems to serve any purpose when one is in possession of a science which explains all phenomena from the vantage point of their social-economic infrastructure, with consciousness being a simple mirror image, as well as an epiphenomenon, of economic reality (a thesis reasserted by Lenin in *Materialism and Empirio-Criticism*).

In skillfully appropriating certain Marxian texts, Lukács hint thats things are in fact a bit more complicated. According to him, the importance of consciousness does not represent a mere prejudice of bourgeois thought - which he criticized carefully but severely in *History and Class Consciousness*, as though to excuse his indebtedness: it is one of the centerpieces of Marxist theory. His thesis can be summarized in the following fashion: revolution is not anchored solely in a mechanical necessity of history, but depends on the class consciousness which it is incumbent upon the working class to develop, that is consciousness which is to become the engine of economic transformation. In other terms, and this lesson has lost nothing of its currency, the economic reduction of consciousness and of subjectivity among Marxist theoreticians is neither more nor less than a hidden form of capitalist reification[9], a uniformization of human reality resulting from generalized rationalization. But, only the "ideological maturity"[10] of the proletariat is capable of responding, which amounts to saying that orthodox Marxism, fixated on economic problems, has still not attained such a maturity.

The title of Lukács' book, hardly very clear by virtue of the "and" which permits several readings[11], could mean that it is futile to expect progress in the history of liberation without counting on the class consciousness of the parties involved. It is not surprising that Lukács chose as the exergue of his central study, 'Reification and Class Consciousness of the Proletariat', the words of Marx: "To be radical is to take things by the root. Now, for man, the root is man himself." Lukács' outstanding feat consists in his relativizing the Marxist economism of his time by resurrecting the ("young Hegelian") humanism of Marx' thought, without being able to rely on the *1844 Manuscripts*, published some years later. In the eyes of Lukács' Marxist contemporaries, humanism, because individualistic, simply masked a bourgeois ideology that had become outmoded thanks to historical materialism which primarily studies class relations. Since then, authors like Bloch, Marcuse, Michel Henry, and others as well, have underlined the humanistic import of Marx' thought, so that Lukács' interpretation can seem to us relatively orthodox. But at the time, an anti-humanist reading of famous texts could be substantiated, in particular of the sixth thesis on Feuerbach, which stipulates that the essence of man resides in the "collection of social relations", and of the Preface to the First Edition of *Capital*. Here one can read that persons will be seen as "personifications of economic categories and bearers of class interests and relations".[12] According to Lukács, the economistic, anti-humanistic reading of Marx' thought - which he does not dare to attack directly - leaves in the shadows the essence of Marxism. This he interprets as a theory of revolutionary praxis whose spearhead must be the class consciousness of the proletariat.

Lukács' argument is built upon an analysis of the sociological phenomenon of reification. Very generally, reification (from the Latin *res, facere*) designates the transformation into a "thing" of what, originally, does not have the mode of being of a thing. Lukács circumscribed in a more precise fashion the process that he had in view at the beginning of his study of *Verdinglichung*:

the essence of the structure of commodities ... rests on the fact that
a relation between persons takes on the character of a thing, and, in
this way, of a 'phantom objectivity' which, by the system of its
own rigid laws, entirely closed and rational in appearance, conceals
every trace of its fundamental essence: the relation among men.[13]

In its essence, the production of commodities incarnates a social relationship, the fruit of a relation among men which assumes the form of a
relationship among things, a relation which finds its very self reified.
Lukács takes up here Marx' theory of commodities in *Capital*, according a particular importance to the short chapter on the fetishism of commodities, where he perceives nothing less than the whole doctrine of
historical materialism.[14]

After having distinguished at the beginning of *Capital* the notions
of use value and exchange value, Marx undertakes the task of making
evident the purely social origin of exchange value: it is the quantum of
human work which determines the amount of commodity value. But if
exchange value is a function of the work invested in an item, how does
one measure in its turn human work? This measure will be equally of a
social order: the price of work, the wage of the worker, will depend on
the cost of its reproduction. It is necessary to grant to the proletarian a
wage which will permit him to maintain his livelihood and to return to
work the next day. The worker thus exchanges the strength of his
work for the necessary means to his sustenance. The capitalist, on his
side, will use the power of work to produce goods which will bring
him profit, "surplus value". According to Marx, the profit which the
owner of the means of production collects arises from the disproportion
between the compensation given to the work-force and the value that it
effectively produces in goods. It is, therefore, on the exploitation of
human work that the production of goods and the inequality of social
classes rest. The role of ideology will consist in rendering this
exploitation invisible by making the begetting of surplus value pass for
a virtue inherent in the value itself. Profit appears to be a "thing" which
flows "physically" from the production of goods. The structure of
commodities appears itself like a "thing" - a "fetish" as Marx ironically
notes - because it is endowed with the "magical" virtue of creating surplus value (it is important to see the relation between this alleged "ma-
gic" and the term "fetish" employed by Marx). Under capitalist ideology - and the expression "ideology" is understood here as a false conception of the real which serves the interests of the dominant class[15] -
the social and "unnatural" origin of profit, the exploitation of the proletariat, must remain hidden, because the elevation to consciousness of
this process would be fatal for the bourgeoisie.

The originality of Lukács consists in showing that the reification of the commodity structure and human work penetrates all the spheres of society, to the point of becoming the "universal category of social being"[16] in the capitalist era. The hegemony of exchange value in our society gives way to a uniformization of all human activities, governed henceforth by the principle of exchange and, thus, the interchangeability of individuals. The production of exchange value represents the common denominator of the real, the fate from which no one can escape, as if it were an eternal law of human affairs. Nevertheless, exchange value sinks its roots in the ideologically concealed reification of men's labor, the proletarian's sale of the substance of his work like something extrinsic to himself, in order to manufacture an object which does not belong to him. Reification is, thus, the fact of a double alienation: the worker is first of all cut off from the substance of his work and then, secondly, from the product of his labor. The consequence of this reification is manifested in the progressive disappearance of the individual, personal, and teleological character of human work, a dehumanization which will command the humanist reaction of Marxism such as Lukács understands it.

Lukács discerns both objective and subjective aspects of reification. On the objective plane, reification brings about the appearance of a world of things and of laws conceived as "so many insurmountable powers producing their total effect all by themselves".[17] Men must bend themselves to the objective fate of economic "laws", whose logic is supposed to escape their control. Thus there is set up a sphere of objectivity for scientific research which will be able to study the so-called economic facts (*Tatsachen*), without bothering to call to mind that those facts embody "facts" in the active sense of the term, that is to say, of historical, reified products of social relations containing nothing immutable. Lukács' most penetrating analyses, which will later permeate critical theory, are devoted to subjective reification, to the reification of consciousness and of personality in capitalist society. The alienation of the worker in regard to the reified substance of his work follows in the wake of a decomposition of his subjectivity. The human being must abdicate the whole affective, or qualitative, side of his person when he works at the factory, where the quantitative imperatives of the rationalized process of production reign supreme. Consequently, the subject loses its active character in order to become the passive spectator of what happens to it. Man no longer appears as the bearer and the accountable source of social reality, as the axle which makes the system turn, but as one of its cogs. Subjectivity is inscribed in a gigantic enterprise of rationalization, which Simmel and Weber - Lukács' teachers in sociology - had already treated in their studies on the spirit of capitalism. But Lukács goes beyond his teachers when he sees in scientific objectivity, scrupulously defended by Weber in the name of the exclusion of value-judgments in science, an ideological lure of capitalist reification.[18] The science which is content with registering facts and with considering their objective laws, or the ideal types of the system, remains at a descriptive and formalist level which does not get to the core of things, that is, does not discover the ideological origin of the reified world, of which it is the reflection and the "good" conscience. By limiting itself to the study of the immutable regularities of the social world, science that claims to be free from prejudices preaches in truth political quietism and resignation. In order to render transparent the material substrate of reification, Marxist theory, as Lukács conceives it, must draw on two central notions, both originally Hegelian, those of mediation and totality.

The category of mediation permits us first of all to penetrate the alleged immediacy of the reified world, to let us take notice of the derived character of the existing order and of formalist objectivity. The objectivity founded on the methodological exclusion of the inquirer's subjectivity is unveiled as the historical result of a conditioning of consciousness by the capitalist system which lives off the reification of human work. The order of things that appears to us evident, "immediate", namely the domination of objectivity, of calculation, in brief of rationalization, only seems that way as the result of a mediation of consciousness secretly dictated by bourgeois ideology. According to Lukács, to trace the historical genesis of the so-called immediacy of the "facts" that characterize the capitalist régime is to furnish for the proletariat the means to liberate itself from reification under all its forms. The theoretical reconstruction of the constitutive mediations of capitalism is therefore linked to a political project, a link which reverses the separation of theory and practice in the self-understanding of bourgeois science.

The critical potential of the notion of mediation can be exercised only in the framework of a really and actually totalizing comprehension of reality. As Lukács observes, the notion of totality has become suspect in an age when positivism reigns, in which one can see the philosophical application of capitalism. A reflection on the real in its totality is today branded as a relapse into metaphysics, on the grounds that it exceeds the limits of scientific objectivity which in principle must restrict itself to immediate empirical givens. According to Lukács, this scientific "modesty" is a by-product of capitalist specialization and reification. The specialization and particularization of scientific research function to prevent a totalizing consideration of the real, which could have subversive consequences. If objective science resigns itself to the study of parts of the real and of its merely formal regularities, it is in order to discredit every totalizing perspective and, thereby, every material perspective which could come to shake its foundations. The limit of capitalist rationalization is encountered in the irrationality of the matter that is removed from its formal jurisdiction (a thesis that Lukács tries to demonstrate through an interpretation of what he calls the *aporiae* of bourgeois philosophy from Kant to Hegel[19]). Lukács unmasks the fundamental incoherence of the capitalist system in the incapacity of scientific formalism to embrace the real in its totality. This only becomes manifest starting from a totalizing conception in which coherence acts as a criterion of truth for the critique of ideologies. Much has been written on the idealist connotations of the notion of totality, but it is, in short, only the result, on the plane of science, of the principle of contradiction to which every theory remains subordinated. The great force of Marxism, its keystone, Lukács thought, is to adopt systematically the point of view of totality, in his eyes that of dialectic, which enabled him to question the material base of current society:

> It is not the preponderance of economic motives in the explanation of history which distinguishes in a decisive fashion Marxism from bourgeois science: it is the viewpoint of totality. The category of totality, the determining rule in every domain of the whole over all parts, is the essence of the method that Marx borrowed from Hegel and which he transformed in an original manner in order to make it the foundation of an entirely new science.[20]

The analysis of commodities in Marx incarnates, according to Lukács, the Archimedean point of a totalizing and coherent reading of the real. Only if this analysis is to become historically effective, and that means subversive, a well-determined subject will have to make its own this totalizing perspective in order to be capable of accounting for all the ramifications of capitalist reification. This historical subject, which takes its very self as an object, will be the proletariat. Lukács contends that the proletarian class is the only one which can become conscious of reification and overcome it. But, one might object, will not the reification of the workers' consciousness end up by preventing the emergence of such class consciousness? Who will assure us that the consciousness of the proletariat will be capable of liberating itself from the ideological bombardment of which it is the target? Lukács seems to be quite conscious of the dilemma. That would explain why he rapidly dropped the Luxembourgian theory of the revolutionary proletariat, dominant in the first essays of *History and Class Consciousness*, in order to rally to the Leninist theory of the Party as the vanguard, entrusted with the mission of instructing and guiding the masses who would otherwise succumb to ideological reification. Variations in Lukács' text have been discussed at length by commentators.[21] It seems to us that, if the argument of Lukács' book is to be faithful to its title, priority must be given to the class consciousness of the proletariat, because the working class must in one way or another give its assent to the Party, hence must recognize itself in the institution which claims to speak in its name. If the proletariat without a Party is blind, a Party without the proletariat remains empty. Unable to be excluded from revolutionary praxis, the proletariat must be in a position to take cognizance of its situation and to resist reification.

In order to establish this capacity for resistance, Lukács must again have recourse to idealist terminology. At the level of being, he writes, the bourgeoisie and the proletariat are both prisoners of reification, dominated by the dictatorship of the quantifiable.[22] But if the proletariat can raise reification to consciousness, it is because, within the working class, quantity is metamorphosed into quality[23]; for it suffers in a qualitative manner from the unlimited quantification to which it is subjected. Because it is to the detriment of the proletariat that reification occurs - because it is the proletariat which in its suffering bears the burden of capitalist exploitation - its social situation must, for that reason, take the form of an objectivity separated from the subjectivity of the worker[24], a brutal objectification of work which will thus be able to be raised to consciousness. Exploitation, which ideology seeks to render invisible, cannot remain hidden over the long run. As Habermas observes[25], Lukács' solution rests in the final analysis on a postulate, notably on a purely theoretical confidence in the "remainder" of mankind and of a sensitivity capable of awaking the resistance of the proletariat. The transformation of quantity into quality and the possibility of a reconciliation of subjectivity and objectivity by reason of an objectification pushed to the extreme, to its human limit, are so many theoretical solutions to the practical dilemma of the ideological integration of the proletariat.

It is on this decisive point that the critical theory of Horkheimer and Adorno distances itself from Lukács. Far from signifying the collapse of Lukács' conception of totality, as Jay has recently attempted to show[26], critical theory accomplishes its radicalization. Reification is now total to an extent that all proletarian resistance appears stifled until further notice. After 1937, Horkheimer was constrained to recognize that the "situation of the proletariat no longer constitutes in this society the guarantee of a correct consciousness".[27] From this fact, critical theory only drew the conclusion implied in Lukács' thesis, according to which reification "has penetrated all the way to the soul of the worker".[28] The subjective reification of consciousness through the intermediacy of mass culture hinders, on the side of the working class, every awareness of the foundations of reification. Critical theory did not, for all that, give up the idea of a totalizing interpretation[29] of the real based on capitalist reification. Contrary to Lukács, the totalizing interpretation was be recognized as a theoretical, and not practical, perspective of the intellectual who seeks to understand the social totality resulting from reification, the totalizing aim of the thinker reflecting, so to speak, that of capitalism in its totalitarian tendency. Conscious awareness became what it was *de facto* for Lukács, that is to say the business of the theoretician rather than of the proletariat, wholly integrated *sans reste* under the ideology of capital. Just as in Lukács, capitalist society is disdained because of its incoherence, because of the contradiction which exists between increasing rationalization and the irrationality of social suffering that it engenders. The incoherence of advanced capitalism resides in the contradiction between the perfecting of technology and the material misery of the masses[30] - an intuition reserved, however, to a handful of intellectuals.

Critical theory was not afraid to take responsibility for the elitist consequences of such a vision of things, even if it claims to speak always in the name of the emancipation of the masses who turn their backs to their own liberation: "Until the great historical overthrow is brought about, it is possible that truth will have to be sought among numerically small groups."[31] Considering itself as one of the last bastions of truth, critical theory must put up with its isolation and with the theoretical utopia of a world totally different, but unlikely. In the context of advanced reification, the idea of an elitist truth reserved to the theoreticians, although dangerous, is not entirely devoid of justification. Since the thinkers of totality are condemned to marginality, it is not unreasonable to believe that one must stand at the margins of the system in order to seize its operation. In *Traditional and Critical Theory*, Horkheimer still seemed to maintain the hope that a critical theory of society will be able to serve as a catalyst when conditions are more propitious for revolution: "History teaches that such groups, hardly recognized even by their opposition to the social order, banished from society, but imperturbable in their perseverance, can, by reason of their more profound political understanding, become at the decisive moment the spearhead of action."[32] In the face of the rise of fascism, the failure of the 1917 Revolution, and the stabilization of capitalism, this hope, the last vestige of Lukács' Messianism, declined more and more in the evolution of critical theory through the course of the Forties.

The persistence and aggravation of reification gave birth to the legendary pessimism of critical theory, once again a consequence of Lukács' thesis, which made revolution depend on men's consciousness. How can one believe in revolution, when every form of critical consciousness is in the process of being liquidated and when all subjectivity finds itself drained under the domination of the principle of exchange?

The optimism of Lukács' philosophy of history was transformed

into its opposite: instead of leading us towards liberation, the progress
of history is made in the sense of the progressive disappearance of the
possibilities of salvation.[33] In the course of this fatalistic reading of
history, reification will cease to represent the *proprium* of capitalism, as
with Lukács, in order to characterize the vice of civilization as a whole.
All of Western culture since Homer finds itself stricken with the taint of
reification. The project of a mastery of nature, which defines our
civilization, is inevitably accompanied by a domination of man by man.
The objectification of nature for the purposes of domination opens the
way to the mutilation of human nature. If he wishes to survive - such is
the tragic lesson of the *Odyssey* according to the *Dialectic of the
Enlightenment* - man must reify his subjectivity, oppose himself to
nature, which, however, will end up by rebelling against him in order
to plunge him back into the barbarism from which he hoped to deliver
himself thanks to his reason. The category of totality, which Lukács
had turned to account in order to understand the social order of his time,
extended to the history of humanity brought under the emblem of
reification. Of course, and somewhat paradoxically, the totalizing and
unilateral interpretation of civilization makes itself seem the reflection of
a totalizing and uniformizing system of oppression that it is precisely a
question of combatting.

The dialectic of totality, essential to theory, but criticized in
practice, is of great subtlety. The condemnation of totality was itself
made in a totalizing manner, as the famous aphorism of the *Minima
Moralia* attests: "the whole is the untrue". This reformulation of the
motto of Hegel's system operates on two levels of meaning. In the first
place, Adorno rendered a very somber verdict on the society in which
we live, where there is, it seems, nothing true following the nearly total
reification of subjectivity. But, in the second place, the text attacks the
very notion of totality (it is the category of totality that is false because it
assimilates all individuality), which it nevertheless had used to condemn
current society *in toto*. This amphiboly flows from Adorno's 'system'
- understood, as is fitting, as an anti-system - which knows it must
fight against ideology by borrowing its own weapons. The negative
dialectic makes itself seem negative in that it takes apart the existing
system and denounces its negativity; but it is also negative because it
refuses to enunciate a positive principle beyond or on this side of the
principle of exchange which impregnates capitalism and, in the final
account, all of Western civilization. Adorno finds himself again in the
delicate situation of having to criticize the totalizing ambitions of
reification by having recourse himself to judgments not less totalizing.
That is why Adorno will acknowledge towards the end of his
anti-system that the "Negative Dialectic is the self-consciousness of the
system of objective blindness (*objektiven Verblendungzusammen-*

hangs), from which, for all that, it has not been rescued."[34]

The criticism of totality even progressed to the point of relativizing the totalizing possibilities of Lukács' notion of reification. The philosopher must not imagine that he possesses a "philosopher's stone" in the dissolution of reification. "Dialectic", continues Adorno, "can no longer be brought to reification nor to any other isolated category."[35] In a characteristic gesture, Adorno refused to rivet dialectic to the notion of reification in a book which, nevertheless, on every page, denounces reification under the headings, more proper to his philosophy, of "principle of exchange" or "principle of identity". Adorno seemed to refuse to make the critique of society gravitate around an Archimedean point, a strategy which would only cause the logic of identity to be reproduced, according to which every form of individuality must be brought back to a universal equalizer. In other words, Lukács himself secretly obeyed the logic of the system that he was denouncing in interpreting society from an identical and universal point of view, which, on the plane of formalism, has nothing to envy in the formal principles for which bourgeois science prides itself.

In addition to rejecting, in theory, the idea of a universalizing principle, with a view to safeguarding the possibility of the totally other, Adorno blamed in particular the notion of reification because it tries to reduce the entire status of a thing to the product of a constituting subjectivity. This tendency, according to him, betrays an idealistic hostility with respect to thingness and to heterogeneity in general. The dissolution of the object's autonomy, or the rejection of a thing-in-itself, serves as a pretext for subjectivity's aspiration to total domination. Against the imperialism of the subject, Adorno stressed the element of otherness and non-identity that the thing-in-itself "contains" in regard to a dominating subjectivity. A truly human world would not be one where thingness would be dissolved, but one where men would know how to live together with things without submitting them to the imperatives of production. The task of philosophy, Adorno concludes, is, therefore, to think what differs from thought - the whole other which marks the limit of the totalizing concept.

On this ground, the later Lukács could certainly agree with Adorno's basic motivation.[36] Not only did Lukács several times recant the idealism of his youthful writings, he saw the necessity of distinguishing alienation (*Entfremdung*) from objectification (*Vergegenständlichung*), concepts which were fatally confused in *History and Class Consciousness*.[37] Objectification inhabits every human expression, and becomes alienation only if it leads to the oppression of man. Certain aspects of the defense of realism and the turn toward ontology in the later Lukács have an echo, essentially in the primacy of the object proclaimed in the negative dialectic, even if the political and practical

conclusions that the two authors would draw from it remain diametrically opposed.

The most recent round of the critical theory debate on the issue of
reification has been conducted by Habermas. At the time of his
university studies, Habermas was seized with enthusiasm in reading
History and Class Consciousness, since he had learned, after the
fashion of several Western Marxists, that it was possible not only to
repeat the doctrine of Marx, but to use it for understanding the
interrelation of political, social, and philosophical problems in our
age.[38] Lukács, who thus opened to him the way to the young Marx[39],
sensitized him to the project of a reconstruction of historical
materialism; but Habermas had to confess with a certain sadness, he
says[40], that it was impossible for him to follow in Lukács' tracks - but
without making clear precisely why. Considering the impact that
Lukács seems to have had on the orientation of his own thought, it is a
little surprising to see that Habermas has never devoted a thematic study
to him[41], that he is, for all intents and purposes, absent from his book
entitled *Toward a Reconstruction of Historical Materialism* [42], and that
he does not figure in the gallery of the *Philosophical-Political
Profiles*[43], alongside Heidegger, Jaspers, Gehlen, Plessner, Bloch,
Adorno, Mitscherlich, Löwith, Wittgenstein, Arendt, Abendroth,
Marcuse, Benjamin, Scholem, Gadamer, Horkheimer, and Löwenthal,
in short, the intellectuals of the twentieth century who have most
influenced the thought of Habermas. The debate of Habermas with
Lukács has really been set in motion only in his imposing *Theory of
Communicative Action*, published in 1981. One must note that this
debate had then become ineluctable, since Habermas proposes in this
summa to define his position with regard to the heritage of critical
theory. One of the principal motivations of this work is to clarify the
normative foundation of the critique of instrumental reason, which
remains hidden, according to Habermas, in the negativism of the
Frankfurt School.

Habermas begins by reformulating the Lukácsian problem of
reification in communicative terms, in order to make precise what is
damaged in the wake of capitalist reification. If critical theory must
make use of a critical standard of which it can also render an account - a
task which sums up the project of a theory of communicative action[44] -
it must be capable of declaring in what name the critique of reification is
conducted. What is it in man that is destroyed through reification ?
Habermas is of the opinion that it is communicative relations among
men which suffer from the objectification of human work:

> To the extent that relations of interaction in the sphere of social
> work are regulated in a traditional manner by organic norms,

individuals maintain, with themselves and among each other, communicative relations that they intentionally contract. That would also be the case if one day social relations succeeded in being determined by a collective will. But so long as the production of goods is organized according to the production of exchange values and the substance of the work of the producers is itself exchanged like merchandise, another mechanism for the co-ordination of activity is in force: the economically relevant orientations of action are dissolved from the context of the life-world and reattached to the medium of exchange value (or money). In the measure that interactions are no longer co-ordinated by the intermediacy of norms and of values, but by the medium of exchange value, the agents must adopt an objectifying attitude among each other (and with their very own selves). It is then that they experience the mechanism of the co-ordination of activity as something external.[45]

Individuals' relations, subject in principle to communicative co-ordination, are frozen into relations among things, ruled by the logic of exchange value. According to Habermas, the critique of reification is carried out in the name of communication, trampled under the weight of a capitalist logic which has become second nature for the social agents - and in the name of a society where communication could be deployed without obstacles. Essentially, it is in the communicative situation, alone qualified for making decisions democratically (and, thus, rationally) about the main orientations of social action, that Habermas perceives the normative foundation of the critical theory of society. Observing the absence of a critical standard in critical theory, Habermas believes that classical critical theory has had to fill in this gap by an idealist philosophy of history, an expedient rendered null and void, he contends, as soon as a theory of communicative action is elaborated.

Of course, Lukács did not himself define the problem of reification in communicative terms; but his thought is not, for all that, devoid of a normative foundation. For him, criticism proceeds from ethical bases in the name of humanity and justice, of which the proletarians are deprived under the yoke of reification. Certainly, these criteria, whose value will always remain intuitive, are very general; but is that not also true of the idea of a communicative reconciliation? Is it really necessary to express the standard of critical theory in terms of communication? For it is not only communication which is impeded under the mode of capitalist production. The most elementary justice suffers also from an unequal distribution of the fruits of labor. With the aid of his theory of reification, Lukács means to suggest that the current situation is not eternal, as ideology would wish, but that it results from a historical conditioning which serves the interests of the dominant class. To recognize this situation - and the proletarians are as capable of it as the intellectuals - is to relativize its domination and to open the way to a possible transformation. The interruption of communication is only one part of what there is to denounce in capitalism, man being more than just a means of communication.

Habermas does not see that Lukács' theory already possesses a normative foundation, which has no need to be made explicit in length and in breadth, so evident is its validity. In the eyes of Lukács - and especially of Adorno - the requirement of making explicit the normative foundations proceeds from what one could call a "reification of ethics", from an objectifying scientism, rehabilitated by Habermas, but from whose domination Lukács and Adorno tried to shake loose. Is a well-defined standard indispensable for condemning exploitation? Is there need, to take another example, of a precise normative foundation in order to rebel against genocide, torture, murder, *etc.*? It is doubtful that the suppression of communication is the most relevant criterion here.

Without recognizing the evidentiary character of Marxist ethics, Habermas attributes the impotence of critical theory to the identification of its normative bases with the limits of the philosophy of consciousness (or of subjectivity). That is why he makes himself the advocate of a paradigm change which will replace the philosophy of consciousness by a philosophy of communication (or of intersubjectivity). This change of model, crucial for the whole of his philosophical enterprise, is defended during his examination of the *aporiae* of the *Dialectic of the Enlightenment* of Adorno and of Horkheimer, which follows the discussion of Lukács. First of all, Habermas rightly denounces in critical theory a generalization without limits of reification, which will be extended to the history of civilization in its totality - to the thought of identity, of which exchange value is only the last avatar - and to every expression of the intellect, reduced to its instrumental function.[46] In this context, Habermas notes, the critique of reification becomes more and more abstract, given that it separates reification from the context of interhuman relations and of its capitalist origins.[47] Reification is conceived by Adorno and Horkheimer as the indelible vice in the subject-object relation, the paradigm of the philosophy of consciousness.

Since thought, from the time of its most distant origins, seems to have always been reifying and affirmative (that is, legitimizing the existing order), according to Adorno and Horkheimer, it appears futile to blame capitalist rationalization in the name of another type of rationality. Such a rehabilitation of reason would perpetuate the reign of the will to dominate. Refusing to identify the criteria of its critique of reason, the theory must be content to evoke the possibility of a new attitude in the face of nature, that of a mimesis which seeks to "imitate" rather than to tame nature. The power of mimesis arises from an "impulse"[48] and not from reason, identified without qualification, under the influence of Simmel, Weber, and *Lebensphilosophie*, with reification. The philosophy of the Frankfurt School, Habermas concludes, consciously assumes the dilemma of a theory which must deny its very self as a theory[49] and which does not fear to yield to art, which it will resemble more and more, the cognitive competence of a critical theory of society. Aesthetic theory, preserving the remembrance of mimesis, will become the refuge of a theory resigned to pure contemplation before a situation without escape.[50] The *Theory of Communicative Action* will have no difficulty in denouncing the *aporia* of a contemplative theory which renounces the rationality claims of a theory by shedding light on the normative inspiration of the critique of society, thus avoiding the quietism underlying the self-renunciation of the philosophy of the Frankfurt School. This political resignation, Habermas emphasizes, contrasts violently with the practical intention of the critical theory of the Thirties, which he tries to reactivate at the end of his *Theory of Communicative Action*.[51]

Habermas' study of the *aporiae* of the Frankfurt School is particularly convincing - and even courageous, since he settles accounts with his own teachers. But the analysis becomes much weaker when Habermas imputes the *aporiae* of the dialectic of the Enlightenment to the philosophy of consciousness (which is defined in a very sketchy fashion). For Habermas, who greatly simplifies, the philosophy of consciousness rests on the subject-object relation, which can be articulated in two ways: the subject is related either to the object as it is, by representing it, or else to the object as it must be, by producing it. The two functions of the mind, representation and production, play, however, a connected part, since the knowledge of objects is related structurally to the possibility of intervention in the world objectified by representation.[52]

Consciousness adopts a theoretical attitude in order to be able to act in the universe of things, which it finds in front of itself. It is in these few words that Habermas sums up the philosophy of consciousness. Then Habermas goes on to assert that the "idea of reconciliation cannot be subsumed in a plausible [?] fashion under the fundamental concepts of the philosophy of consciousness from Descartes to Kant and that it can only be formulated in a superabundant (*überschwenglich*) manner in objective idealism from Spinoza and Leibniz up to Schelling and Hegel".[53] Recent studies have easily demonstrated that such a conception does not do justice to the tradition, most particularly to the thought of Kant[54], who formulated the ideal of reconciliation in the idea of a universalist ethics, of a rule of ends, in the recognition of others as ends-in-themselves, in the theory of the interests of reason, *etc.* Under the influence of Tugendhat[55] and his debate with Heinrich, Habermas erects the philosophy of consciousness into a philosophical bogey-man from which only a turn to communication can save us. He does not notice that communication itself has meaning only for a consciousness or for a subject (the two terms are interchangeable since Habermas speaks sometimes of the philosophy of consciousness and other times of the philosophy of the subject). It is because the individual seeks truth and does not always know how to find it by himself that he appeals to the tribunal of a communicative rationality. If rational communication - whose reality is difficult, if not impossible, to verify - can never be abstracted from this subjective will, it can happen, in return, that the subjects can bypass communication. The whole philosophy of communication and of intersubjectivity, flourishing in our age, is a response to the finitude of the modern subject, who can no longer rely on a metaphysical or transcendent authority in order to attain the truth. Transcendence is sought rather in the direction of inter-subjectivity which promises more universality. Communication offers the possibility of arriving at a truth, which is no longer only individual, but it does so only to respond to a claim of subjectivity. Far from declaring the paradigm of subjectivity obsolete, the philosophy of intersubjectivity derives from it and remains beholden to it.[56] Yet this dependence takes nothing away from the immediacy and the importance of this philosophy of communication, which offers remedies for several problems of our time.

The most obvious weakness of Habermas' view resides in his hasty diagnosis of the *aporiae* of the philosophy of consciousness. An attentive reading of his text shows that Habermas has identified only the *aporiae* of the theory of Horkheimer and Adorno, and that he has contented himself with affirming that the philosophy of consciousness was incapable of positively formulating the idea of reconciliation. Although Habermas speaks, at the very end of his exposé, of the aporetic character of the philosophy of consciousness[57], the reader will have noticed that he has in reality only discussed the *aporia* of critical theory, which is not the sole result of modern thought. If critical theory ends up in an impasse, it is because it assimilates reification and the principle of identity, because it projects reification into the epic of civilization as a whole, and because it consequently sees itself constrained to give up trying to point out a possible salvation, except by invoking the idea of an immemorial mimesis. These theses, unique to the Frankfurt School (and perhaps also to Heidegger), and the *aporia* of a theory which must deny its very self to the benefit of art are not characteristics of the philosophy of consciousness as such. Habermas commits a paralogism fraught with consequences when he transposes the *aporia* of critical theory to modern philosophy as a whole, of which he is in so many respects the heir.

Finally, it cannot be seen clearly how the theory of Lukács can be affected by the critique of Horkheimer and Adorno. Claiming to forsake the sphere of the philosophy of consciousness, Habermas believes he will have to reinterpret the pathology of reification because reification remains a category of *Bewusstseinsphilosophie*.[58] (Indeed, it is modeled on the attitude and conduct of individuals in the face of objects, and not on communicative intersubjectivity). Instead of reification, Habermas will prefer to speak of pathologies of the life-world caused by the illegitimate intrusion of functionalist or systemic reason.[59] According to this interpretation, reification represents a mutilation of the life-world, which appears when an instrumental rationality, that has become autonomous, comes to replace the rationality founded on communicative deliberation at the heart of the life-world. The "colonization of the life-world" by a non-communicative rationalization will be the new name of what the philosophy of consciousness called "reification". The communicative pathologies of our real universe are undeniably genuine, and Habermas has devoted some extraordinarily penetrating analyses to them; but they do not recapture what Lukács was primarily aiming at in the term "reification". Lukács blamed above all else the alleged immediacy of the existing social system, which tends to take on the aspect of a second nature. Reification is the key which permits us to perceive the interests which are at work in official ideology or in any other world-view. Spiritual productions are always the deed of a mediation, whose genesis consciousness, armed with the criterion of coherence, can, in a certain measure, retrace. Habermas is correct to reject the idealism of Lukács' philosophy of history; but he has not seen that this philosophy of history can be detached from the theory of reification: it is not necessary to possess the absolute knowledge that Lukács seemed in effect to claim, if one seeks to eliminate the nonsense in our society by a critique of reification.[60] As that happens to all philosophers, Habermas is perhaps the victim of a philosophical synecdoche: he believes he must spurn all of Lukács' theory, because he refuses to accept a part of it. If it appears improbable today that the proletariat, Lukács' absolute subject, or any other group will be able to resolve the complexity of social problems with the aid of the category of reification, this notion remains no less an indispensable tool in the process of self-reflection[61], constitutive of the Enlightenment, which is not thinkable without consciousness.

Translated from the French
  by David Lang
(Boston College)

NOTES

*   This work was subsidized by the Social Sciences and Humanities Research Council of Canada.

1.   M. Merleau-Ponty, *Les aventures de la dialectique*, Gallimard, Paris, 1955, p. 62.

2.   *Ibid.*, p. 14, 48 ff; M. Jay, *Marxism and Totality*, University of California Press, Berkeley/Los Angeles, 1984, p. 84.

3.   *Klassiker der Philosophie* (2 Vols.), Beck, Munich, 1981.

4   *Geschichte der Philosophie in Text und Darstellung: 20. Jahrhundert*, Reclam, Stuttgart, 1981.

5.   Cf. S. Eorsti, 'Das Recht des letzten Wortes', in *G. Lukács, Gelebtes Denken,* Suhrkamp, Frankfurt a. M., 1981, p. 31.

6.   G. Lukács, *Gelebtes Denken*, p. 176, 179.

7.   Cf. Y. Ishaghpour, *Avant-propos à L. Goldmann, Lukács et Heidegger,* Denoël-Gonthier, Paris, 1977, p. 5.

8.   One should compare with this subject the remarks of K. Korsch at the beginning of his essay *Marxisme et philosophie* (1923), Minuit, Paris, 1964, pp. 64-65; cf. also P. Breines, 'Praxis and its Theorists: The Impact of Lukács and Korsch in the 1920's', in *Telos*, 11, 1972, p. 67 ff.

9.   Cf. A. Arato, 'Lukács' Theory of Reification', in *Telos*, 11, 1971, p.44.

10. Cf. G. Lukács, *Geschichte und Klassenbewusstsein* (abbrev.: GK), Malik, Berlin, 1923, p. 82 (we will cite this first edition, since its pagination in the second volume of the *Werke*, Luchterhand, Darmstadt, 1968, of Lukács is the same as in the paperback edition, Sammlung Luchterhand, Darmstadt, 1970, the two most current editions, but without co-ordination of pagination); tr. Fr. *Histoire et conscience de classe* (abbrev.: *HC*), Minuit, Paris, 1960, p. 95.

11. It is perhaps a significant fact that this word "and", which Fichte called "the least philosophical word possible", because too rhapsodic, shines in a constellation of titles of philosophical works published in the twentieth century, probably a symptom of the relative disfavor of systematic thought and of the romantic tendency to cultivate imprecision and the work of imagination. Here is a sampling from among the most classical programmatic writings: *Matter and Memory, Thought and Motion* (Bergson); *Process and Reality* (Whitehead); *Experience and Judgment, Formal and Transcendental Logic* (Husserl); *Formalism in Ethics and the Material Ethics of Values* (Scheler); *The Protestant Ethic and the Spirit of Capitalism, Economy and Society*

(Weber); *Marxism and Philosophy* (Korsch); *Being and Time, Kant and the Problem of Metaphysics* (Heidegger); *Being and Having* (Marcel); *Reason and Existence* (Jaspers); *Traditional Theory and Critical Theory* (Horkheimer); *Natural Right and Human Dignity* (Bloch); *Being and Nothingness* (Sartre); *Eros and Civilization* (Marcuse); *The Visible and the Invisible* (Merleau-Ponty); *The Open Society and its Enemies* (Popper); *Word and Object* (Quine); *Truth and Method* (Gadamer); *Words and Things* (Foucault); *Voice and Phenomenon, Writing and Difference* (Derrida); *Theory and Praxis, Knowledge and Interest* (Habermas); *Philosophy and the Mirror of Nature* (Rorty); *Aesthetic Experience and Literary Hermeneutics* (Jauss); *Time and Recitation* (Ricoeur).

12. K. Marx, *Das Kapital*, in Marx-Engels, *Werke*, Vol. 23, Dietz, Berlin, 1962, p. 16.

13. *GK* 94; *HC* 110.

14. Cf. *GK* 186; *HC* 212.

15. Cf. D. Held, *Introduction to Critical Theory: Horkheimer to Habermas*, University of California Press, Berkeley/Los Angeles, 1980, p. 186.

16. *GK* 97; *HC* 113.

17. *GK* 98; *HC* 114.

18. In his study on Lukács and Heidegger, L. Goldmann has advanced the thesis that *Being and Time* (1927) could be read as a debate with the problem of reification developped in *History and Class Consciousness* (1923). It is now possible to refute this thesis. Not only has Heidegger acknowledged not having read Lukács (cf. *Martin Heidegger*, ed. L'Herne, Paris, 1983, p. 162), an avowal that one might, to a certain extent, subject to doubt, but also the recent publication of a course dating from 1921/22   (M. Heidegger, *Phänomenologische Interpretationen zu Aristoteles. Einführung in die phänomenologische Forschung*, Gesamtausgabe, Band 61, Y. Klostermann, Frankfurt a. M., 1985) shows that Heidegger already was acquainted with the theme of reification (*op. cit.,* p. 150, 198). Significantly, Heidegger makes an allusion to the question of the *Verdinglichung* raised in Ebbinghaus' habilitation thesis of 1921. Lukács and Heidegger were both dependent on the context of *Lebensphilosophie;* it suffices to point out with Lukács (*Werke*, Vol. II, p. 24 = *HC* 398) that the problem of reification was then in the air.

19. Cf., on this subject, A. Arato, *op. cit.,* and T. Rockmore, 'La philosophie classique allemande et Marx selon Lukács', in *Archives de philosophie*, 41, 1978, pp. 569-595, which draws attention to Lukács' debt to Emil Lask.

20. *GK* 39; *HC* 47.

21. Cf. in particular L. Goldmann, *op. cit.,* pp. 135-138; M. Jay,

'The Concept of Totality in Lukács and Adorno', in *Telos*, 32, 1977, pp. 127-128.

22. *GK* 180-181; *HC* 205.

23. *GK* 182-183; *HC* 208. Cf. A. Arato, *op. cit.*, p. 58.

24. *GK* 184; *HC* 209: "at the same time, however, the split which arises, precisely here, in man objectivizing himself like merchandise, between objectivity and subjectivity, permits this situation to become conscious".

25. *Theorie des kommunikativen Handelns* (abbrev.: *TKH*), Suhrkamp, Frankfurt a. M., 1981, Vol. 1, pp. 491-492.

26. *Marxism and Totality,* University of California Press, Berkeley/Los Angeles, 1984, pp. 241-275.

27. M. Horkheimer, *Traditionelle und kritische Theorie*, Fischer, Frankfurt a. M., 1970 p. 33; tr. Fr. *Théorie traditionelle et théorie critique*, Gallimard, Paris, 1974, p. 45.

28. *GK* 99; *HC* 115.

29. Cf. H. Marcuse, 'La philosophie et la théorie critique' (1937), in H. Marcuse, *Culture et société*, Minuit, Paris, 1970, p. 149.

30. It is on these grounds that Marcuse will denounce the irrationality of the rationality of the mode of capitalist production in *L'homme unidimensional*, Minuit-Points, Paris, 1970, pp. 45, 53, 182, 273, 291, 298.

31. M. Horkheimer, *op. cit.*, p. 55; tr. Fr. p. 78.

32. *Loc.cit.*.

33. Cf. Th. W. Adorno, *Negative Dialektik*, Suhrkamp, Frankfurt a. M., 1980, p. 314; tr. Fr. *Dialectique négative*, Payot, Paris, 1978, p. 250: "No universal history leads from the savage to civilized humanity, but there is probably one which leads from the slingshot to the atomic bomb"; Cf. also M. Jay, *Marxism and Totality*, p. 263.

34. Th. W. Adorno, *op. cit.*, p. 398; tr. Fr. p. 316 (modified).

35. *Ibid.* p. 191; tr. Fr. p. 151.

36. A convergence emphasized, by the mediation of their reading of Hegel, in N. Tertullian, 'Lukács, Adorno et la philosophie classique allemande', in *Archives de philosophie*, 47, 1984, pp. 177-206.

37. Cf. the new preface of *GK* in *Werke*,II, p. 26-7 (= HC 401). On the differentiation of the theory of reification in the later thought of Lukács, cf. N. Tertullian, 'Die Ontologie Georg Lukács", in *Merkur*, vol. 434, 1985, pp. 309-321.

38. Cf. the interview in J. Habermas, *Kleine Politische Schriften* I-IV, Suhrkamp, Frankfurt a. M., 1981, pp. 515- 516.

39. Cf. the article 'Dialektik der Rationalisierung', in *Ästhetik und Kommunikation*, 45, 1981.

40. *Kleine Politische Schriften* I-IV, p. 515.

41. At the very most a few pages here and there, for example in the

preface to the second edition of *Theorie und Praxis,* Suhrkamp, Frankfurt a. M., 1971, pp. 39-41.

42. *Zur Rekonstruktion des historischen Materialismus,* Suhrkamp, Frankfurt a/M., 1976.

43. *Philosophisch-politische Profile,* erweiterte Auflage, Suhrkamp, Frankfurt a. M., 1981.

44. *TKH* I, 7.

45. *TKH* I, 478.

46. *TKH* I, 506-507.

47. *TKH* I, 508. It bears emphasis that this critique does not affect Lukács. Habermas seems to recognize it in his most recent book, *Der philosophische Diskurs der Moderne,* Suhrkamp, Frankfurt a. M., 1985, p. 263.

48. *TKH* I, 512.

49. *TKH* I, 514.

50. *Loc.cit.*

51. *TKH* II, 548-593. Cf. also J. Habermas, *Vorstudien und Ergänzungen zur Theorie des kommunikativen Handelns,* Suhrkamp, Frankfurt a. M., 1984, p. 496.

52. *TKH* I, 519.

53. *Loc.cit..*

54. Cf. O. Höffe, 'Kantische Skepsis gegen die transzendentale Kommunikationsethik', in *Kommunikation und Reflexion,* Suhrkamp, Frankfurt a. M., 1982, pp. 518-539; 'Ist die transzendentale Vernunftkritik in der Sprachphilosophie aufgehoben?', in *Philosophisches Jahrbuch,* 91, 1984, pp. 250-272; W. Lutterfelds, *Bin ich nur öffentliche Person?,* Forum Academicum, Königstein, 1982.

55. E. Tugendhat, *Selbstbewusstsein und Selbstbestimmung,* Suhrkamp, Frankfurt a. M., 1979; cf. TKH I, 527 ff.

56. Cf. already M. Theunissen, *Gesellschaft und Geschichte. Zur Kritik der kritischen Theorie,* de Gruyter, Berlin, 1969, p. 31, who remarks that intersubjectivity is only an expanded subjectivity.

57. *TKH* I, 534.

58. *TKH* II, 557.

59. *TKH* II, 293, 481, 489 ff.

60. This is the meaning of the reappropriation of Lukács by Merleau-Ponty, criticized by Habermas in *TKH* I, 487 note.

61. This Lukácsian spirit is asserted besides in Habermas' conception of philosophy. Cf. *Zur Rekonstruction des historischen Materialismus,* Suhrkamp, Frankfurt a. M., 1976, p. 58: "Die vornehmste Aufgabe der Philosophie sehe ich darin, gegen jede Gestalt des Objektivismus, gegen die ideologische, d.h. scheinhafte Verselbständigung von Gedanken und Institutionen gegenüber ihrer lebenspraktischen Entstehungs- und Verwendungszusammenhangen,

die Kraft der radikalen Selbstreflexion aufzubieten."

WILLIAM L. MCBRIDE

Reification Re-examined

There is no doubt in my mind but that the notion of reification as elaborated upon by Georg Lukács in *History and Class Consciousness*, particularly in the long chapter whose title begins with the word *"Verdinglichung"*, played an enormously important and generally useful explanatory role in the social theory of the mid-twentieth century - roughly the middle fifty years of that century. This is so despite all the fuzziness and "fudging" of which he may be guilty in other writings. This complaint is raised against him by four former students, who have published a short commentary on the *Ontology* that he produced late in life; they urge a return to the treatment of the notion that is to be found in his classic of the 1920s.[1]

At the same time, I have always felt some sympathy with the spirit of the complaints that Feher and the others now raise against Lukács' usage of the term in his later work. My partial agreement with them, however, has been based on misgivings about its meaning in *History and Class Consciousness* itself. I have experienced these misgivings not only in my private readings and re-readings of the book (for which, I repeat, I continue to have great admiration); more significantly (since we are dealing with questions about the social-theoretical explanation of modern society), I have experienced these misgivings in trying to convey, to eager but puzzled students, an understanding of what Lukács or anyone else means by "reification".

Thus I thought that it might be a useful exercise to try to reconsider once again here, despite, but in part also because of, the fact that "reification" has been one of the principal focuses of scholarly attention directed at the exact significance of, and some of the problems related to, this notion. Although I consider this undertaking to have an intrinsic interest, it seems to me also to bear the potential of shedding some light on some more recent thought, of both the specific theoretical and the general *zeitgeistlich* variety. Accordingly, I shall divide this paper into five sections: (1) some preliminary commonplaces and puzzles; (2) divergent perspectives of commentators; (3) the text itself; (4) Jean-Paul Sartre's reference to reification in his *Critique of Dialectical Reason*; (5) concluding reflections on the relevance of the concept to the contemporary scene.

T. Rockmore (ed.), Lukács Today, 108–125.
© *1988 by D. Reidel Publishing Company.*

I. COMMONPLACES AND PUZZLES

Anyone who cares at all about this aspect of Lukács' thought knows that *Verdinglichung* is the central concept of the central essay in his great early philosophical synthesis, published only a few years after his decisive turn to Marxism. The idea itself has its roots in the thought of Hegel and, indeed, before that in the thought of Kant, in a sense *malgré lui*; it has a close connection (precisely what connection is a matter of dispute) with the even better known Hegelian concept of alienation or estrangement. The latter, in Hegel, is a thoroughly trans-historical phenomenon; but already in the thought of Max Weber, the concept of reification appears as a generalization concerning many phenomena that are said to be peculiar to the modern world, to modern culture. The idea of reification is also centrally employed by the political economist, Georg Simmel, whom Lukács respected as a teacher at an early stage in his career. But Simmel makes little or no use of the word, *Verdinglichung*, itself in his *magnum opus*, *Philosophie des Geldes*, and Simmel's focus on the reificatory role of money is very different from Lukács' later emphases.[2]

In *History and Class Consciousness* Lukács draws upon passages from Marx, and most particularly from the chapter on 'The Fetishism of Commodities' in Volume One of *Capital*, to show that the concept of reification, even though not *eo nomine*, is basic to Marx' understanding of how individuals work under capitalism. More precisely, it is basic to understand how they are led to regard the structural components of their economic system, beginning with commodities as defined and treated within that system, as if they were the real and unalterable determinants of their human existence. Lukács then goes on to generalize from this Marxian insight (about the way in which a capitalist economy functions and maintains itself), to many areas of modern thought, the ideological "superstructure" that reinforces capitalism, to which, as Lukács perceives it, the "reifying" tendency has spread. In pursuing this thread, Lukács finds some common ground not only with Weber, but also with elements of the romantic, often idealistic and sometimes politically reactionary, criticism of the "soulless" spirit of dawning modernity that is to be found in abundance in nineteenth- and early twentieth-century Central European thought, including his own pre-Marxist writings. Thus, such terms as "formalism", "quantification", "calculation", and even "rationality" and "objectivity" as understood in dominant modern bourgeois *milieux* are treated pejoratively and shown to play a role, often remarked upon but incorrectly perceived by those who do not share an overall Marxist theoretical framework, in the pervasive reification of our culture. Lukács then points to the "imputed" or "ascribed", as distinguished from the actual, empirical, class consciousness of the rising proletariat as the real agent capable of piercing the illusions of reification, though not all at once, and of bringing about fundamental socio-economic change. But this final turn of thought takes me beyond the scope of the present paper.

Finally, it is important to note, in order to complete this preliminary statement of commonplaces: that Lukács' book evoked considerable criticism from leading Marxist circles from the very beginning; that he later declared himself to have left behind some of its most basic theoretical positions and did not wish to see himself identified with it any longer; but that he permitted himself, in 1967, to write a substantial Preface to a new edition in which - while continuing to insist that *History and Class Consciousness* contains some fundamental errors, most notably a tendency to idealism and a profoundly mistaken identification of objectification with alienation - he furnished a more balanced appraisal of its worth than he had during his time of total self-abnegation. It is important also to note that critics have long appreciated the remarkable extent to which passages in *History and Class Consciousness* seem to anticipate ideas held by Marx in his 1844 writings, which were not known at the time when Lukács composed his classic.

Lukács *nolens volens*, the concept of reification found very sympathetic echoes in existentialist thought, especially French existentialist thought, two decades or so after Lukács' systematic use of it. Instances of the term are still occasionally to be found in his *The Destruction of Reason* and even in his unfortunate *Existentialisme ou Marxisme?*, in which he polemicizes against the entire existentialist movement as "the philosophy of imperialism".[3] Particularly in the person of Jean-Paul Sartre, however, whom Lukács denounces roundly and frequently in that work, the existentialist movement was increasingly coming to terms with Marxism, and it seems to me unquestionable that "reification" served as an important conceptual vehicle to facilitate this development.

Considered in itself, this briefly recounted, familiar story is as replete with historical paradoxes, "counter- finalities", as was Lukács' entire life. A considerable familiarity with the ebb and flow of the intellectual and the political history of our century is required in order to reduce their puzzling surface appearance to some semblance of coherence. If, for a moment, I may make use of an artificial distinction that is not to be found in reality, it is worth considering the fact that the textual, as contrasted with the contextual, puzzles surrounding the concept of "reification" are at least equally striking and interesting.

First of all, we labor under a linguistic difficulty in English, as do writers in French, in that "thingification", like "chosification", sounds alien, if not alienating, like a kind of trick. So we feel obligated to stick, in both English and French, with our respective adaptations of the Latin term. But "*reificatio*" is not to be found in dictionaries of classical Latin, either; while the base noun, "*res*", lives, it would appear a more exciting existence in that language than does "thing" in English: "*res publica*", for example, is the commonwealth, and "*res Romana*" is the Roman state, than which virtually nothing was held in higher esteem in the 'establishment' literature of that culture. To the extent to which, then, we wish to share Lukács' contempt for the phenomenon of *Verdinglichung*, those of us who are sensitive to the etymology of its Anglo-French equivalent experience some initial difficulty. At the same time, we are cut off from the rich associations that the German word bears. To say "reification" is in no sense to conjure up anything in English that resembles the German "*bedingen*", obscurely connected as it may be to certain connotations of *Verdinglichung*, much less to recall the Kantian "*Ding-an-sich*" of which, as passages in the chapter on 'Reification and the Consciousness of the Proletariat' show, Lukács was obviously thinking.[4]

In a portion of the Kantian tradition to which Hegel, Marx, and even Engels, so often the object of Lukács' criticism, were heirs, "things" are opposed to "persons"; so Engels characterizes the decisive moment of future social revolution as that at which the administration over persons gives way to an administration over things. But not all German thought takes an equally negative view, of the sort that Lukács takes, of things. In particular we find in the writings of Martin Heidegger, *bête brune* to Lukács' *bête rouge*, a remarkable paean to "*das Ding*" and a call to reconsider, in a non-calculative, non-representational way, its significance. Heidegger recalls, *inter alia*, that "*thing*", in Old High German, means "a gathering"; he might have mentioned, as added evidence for his argument in favor of thinking of "things" in a more positive way, that the same root word was used as the name for Western history's first on-going parliamentary gathering, at Thingvellir in Iceland. "The thing things", says Heidegger; it brings about nearness, presence.[5] In other words, it makes sense to Heidegger to speak of things as genuine subjects of active verbs, rather than as merely contemptible passive recipients of action. Despite the enormous extravagance of the later Heidegger's language, I do not regard his effort to restore some importance to things in our world as being wholly valueless. It is not irrelevant to an assessment of Lukács' metaphor of "reification".

For we are concerned, after all is said and done, with an elaborate metaphor. True, philosophy, and indeed theory in general, could not survive without metaphors and related conceits, and a richly suggestive metaphor systematically wielded, like "reification", can be, and in this case surely was, an enormous contribution to philosophical thinking.

But it remains a metaphor, with all that that implies concerning the possible limitations of its scope of applicability, its possible abuses, its potentially misleading character, and so on. "Reification" may well at one time have been the most apt available metaphor for the entire bourgeois worldview, but it may not be so any more, and in any case it could never, as a metaphor, serve as a perfect "representation" of that worldview. This point should be kept in mind as we examine Lukács' actual text later on.

II. DIVERGENT PERSPECTIVES

First, however, a brief survey of some clues or guides to interpretation in the recent secondary literature on the subject may be in order. A good starting-point for such a survey is a review essay by George Lohmann, in which the subtle and not-so-subtle differences of approach in four recent works are compared. Lohmann characterizes Michael Löwy's approach as "*Der Anspruch des authentischen Lebens*", that of Andrew Arato and Paul Breines as "*Das Scheitern der Überwindung der Verdinglichung*", Andrew Feenberg's as "*Verdinglichung als kulturelle Kategorie*", and Jürgen Habermas' as "*Verdinglichung als empirische Frage*".[6] What seems to me to be common, at least implicitly, to these and several other contemporary treatments of Lukács on reification is a tendency to see the concept as a *fil conducteur* in a phenomenological description of the modern life-world under bourgeois dominance, rather than as primarily an abstract notion to be tested above all else for logical consistency and rigor. As Winfried Kaminski expresses it: "Thus [Lukács] gives ... a 'Phenomenology of Class Consciousness', a kind of phenomenology of the apparent consciousness of social classes."[7] This seems to me a very healthy interpretative tendency, especially since, as we shall see, from the standpoint of purely formal rigor Lukács' treatment of reification has very serious deficiencies. But then, it must be remembered, formalism occupies a prominent place in Lukács' catalogue of deadly sins!

If the theory of reification is to be taken primarily as a gateway to phenomenological description[8], however, the question arises, as always, as to the exact sense in which we are to understand this "phenomenology". Kaminski, like many other commentators, clearly understands it in a Hegelian sense, as the phenomenology of a certain stage or moment of consciousness, albeit more exclusively linked to a certain historical epoch than the stages of consciousness in Hegel's *Phenomenology of Mind* were supposed to be; and this interpretation finds abundant support in the record of Lukács' intellectual history and in the very title that he chose for his book. Andrew Feenberg, for example, is especially insistent on stressing the Hegelian ontological dimension of Lukács' notion.[9] But is this classical type of pheno- menology that is identified as a phenomenology of a certain form of consciousness really compatible with Lukács' Marxist commitment to avoid idealism? Superficially, at least, it would seem not; hence the appropriateness of any effort to interpret, or perhaps to reinterpret, Lukács' account as a description of a form of life, a term which has more ontologically neutral connotations.

If, however, "reification" is taken to designate a certain form of life, or set of behaviors, one that can validly be identified as a central object of critique within the Marxian tradition, precisely what are they? How is one to distinguish reified from non-reified attitudes and behaviors? What, if any, terms equivalent to "reification" exist at a comparably high level of generality? It is over questions like these that commentators seem most to diverge.

There is, to be sure, initial agreement concerning the Marxian text from which the Lukácsian notion of reification draws its greatest sustenance; it would be hard to imagine a great deal of disagreement on this point, since Lukács himself took such great pains to establish the equivalence. It is, of course, the famous chapter on 'The Fetishism of Commodities and the Secret Thereof', a key paragraph of which Lukács introduces with the words: "Marx describes the basic phenomenon of reification as follows: ..."[10] Marx' central theoretical point here, which Lukács notes, is that, in commodity production, what is in fact "a definite social relation between men ... assumes in their eyes, the fan- tastic [or 'phantasmagoric'] form of a relation between things".

Lukács omitted, no doubt originally for stylistic rather than for doctrinal reasons, since his citation from Marx was already fairly long, the remainder of this paragraph, in which Marx further explains his choice of the word, "fetishism". Marx says that, just as "in [the religious] world the productions of the human brain appear as independent beings endowed with life, and entering into relation both with one another and the human race, so it is in the world of commodities with the products of men's hands. This I call the Fetishism which attaches itself to the products of labor, so soon as they are produced as commodities ..."[11] Marx' debt to Feuerbach at this point, though unacknowledged, is obvious, and no doubt reinforces the impression that Marx is here providing us with another formulation of the basic notion of alienation, which Feuerbach himself employed so heavily. But it is important to note that Marx' elevation of the concept of "fetishism" to pride of theoretical place is novel, and it is a bold stroke. The analogy which it allows him to draw enables him at once to assimilate, by implication, all religious behavior to the attitudes taken towards commodities (and, presumably, towards the marvelous and intricate things that commodities are then fantasized, under capitalism, as doing), by their "worshippers".

Should this notion of commodity fetishism, thus explained, truly be regarded as synonymous with the earlier notion of "alienation", or are there subtle differences in connotation between them? And in either case, should one or the other or both be considered synonymous, in keeping with Lukács' thought in *History and Class Consciousness*, with reification? Lukács himself, it should be observed, makes the parenthetical remark, without further elaboration, in his 1967 Preface that, while reification is indeed closely related to alienation, it "is neither socially nor conceptually identical with it", whereas in the original text "the two words were used synonymously".[12] What interests me more here, however, is what the contemporary commentators have to say about these questions. Lucien Goldmann is categorical: "It was in 1922 that Lukács translated 'commodity fetishism' as 'reification'."[13] So is George Lichtheim: "Save for the employment of the term 'reification' (*Verdinglichung*) instead of the better known 'alienation' (*Entfremdung*) ... Lukács had substantially reverted to the standpoint occupied by Marx in 1844 and 1845."[14] Michael Löwy speaks, in the singular, of "the problem of alienation, reification, and commodity fetishism".[15]

But others are more inclined to raise doubts. Andrew Arato and Paul Breines agree with Lukács' later assessment that reification and alienation are not identical. They point out that alienated labor is only one of several phenomena successively analyzed by Lukács in the classic text; others include "the reification of capitalist society as a whole, and the reification of consciousness in bourgeois science and philosophy". And they further insist, directly contrary to the spirit of the above citation from Lichtheim, that it was Marx' account of commodity fetishism and not any developed theory of alienation as such that inspired Lukács' theory. They also insist on the synthesis that Lukács has presumably effected between Marx and Weber on this point.[16] Laura Boella, on the other hand, characterizing Lukács' theory of reification as "a typical application of the method of totality and of the dialectic of appearance and essence", regards the Weberian application that Lukács makes of this idea as a simple addition; in this context, she criticizes Arato.[17] Boella is no enthusiast of the theory, seeing it as at once one-sidedly economistic and abstract and as reducing ideology from the status of a real historical force, determining the course of institutions, to that of a ghostly emanation of the process of reification.[18] Her fellow countryman, Marzio Vacatello, dismisses the Lukacsian-Goldmannian identification of alienation with fetishism as simply a conceptual confusion.[19]

Kazimierz Sleczka tries to defend Lukács against Istvan Hermann's criticism, strongly supported by elements of Lukács' own later recantation of *History and Class Consciousness*, of the alleged identification of alienation with objectification in that book. He says that no such identification is in fact to be found in the text, but that there does indeed appear to be some ground for thinking that reification is there confused with objectification, of which reification is in fact only a form. He suggests a slight reformulation of Lukács' thesis, whereby it could be maintained that "the liquidation of alienation is closely dependent on [rather than identical with] the elimination of reification" thus rendering dubious the "presumed idealistic character" of the thesis.[20] Finally, Joachim Israel, recalling us to the actual historical sequence of preferred terms, discerns a genuine shift of emphasis and, concomitantly, of meaning from the early Marx' "alienation" through the later Marx' commodity fetishism to Lukács' reification.[21]

The effect of much of this scholarship, which is, generally speaking, of a high quality, is to leave the reader somewhat bewildered about reification. Most readers have, presumably, some initial sense as to what "reification" stands for in *History and Class Consciousness*, but little progress is made in specifying its meaning through the juxtaposition of divergent accounts of its genesis and of divergent formulations of its equivalent terms. In fact, as Boella's remarks imply, focusing too hard on reification may have the effect of removing us further from the life-world and from actual historical forces towards the realm of abstraction. The condemnation of the very real forces of the capitalist economic system which dominate Western culture and act in so many ways to crush the free human spirit becomes reduced to a kind of incantation - "reification - alienation - objectification" that is not so dissimilar in kind to the chants, intended to ward off evil spirits, voiced by the chief fetishists themselves in many earlier societies.

III. THE TEXT

The long chapter, 'Reification and the Consciousness of the Proletariat', is much less focused on the notion of reification - indeed, makes far fewer references to it over the majority of its pages - than one might have expected. It contains, for instance, a most interesting discussion of certain modern philosophies, particularly Kant's, as illustrating "the antinomies of bourgeois thought". Now of course it is obvious that Lukács intends to present these antinomies, along with the culminating Kantian concept of the *Ding-an-sich*, as both symptoms and instances of the general "phenomenon of reification", since this expression and the one quoted in the previous sentence are the titles of the chapter's first and second sub-sections, respectively. These important moments of intellectual history do indeed, we can readily concede, instantiate a group of related phenomena: the tendency to formalism; the identification of an alleged split, not only between subject and object, but even within the human subject (if we set aside the philosophically problematic character of those very terms); the encouragement of a worldview that "valorizes" the natural sciences as supreme sources of truth; and so on. But in the process of elaborating upon these phenomena, Lukács' text progressively moves the term "reification", which is supposed to function as a cover term for these and many other (economic and cultural) phenomena, to a background position. So we are left with a number of ambiguities and uncertainties as to precisely what the concept of reification should be taken to mean.

Perhaps the most straightforward area of applicability of the concept is to be found in one of the central theses of Marx' entire philosophy, namely, that human labor power is and must be treated as a commodity in order for the system of capitalism to function, even though it is radically different from all other non-human commodities, which are things. (For the sake of simplification, let us grant that animal commodities are a special, intermediate case which will not be considered here.) So human labor, reduced to quantitative measurement, is treated as a thing, literally reified; as Lukács says, "the problem of labor-time ... shows reification at its zenith".[22] But the evaluative force even of this fundamental and universal feature of capitalism (I do not for an instant wish to question the accuracy of Marx' description of it) is not quite so simple and unambiguous as it might at first appear, if it is taken in conjunction with Marx' analogical account of "commodity fetishism" that serves as the very *point de depart* for Lukács' treatment of reification. The point of that analogy, it will be recalled, is that human beings collectively and falsely attribute to the things, the commodities, qualities of human social relations. But, *nota bene*, the effect of this development is to impart greater value to commodities than they possess "intrinsically", if one may speak in this fashion. Hence, when human labor power is "commodified" within the capitalist system, it is indeed reified as a commodity-thing, but within a context in which this particular sort of thing, the commodity, has assumed a privileged (fetishized) status. This account, thus elaborated, is, as it should be, highly dialectical, including a central element of paradox. It does not, in all probability, refute any specific claim by Lukács in the text of *History and Class Consciousness*, but it raises some doubts about a certain tone, conveyed both in that text and in a number of commentaries on it, whereby reification is regarded as the absolute and unqualified evil of the modern world.

A further ambiguity arises from the question of whether or not, in fact, reification is to be taken as a phenomenon that is unique to the modern world. On this issue, Lukács wishes to have it both ways: to say that commodity fetishism and reification in general are uniquely dominant in modern times; but he also wants to admit "that Greek philosophy [as well as Greek society] was no stranger to certain aspects of reification, without having experienced them, however, as universal forms of existence. It had one face in the world of reification while the other remained in a 'natural' society".[23] Lukács maintains that the now-dominant status of reification in our society makes this society qualitatively different. He is certainly entitled to say this. But the implication that "natural", as opposed to reified, behaviors occupy a subordinate, but still very real, place within our society does not accord with the apocalyptic conception of reification as virtually all-encompassing and total within our society, and uniquely within this society, that is conveyed by Lukács' critique. Once again, it is more a question of tone, both in the text itself and in its subsequent use by followers and commentators, than of explicit, falsifiable claims. Lukács himself readily acknowledges in conclusion "that there can be no single act that will eliminate reification in all its forms at one blow"[24], hence that the prevalence of reification in the historical future as well as in the past and present is ultimately a matter of degree. But at the same time he relies very heavily, for rhetorical effect, on the principle that quantitative differences turn into qualitative ones in order to support his contentions about the uniqueness of reification under capitalism.

A further problem area is that created by Lukács' references to "natural" relations. It is significant that he so frequently, as in the passage cited above, puts this word within quotations marks. He is clearly sensitive to the enormous ambiguities of this term in the history of thought as, for example, the paragraph in which he refers to Rousseau[25] indicates very well. But that he himself is not immune to such ambiguities is demonstrated by his insistence, on the one hand, that the very concept of "nature" in any given period is a social category, a human product[26], and on the other hand that "the social and economic conditions necessary for the emergence of modern capitalism tend to replace 'natural' relations which exhibit human relations more plainly by rationally reified relations".[27] (Note, once again, the quotation marks.) It is in some of his warm, positive, almost nostalgic references to natural relations that Lukács' critique of reification best reflects the remnant of romanticism in his thinking. (This is made even more clear, not only with respect to Lukács himself but also with respect to Marx and Engels, in another chapter of *History and Class Consciousness*, 'The Changing Function of Historical Materialism'[28].) In short, one of Lukács' principal conceits in thinking about reification as a historical process is the idea of a retreat from what is "natural"; but it is obviously very difficult, if not impossible, to specify just what one means by this term when one is committed to the proposition that the "natural" is itself a social product, historically conditioned.

One way of specifying the direction of the retreat from the "natural" that characterizes the increasing dominance, for Lukács, of reification in the capitalist world is towards increasing abstraction. Formalist and/or quantitative ways of thinking, regarded as "rational" by comparison with the alleged "irrationality" of more qualitative thought-patterns, come to be accorded an ever higher value in the sciences, in economics, in philosophy itself, and ultimately in the life-world of which theoretical enterprises are supposed to furnish explanatory accounts. Now, all of this certainly rings true as a phenomenological description, and in some respects (though not, I think, in all) this general process has only been accelerated since Lukács' time. The difficulty, as I see it, stems from the effort to fit this entire development within the rubric of "reification". For the force of this metaphor seems to depend on the idea of transforming persons into things, whereas the actual processes of intensifying formalism and quantification seem to point in a direction that is very nearly the opposite of any literal, or even semi-literal, interpretation of the metaphor; both persons and things are being transformed (not literally, of course, but in modes of consciousness and behavior that are becoming dominant) into ciphers, into ghostly abstractions. Such abstractions lack the solidity of traditional things; rather, they exhibit some similarity only to the Kantian *Ding-an-sich*. It requires a considerable effort of the imagination - which must of course be brought into play by a metaphor such as "reification" - to identify the overarching malaise of the modern world as one in which things (or what might be called "the spirit of thinghood") attain(s) a position of dominance.

The most fundamental ambiguity in Lukács' treatment of reification, in other words, lies in his initial choice of this summary metaphor to convey the historical trends, much vaster in scope than those (still quite vast) primarily economic phenomena which Marx chose to concentrate upon and systematically to criticize the modern age. It is in fact a very inadequate and in some respects misleading metaphor for the phenomena in question. Yet much of the phenomenological description which Lukács designed this metaphor to bear remains valid and convincing; moreover, ultimate paradox, a more cautious, less colorful trope would not have had nearly the same effect of crystallizing intellectual attitudes along certain critical lines that this one in fact did over the middle decades of our century.

IV. SARTRE'S REFERENCE

Since the epoch of *History and Class Consciousness*, of course, a number of other writers have used the expression "reification" in various ways. One who has employed it with some effect from time to time is Jean-Paul Sartre, although the term rarely plays a central role for him. An interesting clarification, in fact an attempted definition, of "reification" by Sartre is to be found in the first volume of his *Critique of Dialectical Reason*, and it seems to me that a brief reference to this passage will provide for an interesting contrast with Lukács' view.

Sartre has just concluded the presentation of two of his best-known phenomenological descriptions in this work, the historical examples of the deforestation of China and of the impoverishment of colonial Spain through the policy of massive importation of gold. The former practice, carried out by the peasants over centuries, accounts for the recurrent floods which plague contemporary China. It is in the course of his discussion of the counter-finalizing effects of the importation of Spanish gold, an account for which he acknowledges a heavy debt to F. Braudel's book, *The Mediterranean and the Mediterranean World in the Age of Philip II*, that Sartre makes his brief remark concerning reification. Among the long-term effects of the Spanish government's policy were a great outflow of gold from Spain to other European countries, despite the most stringent efforts to keep it within the national borders; a very sharp (67%) decrease in value of the Spanish monetary unit over the course of the sixteenth century; and, finally, a concerted effort by employers in Spain to drive down wages, an effort that met with great success, despite temporary reversals, by the end of the century. (Indeed, wage inflation set in again in 1611, as a result of a steep decline in the population due to the effects of poverty and of epidemics.) In commenting upon this, Sartre says:

> We can also notice, beneath the elementary form, the nature of reification: it is not, as one might too often think, a metamorphosis of the individual into a thing, but it is the necessity which is imposed, through the structures of society, on the member of a social group to live his or her membership in the group and, through it, in the society as a whole, as an atomistic status. What he or she lives and does as an individual remains, at the immediate level, real praxis or human labor. But throughout this concrete endeavor to live, a sort of mechanical rigidity haunts him or her, which subjects the results of his or her act to the strange laws of totalizing-addition.[29]

Sartre is clearly influenced by Lukács' account of reification, but it is equally evident that the French philosopher is aware of some of the pitfalls which the usage of the term can occasion. He, like Lukács, links the notion with phenomena of calculation ("totalizing-addition"). But it is a calculation produced, so to speak, by a sequence of complex socio-economic events, rather than by the philosophical theories and general cultural trends to which Lukács devotes the bulk of his accounts. Sartre's reified individual is forced to live as a victim, like all the others in similar circumstances, of mechanisms and events (*e.g.* wages driven below the poverty level, with all the results which follow from that) over which he or she has no control (the notion of an atomistic status or law, "*statut moleculaire*"). But it is important to note Sartre's emphasis on the fact that at the immediate level, the individual remains fully human, characterized by free praxis. This is not a radical essence/appearance distinction, such as one finds in places in the works of both Lukács and Marx. For Sartre, the lived experience always retains greater relative importance.

Meanwhile, as Sartre implies, the full explanation of what was occurring in Spain was, perhaps, not available to any of the actors of the time in question. Now for Lukács, as a good Hegelian-Marxist, it would not be at all surprising that the workers of sixteenth-century Spain were ignorant of the conditions of their reification, because their era was at best the historical prelude to the era of capitalism. It is only during this era that it has become possible, for the first time, for the underlying conditions of alienation and reification to be made intelligible. In fact, for Lukács, Sartre's very choice of historical example would have been improper, because the impoverished workers of sixteenth-century Spain could at worse have experienced only a modicum of reification. Theirs was not the reified consciousness of the modern world. Sartre, on the other hand, breaks sharply with Lukács and, as the context indicates, he seems to suspect, despite assertions to the contrary, with Marx himself when, in a footnote to an earlier passage, he says: "Thus it is ... that the possibility of reification is given in all human relations, even in a pre-capitalist period, even in family relations or relations of friendship."[30] In other words, reification as Sartre has now defined it is not at all historically specific.

In these brief allusions to reification, then, Sartre has avoided some of the objections to which Lukács' account can be subjected - its vagueness, its dependence on Marx' analysis of commodity fetishism under capitalism with which Lukács initially linked it, the conjoining of its rise with the decline of "natural" relations, which are nevertheless said to be social categories, and so on. Above all, Sartre's understanding of reification is not historically relative, whereas Lukács' is. But Sartre has paid a very high price to avoid such objections: the price of rendering the phenomenon of reification virtually all-pervasive throughout human history, at least as a "possibility". It may therefore be just as well that Sartre, in contrast with the Lukács of *History and Class Consciousness*, did not try to make reification a significant linchpin of his social philosophy.

V. CONCLUDING REFLECTIONS

One area of philosophical criticism in which, as it seems to me, the invocation of the charge of "reification" continues to have considerable value is feminist thought: treating persons as if they were simply "sex objects" is as clear an instance of the actual occurrence of this metaphor as any type of behavior could be. There are ambiguities and pitfalls even in the case of this application: for instance, one possible extreme reaction to reifying sexist practices is to try to suppress sexuality altogether. To make another person an object of one's attentions while taking account of the other's sexual characteristics among his or her other significant aspects is not at all equivalent to treating that other person as a "sex object" in such a way as to reify him or her; but precisely how to draw the desired distinction here is a question to which the answer is not as simple as it may at first appear. Indeed, the looseness with which Lukács, by his own earnest if somewhat exaggerated later account, treated "objectification" in his classic work remains, so to speak, an object lesson here. Despite all these caveats, it would appear that this feminist use of the terminology of "reification"[31] might serve as a means of vindicating and resuscitating Lukács' analysis.

But surely no theorist, no matter how dedicated a critic of the capitalist system he or she may be, would want to claim that sexual forms of reification became significant social practices only with the dawning of the capitalist era. It is certainly true that pornography as an industry exists on a scale never before witnessed in history, and it is probably the case that some people today have a more heightened consciousness of the reality of sexual reification than was common in many past eras. But it cannot be denied that dehumanizing cults of various genital organs, often designated as "things", flourished, along with the general subordination of women to the point of treating them like chattel-things, from very early times. This being so, the identification of feminist thought as an area of contemporary philosophy, in which the concept of "reification" has considerable explanatory and normative force, can hardly be seen as a vindication of Lukács' own version of it. For the latter version, as he so repeatedly insists, sees reification as a salient feature only of modern times.

Aside from its ambiguous but genuine usefulness for a feminist critique, it seems to me, the concept of reification, whether in Lukács' version or any other, has only a limited value for social philosophy today. The contemptuous use by the great powers, especially the United States, of the majority of the inhabitants of Third World countries as their subalterns, dumping-grounds for their products, cheap substitute labor for their transported industries, and bearers of an ever-mounting debt that generates high rates of interest; the ever-shriller efforts of governments of the leading capitalist countries to marshal most segments of their populations behind campaigns in defense of "free enterprise" ideology (matched as it is by comparable efforts on the parts of the so-called "socialist" regimes of state monopoly); the threat of mutual nuclear annihilation as the potential outcome of these global practices and ideological campaigns - these are some of the principal features of the contemporary world to which social philosophy must pay special attention. But it cannot adequately do so any longer by declaring that our society is suffering from an advanced case of reified consciousness, susceptible to cure by the ascribed dereifying consciousness of the proletariat: the situation is too complex, and the highly destructive attitudes, at once self-righteously aggressive and terrifiedly defensive, of large components, even many of those with a proletarian heritage, of the populations of the advanced industrialized countries cannot truly be accounted for by the simple diagnosis that they are reified. Lukács' key metaphor was never perfect, but it more closely reflected the most prominent global realities of the time at which he first presented it than it does ours of the present time.

Taken collectively, we contemporaries may be "worse than useless things". But in any event it seems to me that our dominant consciousness is no longer, or at least not merely, that of the smug, classical bourgeois world-view glorifying in "rationality" and "objectivity" that Lukács discerned in his time and depicted under the heading of reified consciousness. Moreover, we are aware in a way in which his generation was not that being a thing may not be the worst possible outcome. When, as we know empirically from the experiences of Hiroshima and Nagasaki, shadows on deserted pavements may be all that is left of persons after a nuclear exchange, the idea of being a thing may in contrast not appear so bad.

NOTES

1.   "We cannot accept that reification (*Verdinglichung.*) is nothing but the congealing of processes. The problem is not an ontological one. What was said in *History and Class Consciousness* is still valid today in this regard ... Reification. Again, it not clear what this means. It seems to be a stepping out of the process, the rigidification of the process, but at the same time it is also identical with false consciousness, with commodity fetishism, *etc.*". F. Feher, A. Heller, G. Markus and M. Vajda, 'Notes on Lukács' Ontology', in Agnes Heller (ed.), *Lukács Reappraised*, New York, Columbia University Press, 1983, pp. 150 and 151.

2.   Simmel, *Philosophie des Geldes*, 3rd ed., München and Leipzig, Duncker and Humlot, 1920. Interestingly, the one occurrence of the word, "reification", in the Index of the English translation of this book, in which a subsection is rendered as "Money as a reification of the general form of existence according to which things derive their significance from their relationship to one another" proves, on comparison with the original, not to be a literal translation. The original reads: "Das Geld als eine *Substanziierung* [ital.mine] der allgemeinen Seinsform, nach der die Dinge ihre Bedeutung an einander, in ihrer Gegenseitigkeit, finden." (p. x) See *The Philosophy of Money*, tr. Tom Bottomore and David Frisby (London/Henley/Boston: Routledge & Kegan Paul, 1978), pp. vi and 128. The connotations are quite different; and this difference seems to me to have relevance to questions concerning both the provenance and the precise meaning of *Verdinglichung* as used by Lukács. Gillian Rose, in his discussion of Adorno's theory of reification, asserts that there "is only one occasion on which Simmel uses the word 'reify' or its parts". See *The Melancholy Science: An Introduction to the Thought of Theodor W. Adorno*, New York, Columbia University Press, 1978, pp. 34-35.

3.   For instance, he claims that "the phenomena beginning with which it would be possible to unveil the reification of all human relations become less and less accessible to the reflection of the average [type] of people". *Existentialisme ou marxisme?*, tr. E. Kelemen, Paris, Editions Nagel, 1948, p. 28 (tr. from the French mine, *WLM*).

4.   I am ignorant of the equivalent terms in Hungarian, but I do not believe that that matters for present purposes, since it is clear that the young Lukács also thought in German and was influenced by the German etymological associations.

5.   Martin Heidegger, 'The Thing', in *Poetry, Language, Thought*, tr. A. Hofstadter, New York, Harper Colophon, 1975, pp. 174 & 177.

6.   Lohmann, 'Authentisches und verdinglichtes Leben.

Neuere Literatur zu Georg Lukács' 'Geschichte und Klassen-bewusstsein", *Philosophische Rundschau* 3-4 (1983), pp. 253-271.

7.   Kaminski, *Zur Dialektik von Substanz und Subjekt bei Hegel und Marx,* Frankfurt/Main, Verlag Haag & Herchen, 1976, p. 38. Translation *WLM*.

8.   This way of characterizing what Lukács is doing has a solid basis in Lukács' pre-Marxist work, as well. For example, the principal chapter of his *Heidelberger Philosophie der Kunst*, Darmstadt and Neuwied, Luchterhand Verlag, 1974, is entitled 'Phänomeno-logische Skizze des schöpferischen und rezeptiven Verhaltens', pp. 43-150.

9.   A. Feenberg, *Lukács, Marx and the Source of Critical Theory,* Totowa, N.J., Rowman and Littlefield, 1981, p. 78f.

10.   Lukács, *History and Class Consciousness*, tr. by R. Livingstone, Cambridge, Mass., MIT Press, 1971, p. 86.

11.   Marx, *Capital*, Vol. I, tr. by S. Moore and E. Aveling, Moscow, Foreign Language Publishing House, 1961, p. 72.

12.   Lukács, *History and Class Consciousness*, pp. xxiv-xxv.

13.   Goldmann, *Lukács and Heidegger: Towards a New Philosophy*, tr. W. Q. Boelhower, London/Henley/Boston, Routledge & Kegan Paul, 1977, p. 29.

14.   Lichtheim, *George Lukács,* New York, Viking Press, 1970, p. 63.

15.   Michael Löwy, *George Lukács: From Romanticism to Bolshevism*, tr. P. Camiller, London: NLB, 1979, p. 66.

16.   A. Arato and P. Breines, *The Young Lukács and the Origins of Western Marxism*, New York, Seabury Press, 1979, pp. 115-116.

17.   Laura Boella, *Il giovane Lukács*, Bari, De Donato, 1977, pp. 188 and 301 (footnote).

18.   *Ibid.* pp. 194-195

19.   Marzio Vacatello, *Lukács*, Firenze, La Nuova Italia, 1968, p. 65.

20.   K. Sleczka, 'World of Ideas of Gyorgy Lukács' (Some Remarks on Istvan Hermann's Monograph), in *Lukács Gyorgy gondolatvilaga, Tanulmamany a xx. szazad emberi lehetosegeirol,* Budapest, 1974, p. 155.

21.   Israel, 'Alienation and Reification', *Social Praxis* 3(1- 2), 1975, pp. 27-43.

22.   Lukács, *History and Class Consciousness*, p. 167.

23.   *Ibid.* p. 111.

24.   *Ibid.* p. 206.

25.   *Ibid.* p. 136.

26.   *Ibid.* p. 130.

27. *Ibid.* p. 91.

28. See, for example, *Ibid.* p. 233.

29. Sartre, *Critique de la raison dialectique*, Tome I, Paris, Librairie Gallimard, 1960, pp. 243-244, tr. mine. I felt too much dissatisfaction with the English translation (by Alan Sheridan-Smith) of this passage of the *Critique of Dialectical Reason*, London, NLB; Atlantic Highlands, Humanities Press, 1976, p. 176, to cite it here, although I admit that the latter's standard translation of "*statut*" as "statute" rather than "status" seems more appropriate here than in most instances. Note also that I have used the more commonplace English term, "atomistic", instead of the more literal "molecular", for "*moléculaire*".

30. *Ibid.* p. 255, tr. mine (p. 152 in Sheridan-Smith tr.).

31. I owe this allusion to my attendance at the oral presentation of an excellent, as yet unpublished paper by Iris Young at meetings of the Society for Phenomenology and Existential Philosophy, October 1985, in Chicago.

ANDREW FEENBERG

The Question of Organization
in the Early Marxist Work of Lukács.
Technique or Praxis?

Lukács' *History and Class Consciousness* contains one of the most important discussions of organizational questions to emerge from the tumultuous period immediately following World War I. Unfortunately, Lukács' contribution is little studied or discussed today and widely misunderstood by contemporary Marxists. Typically, he is viewed as a proto-Stalinist by critical theorists in Germany and America, and as a romantic irrationalist by many Marxists in France and Italy. Michael Löwy's careful study of Lukács' position in its historical context shows that neither of these interpretations is correct. Löwy argues convincingly that Lukács has something original to offer and that his theory has not yet been entirely exhausted by history.[1] The purpose of this paper is to reconstruct Lukács' position as it grows out of his evaluation of the work of Luxemburg and Lenin, and then to consider the adequacy of the Lukácsian theory of organization.

I. LUKÁCS, LUXEMBURG AND LENIN

In *History and Class Consciousness* Lukács writes that "the question of organization is the most profound intellectual question facing the revolution".[2] Lukács' intense interest in what might normally be seen as technical political problems is connected to the intensity of revolutionary expectations in his day. He writes: "Only when the revolution has entered into quotidian reality will the question of revolutionary organization demand imperiously to be admitted to the consciousness of the masses and their theoreticians."[3] It is in this context that Lukács studied the debates of Luxemburg and Lenin not merely as political disagreements but as indices of the changing relation of Marxist theory to historical reality.

The dispute between Luxemburg and Lenin, in the language of the day, concerned the relative importance of "spontaneity" and "consciousness". These terms refer respectively to uncontrolled mass action and Party-directed activities. It is important not to confuse "spontaneity" in this Second International sense with romantic notions of the uncaused or the unmotivated. On the contrary, in this period economic determinism is implicated in the very definition of "spon-

126

T. Rockmore (ed.), Lukács Today, 126–156.
© *1988 by D. Reidel Publishing Company.*

taneity". Lukács writes, for example, that "The spontaneity of a movement ... is only the subjective, mass-psychological expression of its determination by pure economic laws."[4] "Consciousness", on the other hand, suggests such related concepts as "theory" and "planning", with their obvious instrumental associations but also with all the risks of voluntarism associated with arbitrary action.

According to Lukács, the debate over the relative importance of spontaneity and consciousness goes very deep, to the heart of the Marxist conception of the revolution, for "the question of how to organize a revolutionary party can only be developed organically from a theory of revolution itself".[5] Thus, according to Lukács, Luxemburg's emphasis on spontaneity is due to a certain conception of the revolution as primarily social rather than political, as a product of the laws of motion of capitalism's contradictory economic structure. On the other hand, Lenin's emphasis on consciousness results from his view of the revolution as essentially a transcendence of the determinism of the economy through the intervention of the historical alternative as a political project.

At the time Lukács was writing, Luxemburg's thought was a *locus classicus* among Western Marxists. Lukács started with a spontaneist conception of the revolution, derived in part from Luxemburg, and moved gradually toward a position more nearly consistent with Lenin's actual practice in Russia. *History and Class Consciousness* works out Lukács' changing position on the question of organization in the course of two essays on Rosa Luxemburg, the first written in 1921, the second exactly one year later. The essays differ in tone as well as in content. The earlier essay is a eulogy of Luxemburg, without a single critical note. The second essay expresses the numerous reservations and criticisms that many Marxists came to share with Lukács as Lenin's writings and methods became better known in the West. A remark in the 'Foreword' of 1923 seems to describe the evolution of these Marxists.

A detailed analysis of Rosa Luxemburg's thought is necessary because its seminal discoveries no less than its errors have had a decisive influence on the theories of Marxists outside Russia, above all in Germany. To some extent this influence persists to this day. For anyone whose interest was first aroused by these problems a truly revolutionary, Communist and Marxist position can be acquired only through a critical confrontation with the theoretical life's work of Rosa Luxemburg.[6]

Apparently, Lukács himself passed through this critical process from 1921 to 1922.

The comparison of the two essays is thus instructive not only concerning the evolution of Lukács' outlook, but that of a whole generation of Marxists. In the first essay, Lukács endorses without reservation Luxemburg's critique of the technical concept of organization prevalent in the Second International. Echoing Luxemburg he rejects an attitude "which allocates to the Party tasks concerned predominantly or even exclusively with organization. Such a view is then reduced to an unrelieved inconsistent fatalism when confronted with the realities of revolution."[7] In contrast, Lukács considers Luxemburg's concept of the Party as the "political direction" of the struggle to be "the fount of true revolutionary activity".[8]

In the later essay, Lukács confirms his continued belief in these views, but now qualifies them by saying that "the Russian Revolution clearly exposed the limitations of the West European organizations".[9] The Russian Revolution not only refutes the old technical concept of organization, but also shows the inadequacy of Luxemburg's own alternative concept of political direction, which, Lukács now argues, failed "to go one step further and to look at the question of political leadership in the context of organization. That is to say, she should have elucidated those organizational factors that render the Party of the proletariat capable of assuming political leadership."[10] Lenin's superiority lies in the fact that he did pose precisely these problems and, according to Lukács, solved them.

However, if Lukács finally prefers Lenin's organizational methods to those of Luxemburg, he continues to believe that it is she who "saw the significance of mass actions more clearly than anyone."[11] And as late as Lukács' *Lenin* book, he continues to analyze the phenomenon of the Soviets or councils in pure Luxemburgian terms, as expressing the breakdown of the reified boundary between economics and politics which underlies bourgeois society.[12] His interpretation of Lenin, furthermore, shows an implicit rejection of much of Lenin's own self-interpretation, particularly the theory of "consciousness from without." Thus in his early Marxist works, Lukács seems to have attempted a synthesis of ideas drawn from both Luxemburg and Lenin, which I will try to explain in what follows.

II. THE REFLEXIVE CONCEPT OF SUBJECTIVITY

Underlying Lukács' position on organization, there is a specific interpretation of the relation of theory to practice in the socialist movement. His reflection begins with the question of what ties Marxism as a theory to the revolutionary process. The problem arises because, given its independent "scientific" origin, Marxism's relationship with the movement that adopted it might be merely contingent and conjunctural. Marxism and the working class movement might have joined together through a happy mutual misunderstanding and not be essentially related at all. As Lukács writes:

> The issue turns on the question of theory and practice. And this not merely in the sense given it by Marx when he says in his first critique of Hegel that "theory becomes a material force when it grips the masses." Even more to the point is the need to discover those features and definitions both of the theory and the ways of gripping the masses which convert the theory, the dialectical method, into a vehicle of revolution ... . If this is not done that "gripping of the masses" would well turn out to be a will o' the wisp. It might turn out that the masses were in the grip of quite different forces, that they were in pursuit of quite different ends. In that event, there would be no necessary connection between the theory and their activity ... [13]

Lukács' response to this question is formulated in terms of what I will call Marx' "reflexive" concept of subjectivity.

The concept of subjectivity in Marx' early writings is deeply influenced by Hegel's critique of Kantian ethics and, by implication, of the Jacobin experience in the French Revolution. This critique describes a dialectic of "ought" and "is" that overcomes their opposition in Kant's thought and forms the basis for Hegel's historical standpoint. Hegel argues that the ethical is not a truly independent sphere but only appears to be so to an undialectical consciousness that has not understood the essence of real historical development. Because Jacobin revolutionism is unaware of the deeper level of social reality from which actual development arises, it attempts to impose a moral truth directly and immediately on society. But, Hegel and Marx both argue, morality is a functional element within society and not a standpoint on society. If societies can be ordered in a normative continuum, and both Hegel and Marx believe they can, it must be in terms of standards other than justice and morality.

In the light of Hegel's criticism, Marx is anxious to avoid a purely political moralism that would be based not on the "reality" of proletarian needs but on abstract principles in the Jacobin manner of most contemporary revolutionary sects. Starting from this critique of utopianism, Marx arrives at a general concept of revolutionary subjectivity based on the "reflection" of life in thought.

Marx' original discussion of these problems is found in several early essays, in which he attempted to distinguish his position from utopian communism and Jacobin-Blanquist revolutionism. The proletariat, he argues in his early essay on 'The King of Prussia and Social

Reform', cannot base its revolution on abstract ethical exigencies, for these will always have to be imposed by the state against the real interests they must by definition contradict insofar as they take on an ethical form. But, Marx claims, the proletarian goal is not merely to change the state by infusing it with correct moral principles, but far more radically to destroy the state. Thus the proletariat should avoid politics, except for the purely negative purpose of destruction, and should instead concentrate on social action toward the end of creating a wholly new type of society in which politics will be unnecessary.[14]

In rejecting political revolution for social revolution, Marx attempted to overcome the split between moral community in the state and immoral society at large. Communism, in his view, could not be a utopia imposed from above against private interests, for the very act of imposing "utopia" would reproduce the basic ill, the split between ethics and reality. A revolution which aims to bring morality down to earth, to realize morality in the Hegelian sense of that term, by making it a feature of daily life rooted in the interests and culture of the people, could never succeed on the basis of legal changes and state action. How right Marx was to fear revolution from above may be judged by the results in the existing Communist societies.

In the 1840s, when Marx elaborated this position, he was writing under the influence not only of Hegel, but also of Feuerbach, whose theory of religious alienation he attempted to generalize to include morality and the state. Just as Feuerbach reduced religion to its "human basis" in the alienated community, so Marx projected the "social" as the hidden unity of the contraries into which life was divided in alienated class society. The return to this basis would require not the reform of the state but its abolition and, correspondingly, not the moralization of civil society through an admixture of improvements, but the abolition of the property-based civil society, dialectically correlated with the state.

These concepts had a major and lasting impact on Marx' self-understanding as a revolutionary theoretician. For, if Marxism is not merely a disguised ethical exigency from which the state would necessarily be reborn in case of successful revolution, it must stand in a new relation to the class it represents. Thus Marx' concept of social revolution was connected to his earliest attempt to formulate a theory of the relation of consciousness to history.

Marx introduced the reflexive concept of subjectivity to describe a type of revolutionary theory and consciousness that grows out of historical "necessity" instead of being imposed "abstractly" on the basis of pure moral principle. Marx wrote, for example, that his theory simply explains to the "world" "its own actions" and thus articulates the historically evolved content of the social movement. He writes: "We simply show it (the world) why it struggles in reality, and the consciousness of this is something which it is compelled to acquire, even if it does not want to."[15]

Reflexive subjectivity corresponds to social revolution just as abstract ethical subjectivity corresponds to political revolution. The one emerges from the "social instinct" of the proletariat and articulates the inner meaning of its actions, while the other reflects the essential opposition of "ought" and "is" as they are experienced by the isolated individual in bourgeois society. The Jacobin insurrectional movement is, for Marx, rebellious bourgeois subjectivity writ large and not a way of transcending bourgeois society. He wrote, in fact, that "the more developed and general the political intelligence of a people is, the more the proletariat - at least at the beginning of the movement - wastes its energies in the irrational useless uprisings which are suppressed in blood".[16] As he argued in his essay 'On the Jewish Question', "It is not enough that thought should seek to realize itself; reality must also strive toward thought."[17]

The reflexive concept of subjectivity is developed further in *The Poverty of Philosophy* with the distinction between a class "in-itself" and a class "for-itself".[18] But later writings are ambiguous, conserving only traces of this original concept of subjectivity, as for example in a passage in the preface to *Capital*, where Marx writes of his critical method that "So far as such criticism represents a class, it can only represent the class whose vocation in history is the overthrow of the capitalist mode of production and the final abolition of all classes - the proletariat."[19] This passage continues to suggest that Marxism is somehow rooted in the life experiences of the working class, although unfortunately Marx did not explain exactly how and to what extent. Instead, by this later period, Marx tended to offer programmatic references to "determinism" and "historical necessity" in place of the more precise concept of reflexivity. The deterministic language serves the same function as the earlier theory of reflexive consciousness: both motivate the rejection of political moralism, although with different political consequences.

Lukács' pre-Marxist *Theory of the Novel* recapitulated Hegel's critique of abstract ethics. In that work, Lukács depicted the hero of the novel as the bearer of a degraded idealism necessarily correlated with the degraded reality of bourgeois society. From the ironic standpoint of the novelist and critic, reified society and the nostalgia for meaning are located side by side, on the same level as features of the same desolate spiritual landscape. By the time he wrote *History and Class Consciousness* Lukács was aware that achieving transcendence would require forms of collective opposition that are unavailable to the individual in bourgeois society and open only to the class.

Like the early Marx, Lukács was determined to find a way to renew the theory of revolution that avoids the pitfalls of individualistic moralism. Reflexive subjectivity offers a solution which can also form the critical link between Lukács' interpretation of Marxism and classical German philosophy. Thus, Lukács said that "the deep affinities between historical materialism and Hegel's philosophy are clearly manifested here, for both conceive of theory as the self-knowledge of reality".[20] For Lukács, as for Hegel and the early Marx, consciousness conceived as self-knowledge is the secret of the transcendence of the opposition of thought and being, subject and object, "ought" and "is".

III. THEORY AND CONSCIOUSNESS IN LUXEMBURG

Rosa Luxemburg's theory of mass action recovered the Marxist concept of reflexive subjectivity from the complete oblivion into which it had fallen in the Second International. Her theory was inspired by the 1905 Russian Revolution, the first major mass struggle for socialism since the Commune of Paris.[21] This was an immense spontaneous social movement which quickly passed from basic economic protest to quite sophisticated social and political demands and the creation of a new kind of revolutionary organization, the "Soviet" or factory council.

Luxemburg wrote in an intellectual and political environment in which any form of direct confrontation with the state was viewed as a voluntaristic violation of the principles of historical determinism and a utopian regression. The orthodox position of the day held that only gradual union and parliamentary struggle expressed the historical necessity of the movement toward socialism. Revolutionary subjectivity and the objective historical movement were never more alien to each other.

The Russian experience in 1905 suggested a different way of connecting revolutionary politics with historical determinism. The struggles of 1905 were violent and yet they clearly emerged from the deepest determining forces of the historical process rather than from the insurrectional fantasies of political leaders. In this case, theory and party organization were joined to historical necessity by their expressive, hermeneutic function, which was to grant conscious and explicit form to the implicit content of the spontaneous struggle. In this new theory of Luxemburg, spontaneity serves to reconcile subject and object in history. In the spontaneous struggle, the proletariat at one and the same time realizes the necessity of the historical laws and imposes its will and consciousness on the world.

Luxemburg argued on this basis for a new conception of the relation of theory to consciousness. Against the pseudo-scientific conception of theory prevalent in the Second International, she proposed a historical approach to theory as a prolongation of action, the articulation of its inner meaning. Theory attains its highest development in the reflection of the individual thinker, whose ideas, once they have been developed, may then be propagandized by the Party among the workers. But the result of this propaganda is not immediately an action. In times of social peace, political education can go no further than to produce ideas in the heads of individual workers. This is what Luxemburg calls a "theoretical and latent" class consciousness.

Ideas are the highest product of theory but, as class consciousness, such ideas represent the lowest level of development. Class consciousness achieves full development not in this contemplative form, appropriate to theory, but in the "practical and active" expression of class aspirations and solidarity in revolutionary struggle. Theory must cease to be a mere representation of the inner meaning of class struggle to become consciousness as a historical force in that struggle.[22] As Lukács was later to explain it, "Proletarian thought is in the first place merely a theory of praxis which only gradually ... transforms itself into a practical theory that overturns the real world."[23]

For Luxemburg, as for Lukács, the Party plays a decisive role in the passage from theory to practice, the latent to the active. "Organization", Lukács writes, "is the form of the mediation between theory and practice."[24] To the temporarily latent character of the socialist goal corresponds the historical reality of the Party. In relation to the masses, "the Party is the objectification of their own will (obscure though this may be to themselves)".[25] For, what is latent and theoretical at any given moment must be made present organizationally if it is later to become practical in struggle. Thus, like theory the Party derives its historical necessity from spontaneity in such a way as to overcome utopianism and moralism. Both represent the still latent meaning of struggles that need only achieve sufficient breadth and intensity to express themselves in revolutionary consciousness.

From this Luxemburgian standpoint, political direction no longer has any of the voluntaristic traits Marx rejected. It does not change the fundamental orientation of the movement, but rather expresses the significance of on-going actions, thereby aiding the actors to clarify their own goals.

It (the Party) must immerse its own truth in the spontaneous mass movement and raise it from the depths of economic necessity, where it was conceived, on to the heights of free, conscious action. In so doing it will transform itself in the moment of the outbreak of revolution from a party that makes demands to one that imposes an effective reality. This change from demand to reality becomes the lever of the truly class-oriented and truly revolutionary organisation of the proletariat.[26]

Luxemburg's theory of organization had such a great impact on Lukács because it dovetailed neatly with his own Hegelian interpretation of Marx' reflexive concept of consciousness. But did this theory offer an adequate explanation for the revolutionary movements which followed the First World War? Its intellectual elegance and consistency with Marxism could not, of course, serve as a substitute for this ultimate test which took the form of a confrontation with Lenin's very different approach and with the reality of the Russian Revolution. Lukács' careful re-examination of the debates between Luxemburg and Lenin left him firmly committed to practical Leninism, although we will see that he did not accept Lenin's own self-interpretation and attempted to substitute something quite different for it.

IV. LUXEMBURG OR LENIN

Luxemburg's theory of the revolution is more faithful to Marx' deeper intention than any later contribution. However, just for that reason she cannot accurately describe many important features of the revolutionary process that followed World War I. The world had become so very unlike Marx' that his ideas about revolution, even as developed by Luxemburg after 1905, were seriously misleading. In the concluding essays of his book, Lukács attempts to show that Luxemburg's theory is vitiated by a series of errors that result from the projection of characteristics of the early stages of the revolutionary process into a later stage.

Luxemburg, Lukács believes, has "the illusion of an 'organic', purely proletarian revolution".[27] Her image of the revolution is unrealistically simple in three important respects: her extension of the concept of the proletariat to cover the widest masses of the population; her "over-estimation of the spontaneous, elemental forces of the Revolution;" and her tendency to believe in an "ideological organic growth into socialism".[28] She consistently over-estimates the unity of the proletariat and the proletarian character of the revolution, minimizing the organizational consequences of divisions within the class and the complexity of alliances with non-proletarian strata and classes.

> This false assessment of the true driving forces leads to the decisive point of her misinterpretation: to the underplaying of the role of the Party in the revolution and of its conscious political action, as opposed to the necessity of being driven along by the elemental forces of economic development.[29]

The Party, in Luxemburg's conception, is simply a prolongation of a proletarian spontaneity which, Lukács interprets her to say, points instinctively in the right direction at every stage. Party and class are not two distinct objects for Luxemburg, but dialectical moments of a single collective subjectivity. "The fact is that the Social Democracy is not joined to the organization of the proletariat. It is itself the proletariat."[30]

This view of the Party flows directly from Luxemburg's emphasis on the immanent character of the revolutionary process. What Lenin called Luxemburg's "not-to-be-taken-seriously nonsense of organization and tactics as a process", while by no means nonsense, turns out to be based on a fundamentally Hegelian concept of historical subjectivity. The Luxemburgian proletariat has the undifferentiated unity and the untranscended subjectivity of a world-historical people inventing the future. At first Lukács was enthusiastic about the Hegelian character of Luxemburg's theory, although he later had serious doubts about it because it stood in such flagrant contradiction to the actual function of the Bolshevik Party in the Russian Revolution.

Lenin's Party maintained a considerable independence from the mass of workers and on occasion took initiatives without much regard for proletarian spontaneity. In Luxemburg's theory, the independence of the Party would be the death of the dialectic in which it raises the level of struggle of the masses through articulating the implicit content of class action. Lenin's conception of a disciplined minority as a leadership of the mass movement appeared to her to be a voluntaristic illusion, already transcended by Marxism long ago in the conception of a social revolution.

Lukács describes the effects of these differences on their positions in a number of important domains, including class alliances, the struggle against opportunism, and tactical planning. In each case, Luxemburg's position appears to flow directly from basic Marxian premises, while Lenin's seems pre-Marxist and sectarian. And yet with time it became clear that Lenin's innovations responded to the decisive practical considerations. The split between theory and practice was never sharper than in this debate, and it is toward overcoming this split that Lukács worked.

Let us begin the discussion of the debate with the question of a mass versus a vanguard conception of the Party. Far from supporting the Leninist idea of a formal separation of Party and mass, Luxemburg wanted to go in exactly the opposite direction, toward drawing the entire oppressed population into the Party. Thus she proposed as a partial solution to the problem of opportunism the dissolution of the boundary between the Party and the labor unions, which would be merged in one immense mass organization. Similarly, she wished to convert the Party into a place of refuge and an instrument of struggle not only of proletarians, but of the entire mass of oppressed peasants and petty bourgeois.

Lukács follows Lenin in dismissing this approach because of the confused and chaotic character of non-proletarian movements during great crises. The peasantry and petty bourgeoisie may be revolutionary at one moment and counter-revolutionary the next. Their attitudes are not determined by predictable long-term developmental tendencies of society but by contingent factors. These are, in some sense, classes without strategies, and thus the extension of the crisis of capitalist society to all classes of the population complicates rather than simplifies the revolutionary process. Only sophisticated theoretical leadership of the sort a revolutionary Party can offer, and not mass spontaneity, is adequate to determining the conditions under which class alliances can be made to the benefit of the movement. For Lenin and Lukács, the independence of the Party from the mass corresponds necessarily to the inadequacy of spontaneity in the forging of class alliances.

The disagreement between Luxemburg and Lenin on the best way to fight opportunism within the working class movement is formally similar to this disagreement on class alliances. Luxemburg believed that opportunism would be overcome by the proletariat in the course of the next revolutionary offensive. Lukács interprets her position to mean that "swings to the Right should be and are dealt with - more or less spontaneously - by the 'organic' development of the workers' movement".[31] She seems to believe, as did the young Marx, that the historical solution arises automatically with the problem which it solves.

> Thus ... Rosa Luxemburg starts from the premise that the working class will enter the revolution as a unified revolutionary body which has been neither contaminated nor led astray by the democratic illusions of bourgeois society.[32]

Of course, Luxemburg engaged in a continuous intellectual struggle against opportunism in the interim, but she never believed that this struggle could liquidate its influence in the Party in advance of the revolutionary offensive. Rather, the function of the struggle was merely to maintain majority support for a revolutionary program and leadership during times of social peace or proletarian retreat. Luxemburg's position thus limited her action against opportunism to ideological debate aimed at convincing those wavering between opportunist and orthodox positions. But what more could realistically be attempted in non-revolutionary times?

Lenin, practically alone in the Second International, proposed an outrageous alternative: splitting the movement to create a separate revolutionary organization purged of opportunism from the beginning. Lukács summarizes the difference between their positions on the struggle against opportunism as "whether or not the campaign against opportunism should be conducted as an intellectual struggle within the revolutionary Party of the proletariat or whether it was to be resolved on the level of organization".[33]   To Luxemburg, Lenin's attempt to fight opportunism organizationally appeared completely voluntaristic, a mere bureaucratic device that could never arrest the growth of such an important social phenomenon.   "Such an attempt to exorcise opportunism by means of a scrap of paper may turn out to be extremely harmful - not to opportunism but to the socialist movement."[34]

Yet, despite the apparently voluntaristic character of Lenin's approach, it had the tremendous advantage of clearly defining the differences within the movement. It clarified the issues involved in the struggle against opportunism and enabled the divisions in the working class to take on organizational form.   Ultimately, two coherent strategies emerged, corresponding to the Bolshevik and Menshevik parties, each with significant working class support and a well-defined polemical relationship, of which the entire working class was aware.

By contrast, Luxemburg's methods of struggle could never produce clarity of this sort. She fought opportunism issue by issue within a united Party, through efforts of intellectual persuasion and the formation of tactical alliances with various Party leaders at each congress. But, as Lukács remarks, "A war against opportunism as a tendency cannot crystallize out: the terrain of the 'intellectual conflicts' changes from one issue to the next and with it changes the composition of the rival groups."[35]

Luxemburg was of course anxious to preserve the unity of the movement, and to this end it was essential precisely not to draw the organizational consequences of Party debates. But the price paid for preserving unity turned out to be very high. Opportunism continued to appear to the mass of workers to be a legitimate component of the movement for socialism, and even when the opportunists lost votes of principle, their policies often prevailed by default for lack of organizational teeth in majority decisions. As a result of this situation, the disagreements within the movement "remained differences of opinion within workers' movements that were nevertheless [seen as] revolutionary movements. And so it became impossible to draw a firm distinction between the various groups."[36]   German workers thus entered the crisis of the war totally unprepared for the violent conflicts and betrayals that were to wrack their Party periodically until the final break-up in the aftermath of the defeat.

With the war, the "intellectual" disagreements of the earlier period were suddenly and without preparation translated into practical decisions of immense moment. The long-awaited spontaneous liquidation of opportunism did not take place, and the proletariat entered the crisis not only divided but also confused on the nature of its divisions as well. In fact, the Left social democrats had been so anxious to preserve the unity of the movement that they had never been able to implement their own ideas or organize around them, and so they were not widely understood by the workers.

It had been a fatal mistake to assume that opportunism would be easily defeated by a united working class in a revolutionary crisis when in reality German workers were permanently and deeply divided. In this context Lukács concluded that "Every 'theoretical' tendency or clash of views must immediately develop an organizational arm if it is to rise above the level of pure theory or abstract opinion, that is to say, if it really intends to point the way to its own fulfilment in practice."[37]

The question of the role of tactical planning in the revolution divided Luxemburg and Lenin as deeply and for the same reasons as these other questions. They were, of course, in complete agreement on such basics as the importance of the Party's role in disseminating revolutionary political propaganda in times of social peace, and in the belief that the workers will revolt the sooner and the more successfully, "the more rapidly and more deeply, more energetically the educational work of social democracy is carried out amongst them".[38] And they could also agree on the need for a Party organization to co-ordinate socially or geographically separated struggles. But beyond this minimum the disagreement begins, Lenin holding that the Party can at least try - and sometimes succeed - in directing the struggle according to a tactical plan, Luxemburg dismissing this goal as impossible and indeed harmful to the movement.

Luxemburg believed that the spontaneous tactical line that emerges from class struggle is superior to any plan of the Party leadership. Even when wrong, the class movement's spontaneous choices have the pathos of historical necessity about them and form an integral part of the learning process of the class. "Let us speak plainly", she wrote, "historically, the errors committed by a truly revolutionary movement are infinitely more fruitful than the infallibility of the cleverest Central Committee."[39] She concluded:

> In general, the tactical policy of the Social Democracy is not something that can be "invented". It is the product of a series of great creative acts of the often spontaneous class struggle seeking its way forward ... . The unconscious comes before the conscious. The logic of the historical process comes before the subjective logic of the human beings who participate in the historic process.[40]

These passages show that for Luxemburg the spontaneity of the movement is deeply connected to its historical inevitability. History has the necessity of a real force, an overwhelming power that imposes itself through mass actions often dimly understood by the participants themselves. The hidden forces which produce great events are only revealed in the course of the struggle. The knowledge of the meaning of the events, their objective existence for theory, always follows the act in which historical truth is unveiled bodily. The "owl of Minerva" is necessarily tardy with respect to this mysterious agency.

To the extent that the necessary struggle is the spontaneous struggle and the Party a subordinate product of this spontaneity, the very idea of tactical planning of the revolution is a contradiction in terms. The Party, quite simply, can never take the class as its object, either of knowledge or of action. Rather, the role of the Party is to be the extreme limit of the subjectivity of the class, the prolongation of class action toward self-awareness. If for Lenin the Party should be pictured one step ahead of the class it leads as a vanguard, for Luxemburg the Party is better imagined behind the class, pointing in the direction in which the class is already moving.

The key practical difference implied by this disagreement concerns the role of insurrection in proletarian revolution. Marx' critique of Jacobin methods is prolonged in Luxemburg's theory of the mass strike as the form of movement of the social revolution. Luxemburg argues quite correctly that a revolutionary mass strike cannot be planned and controlled in its technical details by a political party; however, she failed to understand the limitations of the mass strike which, by itself, is insufficient to assure victory. As Trotsky later explained the problem, "Whatever its power and mass character, the general strike does not settle the problem of power; it only poses it. To seize power, it is necessary, while relying on the general strike, to organize an insurrection."[41] In this task tactical planning is essential, as Lenin was the first to understand clearly.

Lukács argued that Luxemburg's theory of the revolutionary process was at least partially invalidated by the practical lessons of the Russian Revolution. Luxemburg had followed Marx in attempting to restrain the political will of the working class so that it would listen to the deeper voice of its social instinct. But in the context of the revolutionary crisis following World War I, political will was an increasingly important condition of social advance. Victory would come only through the co-ordination of the most sophisticated political leadership and the broadest social movement. Lenin appeared to Lukács to have solved the problem of joining the one to the other. The remaining difficulty was to reconcile Lenin's practical methods with Marxism, and this was the task Lukács set himself.

V.   LENINISM OR MARXISM?

Lukács' attempt to produce an independent theory based on Lenin's practice must have been motivated in part by an implicit critique of Lenin's own self-interpretation. Certainly the Russian defenders of Leninist orthodoxy sensed the incompatibility of Lukács' Leninism with their own. If Lukács himself never openly addressed the problems in Leninist theory, it was no doubt because he felt it would be impolitic to do so, and perhaps also because in the early 1920s strictly philosophical disagreements with Lenin did not seem as important as practical agreement.

Unlike Lukács, Lenin had remained faithful to the "orthodox" epistemology of the Second International "center", as represented by such thinkers as Kautsky and Plekhanov. The reified categories Lenin derived from this epistemology penetrate his own self-interpretation, contradicting the revolutionary tendencies of his thought. The chief theoretical positions of orthodoxy included evolutionary determinism, theory as pure science, and organization and strategy as technical applications of this science. These positions had achieved a sort of classical coherence in the Second International where they rationalized the basically reformist practice of the movement. After World War I, these ideas were thrust into the whirlwind of revolutionary action with theoretically confusing results.

Lukács' reinterpretation of Lenin must be understood in the context of attempts in the West to break with the orthodox Marxism in which Lenin still believed, and to devise a version of Leninism compatible with the emphasis on revolutionary subjectivity that had emerged as one of the chief theoretical characteristics of the post-war offensive. These attempts had in common an implicit rejection of the conservative implications of Lenin's technicism, inherited from his orthodox philosophical teachers.

Certainly, Lenin himself was insensitive to these implications. Technicism offered a language in which to articulate his practice in a revolutionary crisis. Lenin's approach was based on the discovery that the revolutionary movement could not spontaneously resolve the crisis it provoked, but merely posed a suspended social potentiality in an explosive contradiction awaiting the action of a conscious minority for its resolution. History would have to become the object of knowledge and control to realize its "necessary" progress. Lenin takes it for granted that the Party could use the laws of history to achieve historically possible ends.

From this point of view the entire society, including the proletariat, appears as an object, relatively predictable and subject to control from above. Historical necessity is not so much discovered in the gigantic power of its unfolding, as it is for Marx and Luxemburg, as grasped technically in the interests of power. So obvious and unobjectionable does this instrumental perspective seem to Lenin that he naively claims that "Marxism ... places at their (the Party's) disposal the mighty force of millions and millions of workers."[42]

This approach to history contradicts the original Marxian reflexive theory of subjectivity, designed to transcend precisely such a voluntaristic political orientation toward struggle. It seemed therefore to revive the Jacobin-Blanquist revolutionary methods which Marx had long ago rejected. The old orthodoxy had never encountered these paradoxical consequences of its technicist interpretation of Marxism because it was linked to a practice of everyday trade union and parliamentary struggle that could easily be seen as expressing the long-range historical necessity of capitalist social evolution. But in an insurrectionary context, no such illusions were possible. The theory revealed its anti-Marxist implications with a vengeance, particularly in Lenin's attempt to use Kautskian views on "consciousness from without" to justify a type of political vanguardism Kautsky would never have accepted. This argument, contained in Lenin's *What is to be done?*, deserves further consideration for what it shows about the doctrine Lukács largely passes over in silence in elaborating his own interpretation of Leninism.

Like his orthodox teachers, Lenin believed that Marxism was a pure science, that it came "from without" and was in no way a product of proletarian class struggle, even if it took that struggle as its privileged object of study. This idea corresponded to a respectable epistemological model of science and assigned revolutionary intellectuals the missionary role of spreading socialist ideas, the source of which was now to be sought in Marxist thought rather than in the spontaneous ideology of the proletariat. However, it does not seem to have occurred to anyone before Lenin to ask seriously what comes "from within" if Marxist thought comes "from without". In justifying his voluntaristic theory of the Party against those who believed socialism was a spontaneous ideology of the proletariat, Lenin posed and responded to this question in a surprising way.

At first Lenin seems to claim that the proletariat's spontaneous ideology is something he calls "trade union consciousness". This is the conscious condition for solidarity in the struggle to defend class interests within capitalist society. It contains no reference beyond capitalism, and is in fact in perfect conformity with the politics of ... opportunism. The success of opportunism can now be explained, and all arguments for reliance on the "spontaneity" of the class assimilated to it.

But on closer examination, it appears that Lenin will not even admit that proletarian spontaneity can produce trade union consciousness.

Trade unionism means the ideological enslavement of the workers to the bourgeoisie. Hence our task, the task of Social Democracy, is to combat spontaneity, to divert the labor movement from its spontaneous, trade unionist striving to go under the wing of the bourgeoisie ... [43]

Spontaneity is now reduced to the simple predominance of bourgeois ideology, "because it is more fully developed and because it possesses immeasurably more opportunities for being distributed".[44] Thus, even trade unionism, even revisionism, is not a properly proletarian ideology. And "Since there can be no talk of an independent ideology being developed by the masses of workers in the process of their movement, the only choice is: either bourgeois or socialist ideology. There is no middle course."[45]

Having denied all ideological creativity to the mass of workers, Lenin proceeds to sharpen the separation between the working class and the theoreticians of socialism. In Lenin's Kautskian view, theory comes from "science" and not from the working class and its struggles. So basic is this distinction for Lenin that to avoid any confusion he calls "the intellectuals", including Marx and Engels, "representatives of the propertied classes".[46] And, at another point, he insists that when workers participate in creating socialist theory, they "take part not as workers, but as socialist theoreticians ... ; in other words, they take part *only* to the extent that they are able, more or less, to acquire the knowledge of their age and advance that knowledge".[47]

Now clearly there is a grain of truth in all this, but there is also a very dubious polemical exaggeration. Lenin believes that the only way he can establish the autonomy of the Party as against his spontaneist opponents is to deny any and all connection between Marxist theory and the proletariat. This explains his forgetfulness of the Marxist theory of ideology, which holds that ideas that come to a class "from without", for example from intellectuals drawn from other classes, may nevertheless belong organically to that class if they reflect its own standpoint on its life conditions and its aspirations.[48]

Once Lenin's argument is pursued to its logical conclusion, the orthodox premises from which he began yield an absurd result. Here "theory seizes the masses" with a vengeance. The proletariat achieves nothing "on its own", for its spontaneous trade unionism has been reduced to bourgeois ideology and its socialist theoreticians are "intellectuals", "scientists", come from an epistemological beyond or from the bourgeoisie. The rigid opposition of "within" and "without" has converted the proletariat into an ideological *tabula rasa*. It has become the first major class in history with no ideology of its own, but only borrowings from other classes and from science.

Why did Lenin push orthodoxy to these absurd conclusions? No doubt because the alternative, within the framework of the debates in which he was engaged, was to accept a theory of the Party he regarded as wrong. At this point, Lenin could formulate only one fundamental philosophical argument for justifying a break with opportunism and the creation of a vanguard Party. Unfortunately, this argument is incompatible with Marxism, for Marxism is refuted on its basis if it cannot find in the proletariat a reality which "strives toward thought" even as revolutionary ideas strive to enter reality as a material force.

Consistency should not be considered a virtue in arguing for a position as overdrawn as Lenin's, and Lenin is not in fact perfectly consistent. Many other passages in his writings show that he did not want to pay the full price of overthrowing Marxism to defend his theory of the Party. Even *What is to be done?* offers an alternative theory, according to which "the 'spontaneous element', in essence represents nothing more nor less than consciousness in an embryonic form".[49] Here the class "strives toward thought" as Marxism requires. But this alternative theory remains undeveloped because within the context of Lenin's orthodox philosophy it constantly risks passing over into opportunist passivity. The conclusion is inescapable that Lenin lacks the theoretical means to develop a properly Marxist explanation for his own practice.

VI. THE "ACTUALITY" OF THE REVOLUTION

Confronted with the success of Lenin's organizational innovations and the incompetence, at least in Marxist terms, of his philosophical explanations for them, Lukács attempted to find an interpretation of Leninism that would reduce the tension between theory and practice. To do so, he reformulated the debate between Luxemburg and Lenin in historical terms, situating their principal ideas with respect to different stages in the revolutionary process.

Lukács' first sketch of such a theory is to be found in an article published in *Die Internationale* in 1921. This paper is a defense of the new insurrectional tactic of the German Communist Party which had been attacked in terms of Rosa Luxemburg's theory of revolutionary spontaneity. Lukács rejected the use of Luxemburg's ideas to preach political passivity, but he could not help recognizing the incompatibility of the new strategy with her views which, as we have seen, had been "theoretically determining" for him from his earliest discovery of Marxism. Confronted with this contradiction, Lukács asks: "Do the relations between Party and mass remain the same in the course of the entire revolutionary process, or is this relation also a process, which actively and passively undergoes the compulsion of the dialectical transformation and overthrow of the total process?"[50]

In reply he suggests the basis of his later theory of the revolutionary process: the idea of a changing relation between spontaneity and consciousness in the course of history. Lukács distinguishes two main stages. Throughout the first and longest stage of the struggle for economic demands and intellectual independence within capitalism, mass action is essentially spontaneous in character. It arises "reactively" under the immediate compulsion of the economic laws, and all the Party can do in this context is to bring the meaning of such actions to consciousness. During this stage, "the economic and consequently the political and ideological process" has "the necessity of a 'natural law'".[51] To this situation there corresponds the "classical" conception of Marxism, as represented by Marx, Engels and Luxemburg, with its emphasis on historical inevitability and the expressive, hermeneutic role of the Party.

But, there is another side to the Marxist theory of revolution which emphasizes the goal of "human control of history", the "realm of freedom". It is true, Lukács admits, that in classical Marxist thought this goal is always discussed in relation to socialist society. But Lukács argues that the realm of freedom is not so much a realm as a process, and one which begins already in the revolutionary movement itself. To draw a sharp line between necessity and freedom, and to call the one capitalist and the other socialist, would be to deny their dialectical relation. Freedom would then appear not as an immanent, historically developing moment of struggle, but as a transcendent ideal. On the contrary, Lukács claims, the "leap" into the realm of freedom discussed by Marx and Engels cannot be conceived as a sudden break in the continuity of history but only as a gradual development in which, with the approach of the revolution, consciousness plays an increasingly important role.

Thus, Lukács distinguishes a second main stage in the revolutionary process, the stage of the final crisis of capitalism, during which the growing role of consciousness and freedom is reflected in a much more active role for the Party. During this stage the Party may have to follow the sort of strategy chosen by the German Communists, energizing the working class by providing an example of a revolutionary initiative to help it overcome its "lethargy".[52]

Lukács did not retain the exact terms of this discussion in *History and Class Consciousness* and his book on *Lenin*, but those works continue to develop the idea of a gradual change in the relation of spontaneity and consciousness in the course of the revolutionary process. Indeed, *Lenin* is based on the theory of the second stage: "Lenin's concept of party organization", he writes there, "presupposes the fact - the actuality - of the revolution."[53] This idea is brought in constantly to explain the differences between Lenin's approach and traditional Marxist strategy and organization.

In *History and Class Consciousness* Lukács elaborates the theory of the two stages in terms of the development of the proletariat. As the theoretician of reflexive subjectivity, Luxemburg is for him the chief interpreter of the organizational implications of the first stage, which implies a theory of the Party he summarizes as follows:

> Its organisation corresponds to a stage in the class consciousness of the proletariat which does not aspire to anything more than making conscious what was hitherto unconscious and making explicitly what hitherto had been latent. More accurately: it corresponds to a stage in which the process of acquiring consciousness does not entail a terrible *internal ideological crisis* for the proletariat.[54]

From this "classical" point of view, one would be tempted to consider the dissolution of the Party with the approach of the revolution, as the entire latent content of the struggle, formerly conserved by the Party, is translated into spontaneous class action.

But the revolutionary period which followed World War I dramatized the crisis and division of the proletariat. The smoothly rising curve of proletarian spontaneity did not carry the class through the revolutionary crisis to power, for the very conditions under which its victory was possible disorganized and confused it. "The crisis involves not only the economic undermining of capitalism but, equally, the ideological transformation of a proletariat that has been reared in capitalist society under the influence of the life-forms of the bourgeoisie."[55] And precisely to the extent that large sectors of the proletariat enter the revolutionary period still "caught up in the old capitalist forms of thought and feeling", the crisis of capitalism is also a crisis of the proletariat itself.[56]

This crisis of the proletariat can only be met by an increasing reliance on theory and class consciousness. As the revolution approaches, the next step on the path to socialism becomes less and less obvious; the spontaneous reaction of the class to the operation of the economic laws is no longer an adequate guide and actions must be based increasingly on the objective potentialities of the society. Instrumental considerations take their place alongside expressive ones in the life of the Party.

The closer this process comes to its goal the more urgent it becomes for the proletariat to understand its own historical mission and the more vigorously and directly proletarian class consciousness will determine each of its actions. For the blind power of the forces at work will only advance "automatically" to their goal of self-annihilation as long as that goal is not within reach. When the moment of transition to the "realm of freedom" arrives this will become apparent just because the blind forces really will hurtle blindly towards the abyss, and only the conscious will of the proletariat will be able to save mankind from the impending catastrophe.[57]

Here is to be found the justification for Lenin's voluntarism. As the theoretician of the final crisis of capitalism, Lenin understood the increasing role of consciousness better than the representatives of the "classical" Left. His break with the organizational and strategic theory of the Marxist tradition looked to many like a return to Jacobin-Blanquist methods out of the distant past, but in fact, Lukács argues, this was no nostalgic, backward glance but a much needed adjustment of the working class movement to the demands of the new revolutionary era.

VII. PARTY, CLASS, AND CLASS CONSCIOUSNESS

This historical justification of Lenin's practice raises a deep theoretical problem; for, even if the sort of Party Lenin created is the most effective in a revolutionary crisis, it remains to be seen if anything more than opportunity links this Party to the proletariat. Lukács' theory of class consciousness is designed to solve this problem by explaining the dependence of the Party on the class even in the second stage, characterized by Party autonomy and conscious initiative. The theoretical issue involved in this discussion has to do with the relation of individual thought to the objectively based class standpoint from which it proceeds. Since this relation is formally similar to that of Party to class, Lukács' theory of class consciousness clarifies much of the earlier discussion.

The Marxism of the Second International situated class standpoint and individual thought on the same ontological level and related them as effect and cause. The result is crude reductionism, the denial of the specificity and relative autonomy of intellectual and ideological processes. Lenin sensed the organizational and strategic risks of such reductionism and therefore employed the idea of "consciousness from without" to distinguish Marxist thought from the class standpoint of the proletariat. But we have already seen the paradoxes to which this view leads.

There is a way of avoiding these paradoxes and preserving the truth of both the concept of reflexive subjectivity and Lenin's objections to a reduction of theory to everyday consciousness. This way requires, however, a difficult distinction between the concept of class consciousness, based on the objective determinants of the everyday activity of the class as these are understood by social theory, and the actual thoughts and feelings of members of the class which, experience shows, may deviate significantly from theoretical expectations. In principle, class consciousness would be the significance of class action represented as "objectively possible" contents of consciousness members of the class might employ to articulate the meaning of their lives. In practice, the objectively possible beliefs described in the theoretical model of class consciousness must compete, and not always very successfully, with ideas borrowed from other classes or developed idiosyncratically from a mixture of sources.[58]

The relation of Party and class can be analyzed on this basis in a way which does justice both to Luxemburg's insistence on the reflexive nature of class consciousness, and to Lenin's insistence on the independent role of theory. The Party can be seen as attempting to interpret the situation of the class in accordance with the concept of class consciousness, understood essentially as the unarticulated meaning of class action. This meaning can be "imputed" to the class in the expectation that, if it is correctly interpreted, the class will recognize itself in the Party's language and acts. The translation of these imputed contents back into action by the class completes the cycle in which class consciousness advances to higher levels. In this model of the development of class consciousness the ideas the Party brings to the class are both "from without", in the sense that they arise from theory, and "from within", in the sense that they reflect the truth of class action.

There is a short passage in Marx' work which comes quite close to suggesting this model of the relation between theory and practice in history. This passage resolves the contradiction of the "within" and the "without" in very much the same spirit as Lukács' theory. Marx writes:

> Just as little must one imagine that the democratic representatives are indeed all shopkeepers or enthusiastic champions of shopkeepers. According to their education and their individual position they may be as far apart as heaven from earth. What makes them representatives of the petty bourgeoisie is the fact that in their minds they do not get beyond the limits which the latter do not get beyond in life, that they are consequently driven,

theoretically, to the same problems and solutions to which material interest and social position drive the latter practically. This is, in general, the relationship between the political and literary representatives of a class and the class they represent.[59]

Lukács' theoretically elaborated version of this suggestion works well in explaining the classical reflexive concept of theory and the Party. But the relation between Party and class in the period of the actuality of the revolution is complicated by the fact that theory can identify instrumentally decisive tasks which are not taken up spontaneously by class action.

It is of course normal that theory contain contents with no immediate relation to class action, for example, abstract ideas about the circulation of money or the schemata of reproduction of capital. These ideas can be called "proletarian" only in the very limited sense that they, like Marxist thought in general, lie under the horizon of the class standpoint of the proletariat. This horizon, Lukács argues, is defined by the possibility of a dialectical transcendence of the reified bourgeois standpoint, both in practice and in theory. But such ideas do not bring the meaning of any specific action to consciousness. They thus "represent the proletariat", in Marx' phrase, only scientifically, not as moments in its self-consciousness. What happens once the success of the movement depends on translating ideas of this type into action? What happens when the mere addition of self-consciousness to action is insufficient, when "what must be done" no longer follows in a smooth continuum along the path of the actualization of the latent meaning of spontaneous action?

For Lenin this situation requires a Party initiative, based on "consciousness from without" and supported by a working class that lets itself be maneuvered like troops on the battlefield. On these terms the Party appears as a historical subject and the masses as just another objective condition it must take into account in pursuing its goals. What is lost in this description is the complex communicative and social dimension of the interaction of Party and class in a revolutionary crisis. Lenin's military metaphor obviously does not explain the authority of the Party, which depends on investments of a wholly different order. It is this aspect of the relation Lukács now tries to reconstruct.

The risk of sectarianism is obvious when theoretically inspired Party initiatives leave the masses far behind in order to respond "correctly" to objective instrumental requirements. Here one can see clearly the dialectical correlation of technicism and ethical idealism: the Party may unconsciously fall back into a moral stance in relation to society, posing ethical exigencies disguised as scientific certainties. Sectarianism can only be avoided where the Party continues to advance proletarian consciousness, because that is the only really fundamental condition of victory it can hope to influence deeply.

With this in mind, it is possible to distinguish "classical" expressive acts of the Party, which follow and render explicit the content of class action, from a new type of exemplary Party intervention which precedes class actions, the necessity of which it makes clear and which it inspires. In both cases the Party's acts are doubly meant, once in function of the particular objective they aim at, and then a second time in function of their expected impact on class consciousness. But in the era of the actuality of the revolution, the passage from latent theoretical concepts to practical and active class consciousness must be immensely accelerated to coincide with the rhythms of instrumental effectiveness in a political crisis. This coincidence can be achieved where, by their exemplary form, instrumental actions also serve to advance consciousness. Lukács writes:

> The struggle of the Communist Party is focused upon the class consciousness of the proletariat. Its organisational separation from the class does not mean in this case that it wishes to do battle for its interests on its behalf and in its place ... . Should it do this, as occasionally happens in the course of revolution, then it is not in the first instance an attempt to fight for the objective goals of the struggle in question (for in the long run these can only be won or retained by the class itself), but only an attempt to advance or accelerate the development of class consciousness.[60]

Here Lenin's scientific-technical self-understanding is completely inverted. The Party does not become the subject of history through its independent actions. Rather, these actions pose the Party as an object before the class. Thus Lukács describes the Party, even at its most active, in the passive mode. He calls it the "visible and organised incarnation of (the proletariat's) class consciousness".[61] And, he writes:

> The Communist Party must exist as an independent organisation so that the proletariat may be able to see its own class consciousness given historical shape. And likewise, so that in every event of daily life the point of view demanded by the interests of the class as a whole may receive a clear formulation that every worker can understand. And, finally, so that the whole class may become fully aware of its own existence as a class.[62]

The Party does not have "at its disposal" millions of proletarians, but on the contrary, it is those millions who have the Party at their disposal, to believe or disbelieve, to accept or reject, to follow or oppose on the basis of its success in discovering and communicating the next "objectively possible" step in the evolution of class consciousness. The apparently contingent technical relation of Party to class in Lenin's theory is subordinated here to a deeper "internal cause" which makes this technical relation possible in the first place. The Party, even in its acts, becomes the objectification of class consciousness. It is not a mechanism of social control in the service of the revolution; it is there to be "seen", and the sight of it inspires the overthrow of the society.

VIII. BREAKDOWN OF THE SYNTHESIS

Lukács' synthesis of Luxemburg and Lenin draws both expressive and instrumental forms of action together under the reflexive concept of subjectivity. Although he lacks the term, Lukács has clearly grasped the concept of exemplary action which supplies the mediating link between the apparent contraries. The synthesis breaks down, however, when Lukács turns from explaining the relation of Party to class in the revolution to a consideration of their relation in the socialist state. Once the Party's acts become acts of state, the informal popular controls under which it developed no longer suffice to insure its subordination to the class and yet Lukács proposes no new controls capable of preventing a regression to Jacobin voluntarism.

Lukács' discussion of socialism is nevertheless interesting as an attempt to sketch the outlines of a public sphere based on a social movement rather than on "politics" in the usual sense of the term. The bourgeois parliamentary public sphere is transcended through the creation of forms of collective action that go beyond mere verbal propaganda addressed to the individual consciousness of the isolated voter. The social basis of this new public sphere is the Soviet or workers' council which overcomes the isolation of the individual and the split between economic and political life on which this isolation is based.

Lukács' description of the Soviets has a distinctly Luxemburgian cast, and reflects her own analysis of similar phenomena in the 1905 Revolution. For both Luxemburg and Lukács, the Soviets represent the point of transition from a reactive spontaneity under the impulse of the economic laws toward a creative social movement capable of restructuring society. To explain this transition, Lukács reframes Luxemburg's analysis in terms of his theory of the transcendence of reification in a proletarian consciousness oriented toward the "totality" of society.

The Soviet system, for example, always establishes the indivisible
unity of economics and politics by relating the concrete existence of
men - their immediate daily interests, *etc.* - to the essential
questions of society as a whole. It also establishes the unity in
objective reality where bourgeois class interests created the
'division of labor' above all, the unity of the power 'apparatus'
(army, police, government, the law, *etc.*) and 'the people' ....
Everywhere, the Soviet system does its utmost to relate human
activity to general questions concerning the state, the economy,
culture, *etc.*, while fighting to ensure that the regulation of all such
questions does not become the privilege of an exclusive
bureaucratic group remote from social life as a whole. Because the
Soviet system, the proletarian state, makes society aware of the real
connections between all moments of social life (and later objectively
unites those which are as yet objectively separate - town and
country, for example, intellectual and manual labor, *etc.*), it is a
decisive factor in the organization of the proletariat as a class.[63]

This description of the Soviets begins to suggest a theory of the
new context of citizenship in socialist society, and as such it marks a
definite advance over most earlier Marxist discussions of socialist
politics, which tend to vary between utopian speculation and
unimaginative appeals to the example of existing bourgeois democratic
forms. And yet it is puzzling that neither here nor elsewhere does
Lukács discuss the institutional aspects of the socialist state, such as
voting, the organization of public debate, competition between parties,
rights of individuals and groups, and so on.

How important is the missing institutional theory from the
standpoint of Marxism? Given Marx' frequent criticism of the
limitations of capitalist democracy, one might imagine that Lukács'
omission is consistent with Marxism and represents a lack characteristic
of Marxism itself. Yet the one text in which Marx examines a workers'
power, *The Civil War in France*, contains extensive discussion of the
institutional structure of the socialist state. This discussion is governed
by the original impulse of Marx' critique of political revolution in his
early work, which is the search for a way of subordinating the new
socialist state to the social movement. Marx judges some means
inherited from capitalist democracy effective for this purpose (*e.g.*
voting), and others counterproductive (*e.g.* separation of powers).

Rather than developing an institutional theory of this sort, Lukács
juxtaposes his theory of the Soviets with a theory of the vanguard Party
derived from the first few years of the Russian example. He writes that
"the Party's role in a revolution - the masterly idea of the early Lenin -

is even more important and more decisive in the period of transition to socialism than in the preparatory period".[64] And he assures us that the apparent contradiction between the authority of the Party and the democratic tasks of the revolution is in fact "the dialectically correct solution to the objective contradictions" of the situation.[65] He seems to claim that the very same mechanisms which insured the subordination of the Party to the class before the revolution will work afterwards to prevent the autonomization of the state.

But the reference to Lenin's idea of the leading role of the Party is deceptive. In the discussion reviewed above, Lukács has shown quite convincingly that before the revolution the Party can lead successfully through exemplary actions that lie at the intersection of instrumental and communicative exigencies. Only in this way can the Party advance the movement politically while retaining and enlarging its base of popular support. But after the revolution the situation has changed and the Party is not forced to find compromises between the instrumental requirements of effective strategic action and the communicative conditions of maintaining a leading relationship to class consciousness.

Instead, the Party focuses on gaining control of a new base of power, the coercitive institution of the state. In relation to this state, the Soviets cannot play the role played earlier by proletarian spontaneity as a corrective and verification of the Party's line. The Party's existence is no longer rooted in the class consciousness of the proletariat, for now it finds itself at the summit of the technical bureaucracies in charge of running an industrial society in which workers appear as simple subordinates. The back and forth movement from Party to class, consciousness to spontaneity, through which both advanced in synergy, is replaced by the command structure of an industrial state. By no stretch of the imagination can the acts of the Party at this point be described as moments in the self-reflection of the class.

One might argue that Lenin had few choices as a leader of a historical movement while still expressing concern about the direction he was compelled by circumstance to take. Certainly the single-party state established in Russia ought to have been a subject for concern among Marxists, if for no other reason, on the basis of a reading of *The Civil War in France*. It seemed obvious to Marx in 1871 that new institutional structures of socialist democracy would be required to maintain the social and emancipatory character of the movement. It is difficult to understand how the passage of fifty years could change the status of that insight. Yet it is not at all obvious to Lukács, nor to many others in his position in the 1920s. Instead, he arrives theoretically at the same contradiction at which Lenin arrived on the basis of practical experience: the assertion of the simultaneous and increased role of both the masses and the Communist Party in a single-party Soviet state. In practice, this contradiction was resolved by the collapse of the social movement and the creation of a new kind of society without precedent in Marxist theory.

The inability of most revolutionary Communists in the 1920s to foresee and forestall the Stalinist catastrophe was due to a deep failure of theory and imagination. The cause of this failure was twofold. On the one hand, thinkers and activists like Lukács and Lenin confused emergency measures taken in the shadow of the revolution with fundamental changes in the nature of the public sphere under socialism. On the other hand, and as a result of this first error, they underestimated the validity of the classic teachings concerning the political and legal preconditions of democracy developed in the course of several centuries of bourgeois and Marxist reflection and experience. The consequences of this failure are still very much with us and represent the inner theoretical limit of the dominant forms of revolutionary Communism down to the present day.

ACKNOWLEDGMENTS

This paper was prepared for the conference on 'Réification et Utopie: Ernst Bloch et György Lukács à l'Occasion du Centenaire de Leur Naissance', March 26-29, 1985, Goethe-Institut Paris. I would like to thank the organizers of this conference, and especially Michael Löwy, for their kind invitation to attend.

NOTES

1.   For examples, see James Miller, 'Marxism and Subjectivity', in *Telos*, no. 6, Fall 1970; Louis Althusser, *et al.*, *Lire le Capital*, Paris, Maspéro, 1967, tome II, p. 104. Cf. M. Löwy, *Pour une sociologie des intellectuels révolutionaires*, Paris, PUF, 1976, pp. 203-225. Another book which helps to correct the image of the early Lukács is Laura Boella, *Il Giovane Lukács*, Bari, De Donate, 1977.

2.   G. Lukács, *History and Class Consciousness*, translated by R. Livingstone, Boston, MIT, 1968. p. 338. This text will be referred to hereafter as *HCC*.

3.   *HCC*, p. 297.
4.   *HCC*, p. 307.
5.   *HCC*, p. 297.
6.   *HCC*, p. xlii.
7.   *HCC*, p. 41.
8.   *HCC*, p. 41.
9.   *HCC*, p. 297.
10.   *HCC*, p. 298.
11.   *HCC*, p. 298.
12.   G. Lukács, *Lenin*, trans. by N. Jacobs, London, New Left Books, 1970, pp. 67-68.
13.   *HCC*, p. 2.
14.   K. Marx, *Writings of the Young Marx on Philosophy and Society*, New York, Doubleday, 1967, p. 350.
15.   Letter from Marx to Ruge (Sept. 1843), quoted in *HCC*, p. 77.
16.   K. Marx, *op. cit.*, p. 355.
17.   K. Marx, *Early Writings*, London, C.A. Watts, 1963, pp. 53-54.
18.   K. Marx, *The Poverty of Philosophy*, New York, International Publishers, 1963, p. 173.
19.   K. Marx, *Capital*, New York, Modern Library, 1906 reprint, vol. 1, p. 20.
20.   *HCC*, p. 16.
21.   R. Luxemburg, 'The Mass Strike, the Political Party and the Trade Unions', in *Rosa Luxemburg Speaks*, New York, Pathfinder, 1970.
22.   *Ibid.* p. 199.
23.   *HCC*, p. 205.
24.   *HCC*, p. 299.
25.   *HCC*, p. 42.
26.   *HCC*, pp. 41-42.

27.   *HCC*, p. 303.
28.   *HCC*, pp. 278-279.
29.   *HCC*, p. 275.
30.   R. Luxemburg, *op. cit.*, p. 119.
31.   *HCC*, p. 287.
32.   *HCC*, p. 285.
33.   *HCC*, p. 284.
34.   R. Luxemburg, *op. cit.*, p. 129.
35.   *HCC*, p. 286.
36.   *HCC*, p. 302.
37.   *HCC*, p. 299.
38.   R. Luxemburg, *op. cit.*, p. 199.
39.   R. Luxemburg, *op. cit.*, p. 130.
40.   *Ibid.* p. 121.
41.   L. Trotsky, 'Les problèmes de la guerre civile', in *Initiative Socialiste*, no. 17, Juin 1968, pp. 9-10. Cf. also V. Serge, *L'An I de la Révolution Russe,* Paris, Éditions de Delphes, 1965, p. 96.
42.   V.I. Lenin, *Essential Works of Lenin*, New York, Bantam, 1966, p. 89.
43.   V.I. Lenin, *What Is To Be Done?*, in *Selected Works*, New York, International Publishers, 1967, vol. I, p. 130.
44.   *Ibid.* vol. I, p. 130.
45.   *Ibid.* vol. I, p. 130.
46.   *Ibid.* vol. I, p. 122.
47.   *Ibid.* vol. I, p. 130.
48.   K. Marx, *The Eighteenth Brumaire of Louis Bonaparte*, in *Marx and Engels, Selected Works*, New York, International Publishers, 1969, p. 121.
49.   Lenin, *op. cit.*, vol. I, p. 121.
50.   G. Lukács, 'Spontaneität der Massen, Aktivität der Partei', in *Geschichte und Klassenbewusstsein,* Neuwied und Berlin, Luchterhand, 1968, p. 136 (my translation *A.F.*).
51.   *Ibid.* p. 137.
52.   *Ibid.* p. 141.
53.   G. Lukács, *Lenin, op. cit.*, p. 26.
54.   *HCC*, p. 304.
55.   *HCC*, pp. 310-311.
56.   *HCC*, p. 310.
57.   *HCC*, pp. 69-70.
58.   For a further discussion of Lukács' theory of class consciousness and the Party, see A. Feenberg, *Lukács, Marx and the Sources of Critical Theory*, New York, Oxford University Press, 1985, Chap. V.

    59.   K. Marx, *The Eighteenth Brumaire of Louis Bonaparte*,
op. cit., p. 121.
       60.   *HCC*, p. 326.
       61.   *HCC*, p. 42.
       62.   *HCC*, p. 326.
       63.   G. Lukács, *Lenin*, *op. cit.*, pp. 67-68.
       64.   *Ibid.* p. 86.
       65.   *Ibid.* p. 87.

ASSEN IGNATOW

Is There a 'Proletarian Standpoint'?

Lukács' criticism of the antinomies of bourgeois thought and the closely related affirmation and presentation of the "proletarian standpoint" belong to the core of *History and Class Consciousness*, the Lukácsian work that marks the beginning and coronation of his Marxist phase (*Zur Ontologie des gesellschaftlichen Seins*, as well as the works in between are clearly not up to its level). The conceptual core of *History and Class Consciousness* is the problem of totality. Lukács uses the ability to grasp the totality as a measure of the intellectual capacity of the social classes that are in conflict. Let us recall the main elements in Lukács' doctrine.

I

According to Lukács, bourgeois thought is subject to a whole series of "antinomies": *e.g.* voluntarism and fatalism, freedom and necessity, is and ought, and contemplation and action. Of particular interest to Lukács is the antinomy of "milieu" and "human activity". "Bourgeois philosophers" of the eighteenth century were faced with the dilemma that, while it seemed plausible that man is a product of the "milieu", of "circumstances", of "education", of "conditions", *etc.*, it seemed no less plausible that this milieu is itself the result of human activity. Lukács wanted to discover " ... the vital ground that is the real basis of this antinomy"[1] which he simply assumed to exist. He went on to reconstruct this "vital ground" as follows: in the era of French materialism, social development had reached a high level, as one can see from the real face of society. It had lost its character of being "beyond man" - a veil that had hidden the face of society in the Middle Ages. It became clear that everything that happens in society is of human doing. By "human" here is meant "bourgeois". For the "bourgeois" thinker - and this is taken for granted - "man" means " ... the egoistic individual, artificially isolated by capitalism".[2] Correspondingly, the consciousness that effects knowledge and activity is " ... an individual, isolated, Robinsonesque consciousness".[3] "Robinsonade" has to be seen as a basic structure of Lukács' theory of ideology, as explicated in *History and Class Consciousness*. It conditions all of bourgeois thinking and is the source of its antinomies. In other words, the bourgeois whose class position is that of the owner

T. Rockmore (ed.), Lukács Today, 157–166.
© *1988 by D. Reidel Publishing Company.*

of private property takes a "standpoint", from which he cannot see social reality except as full of antinomies. He describes this more exactly as follows:

> What appears at first glance as the effect of the sensualistic theory of knowledge of the French materialists - that 'the brain is just a wax to be formed by all the impressions that one wants to make there ... ' and that, on the other hand, only conscious doing can count as activity - proves on closer examination to be merely a consequence of the situation of bourgeois man in the capitalist process of production. What is basic here has often been stressed by us: man in capitalist society confronts the - 'made' by himself (as class) - reality as a 'nature' that is essentially different from him; he is irresistibly delivered over to its 'laws' and the only thing he can do is to exploit individual laws for his own (egotistic) interests. But, even in this 'activity' he remains essentially an object and not the subject of the phenomena. The range of his activity is thereby forced completely inside: it is, on the one hand, the consciousness of these laws and, on the other, the consciousness of his internal reactions to the course of events.[4]

In this way, according to Lukács, the social nature of bourgeois thought condemns it to remain drawn between polar and unmediated determinations: necessity and freedom, consciousness and society, activity and external circumstances. Oscillating between them, bourgeois philosophers cannot reconcile them. Therefore, bourgeois thought knows no freedom or creativity that is not internal and no law that is not external. Bourgeois thought cannot overcome these one-sided aspects, each of which is but a reflection of the other. Accordingly, every important domain of reality is diminished: morality is reduced to inefficacy, and politics and economics are robbed of their cultural content. Lukács traces the effects of these antinomies on the development of "bourgeois" philosophy from the eighteenth century up to his contemporaries, and reacts negatively to all the most important philosophic, social-scientific, and cultural debates of the first two decades of the twentieth century. According to Lukács, all of these disputes are based on false oppositions. He is particularly sharp in his criticism of the fact-value split in the philosophies of neo-Kantianism, Max Weber, and the Marxists of the Second International, and of the division of philosophy into "disciplines", *etc.* - in other words, in a whole series of theoretical domains which, according to Lukács, all result from the same undialectical structure of antinomic bourgeois thinking. German Idealism was the sole bourgeois philosophic current to come close to the problem of totality and to anticipate the correct answer. But even German Idealism could not escape the strictures that are organically inherent to bourgeois thought.

The true bearer of revolutionary change is the proletariat. The opposition between bourgeois and proletarian standpoints is described by Lukács, in a first approximation, as an opposition of method. Two methods stand opposed to each other: the bourgeois principle of immediacy and the proletarian principle of mediation. These two approaches to reality evolve from the social situation of the two classes.

Lukács' long discussion may be summarized as follows: precisely because of his social position, the bourgeois is forced to remain a prisoner of immediacy (*i.e.* of the reified social world which generates the illusory vision of reality as a foreign externality and of our subjectivity as the sole medium of freedom and activity), and not to see the masked social relations, or the genesis and social development that lead to the reified capitalist world.

On the contrary, the "proletarian standpoint" - to the extent that it has undergone an autonomous development - means "overcoming the immediacy of bourgeois relations and acquiring an insight into mediation"; *i.e.*, into the human, subjectively caused activity, and into the processes and relations that bourgeois society has occasioned. In Lukács' words: "Since it [bourgeois thought, *A.I.*] is incapable of discovering further mediations, or of grasping the being and origination of bourgeois society as product of the same subject that 'created' the conceptual totality of knowledge, its ultimate standpoint, that is decisive for all of thought, is that of pure immediacy".[5] "To the contrary, these limits of immediacy serve for the proletariat at the point of origin, at the moment of taking the standpoint, as what is to be internally overcome ... . For the proletariat, the limitation of immediacy has become an internal limit."[6]

This clearly has to mean - at least in the final analysis - that the bourgeois finds himself at home in his "immediacy" since this privileged position is justified as "natural". But the proletarian, in order to emancipate himself, has to go beyond the apparent self-justifiability of immediacy, since it is just this immediacy that oppresses him and imprisons him. This is - or so it seems to us - a plausible reading of *History and Class Consciousness*.

We can be even more concise: the revolution in theory, that the proletariat has to carry out along with the social revolution, consists in the unlocking of the rigidified conceptual reification and in the discovery of the processual and relational character of what is apparently reified, the subjective source of the quasi-natural.

Of course, the reader's interest is aroused, in particular because this intellectual revolution - as the "reversal" of another standpoint - seems far more interesting, detailed and fruitful than Engels' effort at "putting

it [the dialectic, *A.I.*] on its feet". The most obvious question that
emerges here is how and when does the proletariat reach "its"
standpoint?

It is precisely at this point that Lukács' explanations become unclear
and equivocal. Here in *History and Class Consciousness* something
occurs that will constantly recur in the future: Lukács is more
convincing in his negations than in his affirmations. Though often
one-sided and narrow, his accounts of "bourgeois" poets are always
sensible and relevant. However, the Western public was speechless
when it heard Lukács seriously make the claim that Makarenko and
Sholokhov are superior to Kafka and Proust. Quite similarly, in the
present case, the result is disappointing, although without the
catastrophic character that Lukács' thought had in the Stalinist era. The
whole process of reasoning here is unclear and confused.

The proletarian experiences in his own body that he is ruled by a
reification and that he is only a quantified thing, " ... a mere token
reduced to abstract quantity ... ."[7] Of course, the capitalist is also
reified, but he has the illusion that his activity is a freely exercised
unfolding of his subjectivity. This is totally lacking in the proletarian.
As if with elementary force and clarity he understands the brutal
inhumanity of the capitalism that oppresses him and turns him into a
thing. Here is a very significant passage:

> He (the proletarian, *A.I.*) is therefore obliged to undergo his
> 'commoditization' and reduction to quantity. Precisely thereby is
> he however projected beyond the immediacy of this situation.[8]

But, how can a total and acutely experienced transformation of the
proletarian into a mere commodity simultaneously "project" him over
the immediacy of this situation; more, how can the proletarian be
precisely "projected thereby" over this misery? The two situations
exclude one another. To become aware of his reification, the proletarian must be freely subjective. But, according to Lukács, he cannot
be; nor can the bourgeois, although he thinks himself into thinking he
can.

Lukács has no answer to this dilemma. It is true that he tries to
imagine many of the stages in the process. For example, the proletarian
must have experienced work time, leisure time and the fight to shorten
work time in order to overcome fetishistic immediacy. From the
standpoint of bourgeois consciousness, the shortening and lengthening
of work time are purely quantitative processes. For the proletarian,
however, they are above all qualitative phenomena, since they directly
affect his style of life. Becoming conscious of work time, however,
does not completely overcome reification. The stark opposition of

object and subject is not yet overcome. On the one hand, it "... appears directly as an object and not as an actor in the social process of labor".[9] On the other hand, this objectification is not complete: "Through the separation that occurs here between the objectivity and subjectivity of the man transformed into a mere commodity, the latter is made capable of becoming conscious of it."[10] The worker comes to see that it is he who stands behind the commodity. The proletarian completes the self-consciousness of the commodity; and this self-consciousness leads to fundamental changes in his social situation. The change in the proletarian's knowledge and consciousness is simultaneously a change in his being: " ... since consciousness here is not the consciousness of an object standing over against him, but is the self-consciousness of the object, the act of becoming conscious changes the form of objectivity (*Gegenständlichkeitsform*) of its object".[11] In other words, in full conformity with Lukács' principle of the identity of subject and object, the becoming conscious of reification implies - at least to a certain degree - an overcoming of this reification. But, the critical reader must ask: as long as the class-conscious proletarian remains under the capitalist "yoke", how can the "form of objectivity" of the proletarian be changed? and does not "form of objectivity" here mean just the reification? Be that as it may, it turns out that the real point of transition does not lie in the worker coming to consciousness of his status as a commodity:

> When it is a matter of mere commodity relations, the proletarian can become conscious of himself only as the object of economic processes. For, the commodity is produced and the worker as commodity, as immediate producer, is in the best of cases, a mechanical spoke in the machinery. If the reification of capital resolved in a continuous process of its production and reproduction, one can become conscious from this standpoint that the proletariat is the actual - if bound and as yet unconscious - subject of this process.[12]

The last chord in this enthusiastic, but not always harmonious, hymn to the proletariat is:

> Only one class can have a transformatory practical effect on the totality of reality. This class can do this only when it can see its own fate in the processes of the world before it.[13]

Thus, for Lukács the proletariat is a Prometheus not only on the social-political level but also on the intellectual level.

Let us now turn to a critical analysis of Lukács' theory.

One basic premiss and an essential pillar of Lukács' whole theory is, of course, class war - that is, the sharp conflict between a reactionary bourgeoisie and a revolutionary, heroic proletariat, who is called upon to liberate not only society and the workers but also human thought. This is why in Lukács we find most tightly connected with each other, on the one hand, the critical analysis of bourgeois, reified, undialectical thought of the isolated individual, blind to totality and enslaved to immediacy and, on the other hand, the enthusiastic and pathos-filled analysis of proletarian thought which alone is able to ground totality, process, becoming and mediation. The two analyses are of unequal value.

His analysis of bourgeois thought is - at least as a first approximation - not only coherent and sensible, but even plausible. From a certain point of view, it is an acceptable interpretation of modern thought. One finds little factual error and no serious logical problems.

The same is not true of his analysis of the proletarian standpoint. In the first place, the difference between consciousness of commodity status and consciousness of being the subject of history is not clear. If becoming conscious of commodity status projects one beyond reification, it should also reveal to the proletarian his intellectual role and lead to his spiritual emancipation.

The main weakness of Lukács' notion, however, lies in its inability to answer an absolutely essential question that he ignores: how and when has the proletariat raised itself up to overcoming reified immediacy? In fact, has the proletariat ever done this? The answer comes out clearly in the negative. From the proletarian standpoint the category of totality (consciousness of which is needed for overcoming reification) is hard to see because any category is hard to see from this viewpoint. A Marxist author should know precisely that the proletariat is frozen at the lowest level of daily consciousness. For example, Lukács says that proletarian consciousness is free from the illusions, *e.g.*, of the bureaucracy that thinks it is doing interesting and dutiful work. So, it well may be that - from a Marxist perspective - proletarian consciousness is free of a certain obstacle; it is not free, however, from the obstacle of intellectual underdevelopment, which allows no theoretical thought, be it 'adequate' or 'false'.

Note these words from Lukács: " ... the reification process, the transformation of the worker into a commodity ... cancels (him), disturbs and cripples (his 'soul'), [but] does not (change), however, his human spiritual essence into a commodity".[14] This assertion does not prove what it was supposed to prove, *i.e.*, the privileged position of "proletarian thought". It is not clear why the "crippled" and "stunted" proletarian soul should be better adapted for knowledge. The intellectual poverty of the proletariat - overlooked by Lukács - is equally responsible for the transformation of human beings into commodities. While his muscles are sold directly, the proletarian's mind is reduced to a level where it cannot resist this sale.

In Lukács' understanding of ideology, the proletariat is a sort of incarnation of the absolute spirit, since only the latter is the genuine totality of object and subject that knows and understands itself as such. It seems, however, that the absolute spirit had bad taste in incarnating itself in the proletariat; for only a miracle could combine the indubitable Messianic role of the proletariat with the equally indubitable misery of the proletariat under capitalism.

The totality that, for Lukács, is the truth was discovered not by proletarians but by the "bourgeois" intellectuals, Marx and Engels. The social situation of these thinkers (their, so to speak, "observation tower") was that of stable intellectuals who were not in danger of having their intellectual powers atrophied by the daily struggle for their daily bread. What is more, both Kautsky and Lenin (the former rejected by Lukács and the latter praised but not fully accepted by him) knew that, left to themselves, the proletarians were capable only of a "trade-union consciousness" and that revolutionary consciousness can be brought in only from the outside, namely by bourgeois intellectuals like Marx and Engels.[15] If this is the case - and it is hard to see how it could be otherwise - the whole unclear, but intensive Lukácsian drama of the emergence of proletarian consciousness falls apart. Since it was not the proletariat or a single proletarian, but two bourgeois intellectuals, namely Marx and Engels, who created the "proletarian standpoint", there was clearly no question of a transition by them from reified subjectivity into free subjectivity. If Marx and Engels had not created this standpoint, they could have enjoyed a secure life and even reached the summits of society. This would, of course, have also been a reification, but not one that involved questions of life and death.

A further question, that is the Achilles heel of Lukács' theory, is: how could the ideas of these two thinkers form a "proletarian standpoint"? The proletariat itself could not develop such a "standpoint". What is "proletarian" in these ideas of Marx and Engels, the bourgeois intellectuals? That these ideas are favorable to the proletariat is not enough to establish their "proletarian" character. There were other ideas that called upon the proletariat - such as those of Lassalle, Proudhon, Weitling, *etc.* Why should not the latter express the proletarian standpoint, since the majority of proletarians (especially in

highly developed industrial countries) followed these and not the
Marxist ideas?

To deal with these difficulties, one has to deal with two other
highly suspect conceptual operations. First, one has to assume that the
factual support of a given standpoint by one class or another is
irrelevant for the class character of this standpoint. Second, one must
presuppose that there is a "hyper-empirical" link, that is, independent of
the factual indifference of the proletariat *vis-à-vis* Marxism, between
Marxism and the proletariat. It is as if Marx and Engels had turned into
proletarians and, unbeknownst to themselves, had become incarnations
of a "higher consciousness" with a secret "mission" for the proletariat.
It is easy to see that both of these conceptual operations belong rather to
mysticism than to verifiable social science.

The usual Marxist reply to such objections is that Marx and Engels
correctly recognized the fundamental (strategic, so to speak) interests of
the working class, while the other "petty bourgeois socialists" aimed
not at the radical liberation of the proletariat, but at a compromise with
the bourgeoisie. However, who decides on the correctness or
incorrectness of Marxist doctrine, *i.e.*, on its conformity with
proletarian interests? According to the Marxists, once again: this is a
process where one of the participants declares himself to be the judge.
To support the contention that they are legitimate thinkers of the
proletariat, Marx, Engels, Lenin and Lukács used their own
self-assessment. As incoherent as these self-consecrations may be,
they seem coherent to the Marxists who are dealing not with a real
proletariat that exists only in an empirical way but with an idea of the
proletariat that can, like any conceptual thing, be transformed as one
likes.

Lukács' failure to demonstrate the existence of a proletarian
standpoint which would be completely superior to the "bourgeois" one
and would solve the "antinomies of bourgeois thought" has
consequences for the whole theory of ideology to be found in *History
and Class Consciousness*, the main elements of which are - as we said
above - closely inter-connected.

*   *   *

Our results are:

1. There is no proletarian standpoint.
2. The overcoming of what Lukács calls the "bourgeois standpoint" (the isolated, Robinsonian individual, fixed in immediacy and
unable to see the dialectic and totality of subject and object) occurs not
in the thinking or consciousness of the proletariat but in the thought of

"bourgeois intellectuals" - *i.e.* in "factions", rebelling against the bourgeoisie itself. That they chose to call this "proletarian" without any authorization from the proletariat is irrelevant for the class character of their doctrines. This shows only their claims and readiness to serve as the instrument and the voice of history. It is the conduct of men who want to control thought - and we could show them to be totalitarian.

3. It is clear that the thesis that the social position of one's class determines one's view or perspective is false in this strong formulation. When, for example, Heinrich Rickert, who came from a bourgeois context (and who was strongly criticized by Lukács), does not see the subject-object unity and the equally bourgeois Georg Lukács does see this unity, this means that social position does not constitute a necessary determinant of thought. Rather there is only one factor, from the influence of which the thinker can withdraw, without changing his social position.

Lukács' theory of ideology does contain a spark of truth, which he - to use a Marxist expression - proceeds to absolutize. To reduce the - to use another Marxist expression - "rational kernel" of his thought, we might say: the knowing subject's inclusion in the bourgeois class serves to encourage certain one-sided and, therefore, false ideas in him, but does not force these ideas on him. It is only a tendency, not a causal link. The subject can overcome this error without changing his social position.

On the contrary, to belong to the proletariat does not work in favor of any ideas, either true or false. What is more, to belong to the proletariat encourages a lack of ideas that, again, is only a tendency and can be overcome, with great effort and material sacrifices.

In other words, the truth is not bound up with any class. If it is socially bound, then - to use the language of Karl Mannheim, Lukács' fellow countryman - it is bound up with the "free intellectuals" (*freischwebende Intellektuelle*). Most of the latter come from the bourgeoisie; but they tend to take a critical attitude, not only toward their own class, but toward any other class. Only untruth is bound up with classes: not as a necessity but as a tendency that does not have to be actualized.

Thus, the meaning of Lukács' thought comes down to the idea that the class-conditioning of thought, where it exists, can only be harmful because it sets - although not obligatorily - certain limits to thought. This belongs more to the *Wissenssoziologie* of Scheler and Mannheim than to that of Marx.

Translated by
Thomas J. Blakeley
(Boston College)

NOTES

1.   Georg Lukács, *Geschichte und Klassenbewusstsein*, 6.Aufl. Luchterhand, Darmstadt u.Neuwied, 1979, S.245.
2.   *Ibid.* S.246.
3.   *Loc.cit.*
4.   *Loc.cit.*, italics by Lukács.
5.   *Ibid.* S.277, italics by Lukács.
6.   *Ibid.* S.289, italics by Lukács.
7.   *Ibid.* S.291.
8.   *Ibid.* S.292, my italics, *A.I.*
10.   *Loc.cit.*
11.   *Ibid.* S.309, italics by Lukács.
12.   *Ibid.* S.313-314, italics by Lukács.
13.   *Ibid.* S.332.
14.   *Ibid.* S.300.
15.   Cf. V.I. Lenin, *Ausgewählte Werke*, Bd.1, Dietz (Ost-) Berlin, 1982, S.166, 174-175.

J.M. BERNSTEIN

Lukács' Wake: Praxis, Presence and Metaphysics

It has become a standard practice, almost a narrative habit, when writing about Lukács to displace his efforts in *History and Class Consciousness* by placing them into a comfortable history, above all that history which leads through his early work to the critical theory of Adorno, Horkheimer, Benjamin *et al.*, which terminates, ironically, in the neo-Kantian locutions of Habermas. There is also that other history which traces the trajectory leading from *History and Class Consciousness* to Lukács' *Lenin*, and from there to Lenin, to Stalin and thence to the wax fruits of dialectical theory in Soviet practice. Consigning Lukács his place in this way certainly eases the burden of reading him, but must do less than justice to his text. Of course, there is a 'history' which allows these histories to be written; but we should be uneasy about a telling of the past that allows Lukács to be indicted for his deviation from the truth of Marxist science, for his incipient humanism, and held responsible for the reduction of class praxis to Party dictatorship. Nor can we avoid the complacent irony of a history that commences with Lukács' insistent, penetrating critique of Kantianism in all its forms and culminates in what is but the most recent avatar of Kantian, transcendental philosophy. Should we not concede that *History and Class Consciousness* could not have been so germinative, so influential, so decisive for Western Marxism if its writing did not exceed the silencing gestures of the histories into which it is written? And should this insight, this concession, not lead us back into the labyrinth of that text, much as we are led back into the texts of Marx after each attempted silencing of them?

In order to begin to tap the radicality of Lukács' text, above all the radicality of its central moment, the essay 'Reification and the Consciousness of the Proletariat'[1], it is necessary to provide an acute angle of focus capable of bypassing the conceptual markers which have governed its reception. This angle of vision can be achieved through the establishing of a claim and the making of a comparison. The claim is that Lukács' philosophy of praxis, as adumbrated in *History and Class Consciousness*, intended a supersession (a sublation, an *Aufhebung*, a *relève*) of (modern) Western metaphysics.[2] This supersession effectuates itself, is to be effectuated by, the displacement of those components of the metaphysical tradition that are bound together under the name of 'presence'. If presence is indeed Lukács' target, then it becomes philosophically pertinent to bring his discourse

T. Rockmore (ed.), Lukács Today, 167–195.

into proximity with the writings of Heidegger and Derrida, since their work appears to be analogously targeted.[3] The point of urging such a dialogue (or con- frontation) is to clarify what might be intended by the overcoming of the metaphysics of presence. And while what is at issue here might be uncertain in Heidegger and Derrida, in Lukács' case the overcoming of the metaphysics of presence as a question is directly affiliated with the question of the possibility and intelligibility of socialism.

I. REIFICATION AS PRESENCE

What Lukács designated as the antinomies of bourgeois thought - always approached through the antinomies of Kantian philosophy - can with equal validity be designated as the antinomies of the phi- losophy(ies) of presence. Lukács regarded the sovereignty of presence as either a consequence of, or as underwritten by, societal reification, where reification represents the social generalization of commodity fetishism, the coming to appearance of relations between men as rela- tions between things (commodities).[4] As a consequence of reification, society (=social structures and practices) comes to appear as an object, or a collection of relatively autonomous and discrete object domains (the economy, the judicial system, the political sphere, the family, *etc.*) existing 'out there', external to men, obeying laws impervious to the will of individuals, capable of being viewed, investigated and re- presented in social theories of various kinds.[5] Now while it is not true that these (relatively) discrete object domains are autonomous in this way - they are produced and reproduced as the unintended con- sequences of intentional social practices, and hence are ultimately subject to collective control - what appears as an object for representation is nonetheless no illusion, no *mere* appearance for Lukács; rather, the social processes in accordance with which society is objectified in this way produce and constitute the "basic categories of man's immediate attitude toward the world". (89) Where philosophers regard the categories in accordance with which we interpret the world as mental products or constructs, Lukács takes these same categories to be existential forms inextricably bound to the dominant principles governing social reproduction under capital.

Lukács denominates the categorial stance between man and world, and man and man, engendered by these principles as "contemplative". (89) "Categorial contemplation", then, signifies "the fundamental existential structures of social life under capital"; under its sway social processes appear as social systems governed by natural or quasi-natural laws; the historical specificity of the categories of social life under capital come to appear as natural and non-historical, and individuals become spectators in a world they can only view or instrumentally manipulate. Men and women are here 'subjects', present to themselves in self-conscious acts of reflection, gazing on objects only derivatively non-present, that is, objects which will be fully present to them in representation (theory) once the laws governing them are fully known.

All philosophies which work within the governing parameters of categorial contemplation are philosophies of presence. So all philosophies which begin with a subject-object dualism (empiricism, positivism, scientific realism), or are metaphysically individualist (social contract theories, Sartrean existentialism), or take the world to be only derivatively non-present (utopian socialism, Hegelian rationalism), or reduce reason to a means-end rationality (utilitarianism) are philosophies of presence. All these philosophies turn social appearance into philosophical truth. Because, however, they are grounded in the existential categories of the social world they should not be regarded as simply false, as ideological dross, for they contain social truth. This is also to say that we can no longer talk of theories being simply true or false, since this discourse presupposes a representational construal of the relation between man and world, theory and object, and hence itself belongs to categorial contemplation; further, the comprehension of the relation between man and world as being fundamentally one of a relation between a representation and what it represents, and the dominion of the correspondence theory of truth that goes along with this understanding, form the *foci* of categorial contemplation in its philosophical moment.

Lukács' philosophy of praxis marks a refusal of the conceptual apparatus of the metaphysics of presence, its tropes and rhetoric. As a refusal of presence, theoretical praxis - which, as we shall see, cannot be interpreted as a 'theory' in any of the usual senses of that term - operates by showing how the theoretical limits and antinomies of a philosophical theory are displacements, or reinscriptions, of reified social relations, of the existence forms inscribing the categorial appearance forms of society. So, for example, the antinomic duality of 'is' and 'ought' reinscribes the neutralizing of economic relations which occurs as a result of the domination of use value by exchange value. When this occurs - and for Lukács it occurs only under capital since only there is all production for the market - the economy does, in a sense, become 'value-free', since the laws and forces of the market determine things' value; simultaneously, moral value retreats inward, coming to reside in the awarenesses of isolated subjects. 'Ought', Lukács contends, signifies a refusal of empirical reality which at the same time must consecrate and affirm it: "'ought' presupposes an existing reality to which the category of 'ought' remains inapplicable in principle" (160).[6] Of course, the duality of 'is' and 'ought' can itself be displaced by reducing the latter to the former; but this simply consecrates empirical reality more directly. Hence the displacements of Kantian morality (*e.g.*, into the 'beyond' in the 'Postulates of Pure Practical Reason') and the paradoxes of utilitarian morality (represented, for example, in Mill's differentiation of higher and lower forms of happiness) reinscribe the dislocations of reified social life through their categorial placements and displacements.[7]

Tracing backward and forward categorial contemplation in its practical and theoretical forms does not amount to a supersession or even to a critique of it; in bringing the laws of form of capital to view in this way, they are not overcome but recognized. They are recognized and not overcome because categorial forms are existence forms. Hence the supersession of presence - Marxianly: reification and categorial contemplation - requires the submerging of what was philosophy - the becoming present of the categorial determinations of existence - back into historical practice, which is called 'praxis' only if it possesses this now submerged or relocated philosophical dimension, and precipitates the appropriate transformation of the existence forms of capital. Whether this transformation can be conceived without relapsing into the tropes of presence is a matter of some debate. The debate turns on, at least initially, some of the details of Lukács' theory, above all his theory of proletarian class consciousness, and on the particulars of our understanding of the scope and sense of the metaphysics of presence. As a preparatory constraint on our further elucidation of Lukács' position, it is to the latter we now turn.

II. METAPHYSICS OF PRESENCE

A. Absence and Epoch.

In his now familiar analysis of presence-to-hand and readiness-to-hand (*Vorhandenheit* and *Zuhandenheit*) in *Being and Time*, Heidegger attempts to demonstrate how the appearance of an object as merely out there, before one and open to one's look or gaze, can occur only on the basis of a prior (tacit) awareness of the object as bound up in a circuit of signifying references - say, of a hammer, to nails and other tools - which condition and make possible the object's being an object of awareness in general: "an individual piece of equipment, as individual, is handy and extant only within an equipmental contexture. The understanding of equipmental contexture as contexture precedes every individual use of equipment".[8] Further, in our employment of equipment, when equipment is handy, it has "in a pre-eminent way the character of unobtrusiveness",[9] that is, things are properly useful to the degree to which their singularity, there being a 'this object here', does not obtrude on our awareness. Conversely, things obtrude, and hence have a diminished usefulness, when they are defective (the pen that runs out of ink, the shoe that rubs) or, at the extreme, when they are missing ("Where's my hammer!?"). Paradigmatically, in the order of their existential determination, it is missing and defective objects which are present-to-hand, that is, objects in space and time as normally understood. However, this understanding of objects as presence-to-hand is our and the philosophical tradition's conception of objects, as things out there in space and time, to be viewed and represented. Hence the traditional ontology of objects as for and of representation, our paradigmatic conception of a thing as an object of vision, is based on the paradigm of missing or defective things; and our awareness of things as present-to-hand involves an essential covering over, a repression of their constitutive equipmental contexture.

Heidegger continues his analysis by referring the equipmental contexture back to the phenomenon of the world, and thence referring the world to the temporality which makes anything like a world possible. These extensions need not concern us; what is important here, for our purposes, is the thesis that for anything to become present it must have ineliminable absential dimensions; that is, the presence of a thing makes tacit, but necessary, reference to what is not present: the referential totality and the categorial determination of that totality to which the object belongs, to the world to which that totality belongs, and so on. Presence-to-hand is founded on readiness-to-hand, presence is founded on absence, and, why not, identity on difference.

If we were, prematurely, to let the Heideggerian and Lukácsian analyses be drawn into proximity at this juncture, then the following might be said. Reification is a process whereby the world as world comes to appear as present-to-hand. Categorial contemplation, as product and component of the reification process, involves a determination of the dominant categories of signification whereby the absential dimensions of objects are (categorially) covered over. Conversely, presence-to-hand can now be regarded as an appearance form of the handy, of what is ready-to-hand. Yet, and here the premature character of the comparison becomes evident, while Heidegger would have the referring back of a thing to the relational totality of its signifying references be a way of *restoring* to an object its 'proper' place, the beginning, perhaps, of an "authentic" engagement with it, for Lukács the referring back of a phenomenon to a totality does not restore it but rather reveals it as reified. To put this same point otherwise: there appears in the early Heidegger to be a presumption that through a recursive analysis of the conditions for a thing being present we can make present to ourselves the entire dynamic, disclosive process whereby they become present (out of absence). Consequently, the early Heidegger overlooks the possibility that the categorial determination of the relational totality of which we are co-aware in being aware of a thing, *e.g.*, the category of equipment, might itself be subject to historical mutation and alteration. And if this were to be the case, then no one categorial structure, or its essence, could be employed as a guide to the process whereby things come to presence (out of absence) generally.

Now the later Heidegger does take account of the historical relativity of categorial structures. While for the early Heidegger being was mistakenly interpreted by the tradition in terms of presence, on the model of things present-to-hand, and could more appropriately be interpreted in terms of the structures of (ecstatic) temporality, in the later Heidegger things become present in accordance with some epochal (historical) determination, which is to say that being 'works' epochally, where an epoch is conceived of in terms of a way in which being, the disclosive process, withholds itself, remains concealed. Heidegger's guiding thought now appears to be this: being, which is self-concealing, intrinsically privative, has an essential absential moment, and works epochally by giving forth forms of presentness (*idea, energeia, esse, subiectum, etc.*), these being the traditional philosophical interpretations of being as presence; the history of being, the history of metaphysics, is the history of these forms of presentness, seen as ways in which being has withheld or concealed itself. Because throughout metaphysics being has only been present in various forms of absence, the meaning of being, the question of being has been forgotten. So to read the texts of the tradition now, at the end or closure of that history, now that we are aware of the oblivion and forgetting of the meaning of being, requires a double reading: first we must read those texts as instantiating a form of presentness, as providing an interpretation of being as presence, and then as exceeding that form, as having a moment of excess, or absence, which marks the test as a site in which being has been withheld.

From this plateau of analysis, two consequences follow for Heidegger's position. First, no one categorial structure, like that of equipment, can be employed as providing access into the process of presencing in general. Rather, insight into the being process now requires going through the historical formations of presentness, which, of course, is accomplished through the double reading of the texts of the tradition. Secondly, since each historical formation of presentness inscribes the categorial determinations in accordance with which objects can be comprehended and practices proceed, then there exists no interpretative-hermeneutic route through which objects can be grasped 'properly', *i.e.* restored to their proper place. As in Lukácsian analysis, philosophical-theoretical practice provides recognition - of the regimes of presentness as withholdings of being - but not overcoming or restoration. This is most radically so in our own epoch, the age of technology, where being has withdrawn so completely that not even a (revealing-concealing) name for it remains. We, so to speak, have been left with only ourselves, without a hint of excess, of absence, of non-identity marking the (dominant) forms of discourse in which we engage; which, perhaps, explains why our access to the meaning of being must occur through a thinking of the tradition of metaphysics.[10] In short, and crucially for our purposes, the recognition of epochality provides for the possibility of a fuller recognition of the historical intransigeance of present forms of practice to transformation or overcoming. There remains the large question here of what overcoming could possibly mean or be for Heidegger; this problem we shall pick up shortly.

B. Deconstruction and Anti-Humanism

Derrida's practice of deconstruction inaugurates a "repetition"[11] of the Heideggerian double reading, where the programmatic elements of the Heideggerian project are retained but their site altered from the epochal manifestations (withholdings) of being in texts to texts, in their linguistically constituted textuality, themselves. Since for the later Heidegger "language is the house of Being", then nothing could be more natural than to reveal how the fatalities of language itself take on the work of being.[12] Deconstructive readings, then, are double readings which record a text's (textual) compliance with the metaphysics of presence and its exceeding that metaphysics. Derrida's terms of art, like "différance" (with an *a*), are employed to mark places in a text where presence must be and cannot be, but whose excess beyond the logic of presence is what permits the text to work, to do its work of presencing. Difference, and its substitutions, are non-concepts because conceptual thinking (meaning), in the only forms available, always presupposes a presence which cannot - the mark of difference - be had. Difference does not name a different, more primordial presence; nor does it name an absence (like the Sartrean "lack"); it (materially?) marks a text's own excess, its transgressiveness, its non-equivalence with itself.

      Humanism, as generally conceived, involves the turning away from God toward man, man's reappropriation of himself, his essence out of the projections of religious thought. For humanism the rejection of

God as the being through whom all beings must be understood, the rejection of eternity as the model (ground) of time, and the rejection of a necessary existent being as the model and ground of finite, contingent existence intends a rejection of what could be called the metaphysics of presence. For Heidegger and Derrida, this rejection and reappropriation, in Marx or Nietzsche or Sartre, also belongs to the metaphysics of presence and, hence, also involves a covering over, a repression of absence, of what is other than 'man'.[13] Yet releasing this repression is not something we can do, first because the assumption that the meaning of being depends on us, is at our disposal and within our purview and control is what makes humanism an avatar of the metaphysics of presence; and, secondly, the double movement of presence and excess will figure (or dis-figure) even the most determinately anti-humanist texts. In his 'The Ends of Man', Derrida traces the central movements of Heidegger's 'Letter on Humanism', demonstrating how the very torsions through which the Heideggerian text escapes the humanist impasse, as inscribed by the metaphysics of presence, irrevocably draws it back into the ambit of metaphysics.[14] A brief, synoptic look will have to stand in here for an examination of the text as a whole. In the 'Letter on Humanism' Heidegger claims that, though refusing humanism as portrayed within metaphysics, his essaying in the history of being, his turning away from beings (including men) toward the disclosive process (of being) itself, engages the question and worth of humanity even more emphatically than does humanism. The demonstration turns on revealing the (ontological) proximity of man and being. Derrida's interrogation of the metaphorics of proximity used by Heidegger reveals how

(i) despite the evident ontic reverberations and metaphysical temptations of this metaphorics, it does escape the dictates of the metaphysics of presence - Heidegger's terms of the "near" and the "far" marking a difference - and

(ii) it does, eventually, collapse back into another configuration of presence.

(i) The near and the far are thought here, consequently, before the opposition of space and time, according to the opening of a spacing which belongs neither to time nor to space, and which dislocates, while producing it, any presence of the present.

(ii) The proposition of the proper, certainly, is not to be taken in a metaphysical sense: the proper of man, here, is not an essential attribute, the predicate of a substance, a characteristic among others, however fundamental, of a being, object or subject, called man. No more can one speak in this sense of man as the proper of Being. Propreity, co-propreity of Being and man, is proximity as inseparability. But it is indeed as inseparability that the relations between being (substance, *res*) and its essential predicate were thought in metaphysics afterward.[15]

The inseparability of substance and (essential) predicate is grounded, then, in an anterior inseparability, the proximity of man and being. Derrida's emphasized "afterward" hence is scoring proximity as inseparability as an operation of metaphysical grounding, with the further suggestion that Heidegger's presentation of proximity insinuates a temporal ordering whereby primordial proximity historically precedes and grounds the later history of metaphysics where the logic of substance and predicates reigns. Having thus followed Heidegger so far, Derrida can but point to the possibility of another site of escape: "Is not this security of the near what is trembling today ... ?"[16] If there is a trembling, what else could it be but the recognition of the logic of presence governing the discourse of anti-humanism?

Derrida reinscribes the Heideggerian experience of the intransigeance of our epochal present into a textual fatality whereby the locutions of presence recur, silencing thus both epochal history and the nostalgic search for primordial proximity. On this accounting the overcoming of metaphysics becomes, apparently, literally inconceivable.

C. Overcoming and Historical Formations

At this juncture, before returning to Lukács, the question of the meaning of "overcoming" must be raised. If we take seriously Heidegger's conception of epochal history as the history of being, we are confronted by a paradoxical dénouement. For Heidegger epochal history, again, is constituted by the various formations of presentness, where each such form signifies a particular withholding of being. Hence, the overcoming of that history would entail the coming into being of a formation that was not a historical formation, since historicality is equivalent to epochality, and epochal formations are formations of presentness, *i.e.*, formations which partake of the oblivion and forgetting of being. Overcoming metaphysics for Heidegger is only comprehensible as an overcoming of epochal history.[17] Derrida's analysis of Heidegger confirms this way of stating the position: if what comes "afterward" is metaphysics, then overcoming metaphysics looks to entail a return to origins, to a primordial inseparability and proximity of man and being *without the opacity of a formation of presentness*.[18] It is this, one suspects, that leads Derrida to place a trembling of that proximity on the agenda, to insist upon a trembling; for even if we grant that the originary proximity involves an acknowledgment, an acceptance of an irretrievable absence, of a self-concealment that cannot be made present, nonetheless the thought of an *enduring* acceptance/acknowledgment is the thought of what would *hold* that absence in presence.[19] In sum, Heidegger conceives of the overcoming of metaphysics as involving a double revealing: a revealing of the disclosive process as a series of withholdings of being, that is, the workings of epochal history, and the consequent revealing of the disclosive process itself as what comes after epochal history. Surely, however, this programme is metaphysical, since in it absence is held in presence as a component of a complex, but unitary, process of disclosure. Being, as a disclosive process, gathers the radical excessiveness of historicality into a complex unity. Conversely, this implies that it is only through formations of presentness, as formations, that the experience of absence can be sustained, for it is only in terms of formations that presentness comes to entail an irrecuperable opacity. Nietzsche called this acceptance of formations of presentness "active forgetfulness". Active forgetting writes the forgetting of the meaning of being in difference.

Now, there is a way in which we can understand why this should be so, why, that is, the acceptance of presentness in terms of historical formations should be required for the preservation of absence and alterity without metaphysics. It begins with something Derrida says, namely, that the concept of presence is not univocal, or better, we cannot translate the diverse concepts of presence thrown up by the tradition of Western metaphysics into a semantically unified concept of "presence"; that term alone cannot stand in for, or be treated as containing, that over-determined and complex history.[20] Whatever regularities might be discovered here, they do not compose a history. If this is the case, then it would follow that the overcoming of the metaphysics of presence would be plural, not singular, indefinite and on-going, not permanent and achievable. Heidegger's late conception of thinking sometimes appears to have this flavor. However, we can read the significance of the equivocity of presence differently, in terms of what in particular is repressed, denied, reduced as a consequence of a formation of presentness. While what is other than presence is, at least, a disclosive process, it is also particulars demanding, calling for acknowledgment: the formation of patriarchy and the call of women; the formation of racism and the call of the races of man; the formation of technology and the call of nature; the formation of capital and the call of workers. There is a politics as well as a metaphysics of presence, or better, because of the equivocity of presentness, the metaphysics of presence is, always already, political. This is not to claim that "forma-tion", as employed above, is equivalent to formation as a formation of presentness; a formation of presentness defines, constitutes, signifies the 'being' of things in general within an epoch, *e.g.*, to be a thing (exist) is to be created (by a god), or perceivable by a subject, or an idea, *etc.* Nonetheless, since each formation of presentness involves a withholding of being, then each also involves a denial of absence, alterity, excess with respect to what exists; and this repression of alterity cannot but have implications for individuals' comportment toward themselves, others, and their natural and social environment (nature and society). It can be no accident, then, that systems of slavery, patriarchy, racism, technology and the like, institute refusal of difference. And would the question of presence make a difference, matter, if this were not the case? Does not the question of presence matter only because others matter?

III. PRAXIS, HUMANISM AND CLASS CONSCIOUSNESS

If reification signifies "an epochal dominion of presence"[21] then the philosophy of praxis should instigate the overcoming of the contemplative philosophies which accord with the regime of reification. Yet Lukács' theory cannot be so quickly drawn into the ambit of the post-metaphysical discourse of absence, and absolved of ambitions for presence. Three charges in particular stand in the way of reading Lukács as a post-metaphysical thinker: (i) the claim that his identification of the proletariat as the subject-object of history "images" an explicit reversion to a rationalist philosophy of history; (ii) the contention that the proposal for a collective class subject to be the bearer of overcoming involves both some form of humanism and a denial of non-class forms of self-comprehension - a denial of difference; and (iii) praxis itself, as a form of practical activity, can be theorized only through a teleology which reverts to a conception of reason which is fully metaphysical. Charge (i) can be shown to be a straightforward misreading of Lukács' text; charges (ii) and (iii), however, because they carry some weight, will force us to the limit of Lukács' thought; but this limit is not unambiguous. It is not a limit that can be simply passed over into some other terrain, for it invokes issues about limits, about overcoming them, which equally question the standards of post-metaphysical thinking which are here challenging, delimiting the possibility of praxis.

Although it will not be possible to keep consideration of the charges against Lukács' text separate, or even in focus (since answering them involves changes in focus), still beginning with the easily dispatchable misreading (providing as it does a known and familiar quantity), will prove provident for what follows. Lukács' tracing of the antinomies of bourgeois (Kantian) thought (through their reception and proposed untying in German Idealism) ends with the recognition that history is the locus of the genesis of both subject and object; history, we might say, is the indeterminate ground of their being what has come to be called subjects and objects (142-4). Why this ground must remain indeterminate, cancelling the grounding function in the very gesture through which it is proposed, will be returned to. What Lukács deduces from this recognition is the thesis that there can be no apriori or transcendental accounting of subject or object, for they are delimited, given form, become subjects and objects through the discontinuous development of historical, structural forms; and it is within these structural forms that the essence of history lies (153).[22] For Lukács, "man himself is dialectical" (187), man himself is a precipitate of the structural forms of history, his being inscribed and reinscribed by formations which articulate his categorial possibilities of action and passion. With this, Lukács intends a rejection of all reductive forms of humanism and anthropology which would permit man's being to have an ahistorical essence, and human nature to form a perduring standard against which history (historical progress and/or regress) could be measured; hence a rejection as well of all philosophical practices which attempt to comprehend human existence apart from the particulars of the structural forms of history. These rejections are sufficiently evident in Lukács' text and would appear to belie any attempt to project onto it a rationalist core; on the contrary, the natural assumption is that he is essaying a hermeneutical philosophy where historical meanings, the meanings of history, are epochally differential comprehensions of the velleities and possibilities of historical practice.

And yet. Lukács does ask the question, who is the we which is the subject of history, the we whose deed is in fact history (145)? And he does answer the question: the we of the genesis is the proletariat. Do question and answer revoke his earlier rejection, or have we misunderstood what was at issue in his questioning? That the latter is the case is demonstrable. First, to read the question as part of a rationalist attempt to comprehend the meaning of history presupposes that history has a meaning, a telos or end, or functions in accordance with specifiable principles; but Lukács explicitly denies that history has an end, and indeed claims that within dialectics such an assumption is "scarcely comprehensible" (147). Dialectic, for Lukács, is forever immanent since "historicity" invades "all categories". Secondly, to consider the we of the proletariat to be a privileged site through which the meaning of history is understood presupposes that the question of history can be answered from the outside, from a place beyond history. It is this assumption which governs speculative/contemplative philosophies of history; such philosophies of history, philosophies which refuse to suspend their own workings in history or do so only momentarily, relapse "into the contemplative duality of subject and object" (148), the very duality which instigated the turn towards history as an indeterminate ground of genesis for its overcoming. Finally, and quite straightforwardly, Lukács denies that the dialectical discourse, which provides the structural clues for making the overcoming of the present intelligible, should itself be regarded as having a historical validity. On the contrary, its present validity, its being valid for this present, does not preclude the "emergence of societies in which by virtue of their different social structures other categories and other *systems of truth* prevail" (228; emphasis mine); and by "systems of truth" here Lukács intends more than conceptions of truth; systems of truth designate ways of being true. Hence the dialectical discourse of Marxism is not ahistorically privileged; given the historicity of all categories, it does not reach beyond the present into either post- or pre-capitalist (237-8) social formations. And this is to say that readings of the 'Reification' essay which construe it as proposing the proletariat as a historically produced Fichtean absolute subject, as proposing the proletariat as a historically generated transcendental key to the meaning of history, as proposing a realization of some ahistorical logic of history in socialism contravene the letter and spirit of Lukács' project.

A rigorous immanence governs Lukács' interrogation; his question of who the subject, the identical subject-object, of history is relates not to a speculative concern for the meaning of history in general, but to the intersection where his autocritique of the representational com-prehension of Marxist theory meets his reconstructed history of (modern) philosophy.[23] This intersection marks the place where the problem of reification and the antinomies of bourgeois thought, the disabling dualisms of the philosophies of presence, meet. Their meeting and intertwining - the suspension of the Marxist philosophy of history within the history of philosophy, and the equivalent suspension of the history of philosophy in the Marxist philosophy of history[24] - binds the history of philosophy to its historical contexture and raises the analysis of that contexture, of societal reification and rationalization, beyond sociological generality to philosophical significance. The point of convergence between the two lines of analysis, the dialectical interaction of philosophical meta-critique and theoretical auto-critique, precipitates the meaning of history for now, for us; and makes of Marxism the philosophy of the present.

Now if the proletariat is not to be interpreted along transcendental lines, then how is the question concerning the we, the subject of history to be read? And we must begin by keeping in mind the disclaimer that this question pertains to a unified subject, to some one, to a collective subject who produces and realizes itself in history.[25] We are speaking, rather, of a subject who is the bearer of the meaning of present history;

and while this does entail that a certain level of contingency is in operation here, it remains unclear whether the dialectic through which the identification of the proletariat is made can relieve that contingency of arbitrariness (without passing over into a dialectical mechanicism which would transform contingency into necessity). For we remember that the transformation of a historical dialectic into a dialectical logic, which would make such a necessitation possible, is just what Lukács found "scarcely comprehensible".

Lukács' identification of the proletariat as the bearer of overcoming turns, as suggested above, on an intersection of different lines of analysis. In the first instance, these are a feature of proletarian experience, the Marxist philosophy of history and the analysis of societal reification and rationalization. Proletarian experience, within industrial capitalism, was one where workers discovered that features of social life that appeared to be within subjective control, areas where workers presumed themselves to be agents of a process, were in reality objective social processes (165-7, 225-8); in particular, within the work process itself, the worker discovered himself to be both producer and commodity, both subject and object. The significance of this experience lies in the fact that, through workers becoming self-conscious of themselves, commodity relations reveal themselves for what they are: social relations between men transfigured into quantitative (exchange) relations between things (168-9). Now the operation whereby labor is transformed and figured into quantities is through the reduction of living labor into abstract labor, and that reduction is carried through, concretely in reality, by means of the rationalization of the work process itself. Hence the commodity form becomes increasingly (tendentially) determinable as an objectification of abstract human labor; the determination being made, of course, in terms of labor time. As quanta of embodied/abstract labour time, commodities are objectifications of a quasi-natural determinant.

Intersecting with this is what Lukács regards as the center of the Marxist philosophy of history, not historical materialism as ahistorical logic, but what capitalism brings to light as a social formation, its civilizing influence: "the uniqueness of capitalism is to be seen precisely in its abolition of all 'natural barriers' and its transformation of all relations between human beings into purely social relations" (176).

If these confluences are now suspended in the history of philosophy, if, that is, we raise the analysis of capital's socializing function to the level of philosophical understanding through which we comprehend ourselves in categorial terms, then the socializing function of capitalist development is its philosophical significance, realizing historically what philosophy, in Hegel, realized theoretically; and it is the frustration of that development which proletarian experience unearths.[26] However, there is nothing either sacrosanct or necessary about the identification of the proletariat here; on the contrary, the argument turns on a contingent, albeit structurally explicable, de-reifying aspect of working experience in industrial capitalism. Nothing guarantees that these de-reifying features of experience will continue unabated or will not become subject to countervailing (ideological) forces. What Lukács' pattern of analysis privileges is a space where social processes take on the form of natural determinations as it intersects with the socializing function of capital. This dialectical intersection, significantly repeated in recent times in the experience of women and racial minorities, marks the contingent, socially embodied coming to presence of our epochal fate.

Two points of clarification. First, if this is correct, then Lukács cannot be read as prescribing that the overthrow of capital must be through a proletarian revolution. At best it could be said of industrial capital that, were a revolution to take place, it would most probably take that form. What he does insist upon, of course, is that given the structures of capital production, and their corollaries in societal reification and rationalization, a necessary condition for realizing the socializing function of capital would be the overthrow of capitalist relations of production. Socialism is a necessary, but no longer sufficient, condition for realizing this end.[27]

Secondly, the agents of transformation, the collective subject(s) of change are not identified through the descriptive identification of the agents of intersection. The question of the we is a question about where in actual experience the historical meaning of the present has become self-conscious (even if in a distorted form). Theory's task is to explain and interpret given experience of a certain sort, not to prescribe the having of an experience or to legislate a political project.[28] To suppose that the quasi-naturally determined objects of reification are the same as the collective subjects of transformation is to reduce the agents of change to their natural determinations, what the congealing processes of capital have made them. The collective subjects of social transformation are formed (become such subjects) through praxial action. Praxis is action escaping from the quasi-natural reductions of meaning which are the consequences of societal reification. Praxis is action without (transcendental) presence.

IV. PRAXIS: RISK AND REVOLUTION

In brackets we find 'transcendental', then outside of the brackets 'presence'. Is a parenthetic bracketing sufficient to retrieve praxis from the metaphysics of presence, or does praxis presuppose the very terrain from which it is departing? This, as anticipated earlier, is the limit of Lukács' dialectic where the question of the limit, as posed by post-metaphysical discourse, comes to interrogate and be interrogated by the very idea of revolutionary praxis. Revolutionary praxis 'intends' a rupture, the installation and institution of new spaces where praxis can displace 'action - 'action' signifying forms of practical activity under the governance of the metaphysics of presence.[29] Praxis is practical activity oriented toward the totality as totality; as such it cannot operate by reasoning from a determinate end to the means of achieving that end; rather, the ends of praxis - the institution of a new totality, a new system of truth, hence new institutional forms and new collective identities - are specified in and through praxial activity itself. It is a reasoning toward the end where the end, a new meaning of being, is neither given nor posited. Hence praxial doings are neither practical nor theoretical nor expressive, but all three together; its knowing is a doing, and its doings continually reinscribe, reveal and express what knowing, what truth means. The world is no longer an object of representation; for what it is to be, or have, a world is part of what is interrogated through praxis. "Reality", Lukács says, "is not, it becomes - and to become the participation of thought is needed" (204). So, for example, for collective subject(s) who can be subjects to become, it might be necessary, at first, that being true come to mean 'solidarity', where solidarity expresses or evokes the negation of the economic, political and social forms of dispersion and isolation that are consequent upon the forms of rationalization and reification under late capitalism. However, what solidarity 'means' can only be determined by the forms we discover to be adequate for overcoming the quite specific insti-tutional derangements of capital. Because reality, the world itself, the meaning of being a world is put into question by praxis, revolution becomes an ontological experiment.[30]

Stated even so briefly, suspicions arise: is not solidarity, as employed here, another exemplar of transcendental presence? And does not the very idea of praxis, as involving concrete doings which are metaphysically interrogative, assume that it will be some future we who make or constitute this new world? And would this not entail a massive return to humanism? Finally, must we not recall Derrida's explicit warning against the discourse of revolution and rupture: "I do not believe in decisive ruptures, in an unequivocal 'epistemological break', as it is called today. Breaks are always, and fatally, reinscribed in an old cloth that must continually, interminably be undone."[31]

Let us begin addressing these questions from the end, with the Derridean warning. To be sure, as a statement of a policy of prudence about what might be achieved, Derrida's statement is well taken: we may always discover an intended rupture recuperable, the sought after break in reality a repetition; and new forms of the metaphysics of presence may well shadow new ontological spaces. Further, if historicality requires active forgetfulness, then no rupture can be decisive, for a system of truth can fall into presence, become metaphysical through the way it is adopted, reproduced and transmitted. However, no further or stronger thesis would directly contradict some of Derrida's own practices as he understands them. In a recent interview, Derrida has said that the founding concepts of metaphysics are instances, not of metaphor as is often claimed, but of catachresis, the improper use of words which violently, without antecedent or norm, produces new meanings, or even new meaning forms. His intention, in works like *Glas*, is to write in a way which might produce a new catachresis.

> In a work such as *Glas* ... I am trying to produce new forms of catachresis, another kind of writing, a violent writing which stakes out the faults (*failles*) and deviations of language; so that the text produces a language of its own, in itself, which while continuing to work through tradition emerges at a given moment as a monster, a monstrous mutation without tradition or normative precedent.[32]

Not only does this statement align deconstruction with the discourse of rupture, the hope for monsters (which are what, perhaps inevitably, new formations look like from here), but concedes that the product to be produced be "a language", that is, can only be, a site of sense making. So Derrida accepts that anything that could count as displacing the metaphysics of presence will involve form, a language, a formation of presentness. And if we ask how such a formation as a formation could be such without repeating metaphysics, then the only plausible answer is that it does so by acknowledging, in its inception, its status as a formation, hence its historicality, its finitude, its materiality and mortality. Of course, one could respond to this by saying that it presupposes a traditional metaphysics, a metaphysics of history or becoming, not unlike that suggested in the early Heidegger. But that is not what is being proposed; to do so would anticipate, attempt to determine now what the new site of meaning will be like. If a rupture occurs, if the revolution is ontological, if a new system of truth is inaugurated, then we cannot now ground it, as it were, in a metaphysics of becoming. The indeterminacy of history as ground cannot be withdrawn by us.

This result is at least logically possible if one argues for the discovery of historicity as a generality in the modern epoch while simultaneously contending that the meaning of being as becoming reaches determinacy, will reach determinacy, only afterwards. And this is more than plausible, given the most obvious interpretations of what the components of a formation of presentness are: a system of truth; a categorial determination of objecthood; the establishment of subject-object relations; the institution of a demarcation between *physis* and *nomos*, *etc.* - each of these having the peculiar characteristic of being grounds which are here taken to be instituted, established, produced, *etc.*, hence grounds that are themselves groundless, too late; grounds whose validity is retrospective, available only within what they establish. Post-metaphysical formations, hence, will 'post-' in virtue of their working within the horizon of historicity, but the meaning of historicity itself can reach determinacy only within a formation of presentness. The meaning of being, it might be said, has become onto-logically interrogative.[33]

And yet, this does not go nearly far enough; for it leaves open the thought that a socialist formation of presentness, say, could be a human construct, an intentional human product, something made. To conceive of socialism in this way, as something as such makeable, fully within our power to make, entails a return to humanism, making history masterable, something of which we could be the masters and possessors. This mistakes the nature and possibility of praxis. Praxis, as the form of activity appropriate, even 'proper', to the revolutionary overcoming of the present, is groundless, a release, a letting go of presence. Praxis is risk, the risk, above all, of one's social identity, where to have an identity is to have (possess) an account of who one is in relation to one's others, including the institutional forms within which those relations are sustained. It has already been suggested that given social identities - of women, workers, blacks, *et al.* - are reductions to presence, which refuse alterity either directly through reification or in a manner which complements and re-enforces capital's delimitation of its own socializing function. Hence collective praxis must be, in the first instance, the refusal of these imposed and objectified identities and the formation of new ones; and these new social identities will be instances of and/or dependent upon the formation of a new collective identity, some new inscription of who 'we' are. Again, the we who are the objects of (present) history are not the same as the we who are the subjects of (future) history. However, I now want to argue, new collective identities cannot be formed without risk, a risk which is absolute, a risk of the complete loss of self, indeed a risk of life. The demonstration of this will proceed in two stages: first through a brief, descriptive account of the phenomenon of risk, and then through a critical engagement with Derrida's deconstruction of dialectic and risk in his well-known essay on Bataille, 'From Restricted to General Economy: A Hegelianism without Reserve'.

In forging a radically new identity one must, of course, surrender one's old identity; but a social identity, the sort of identity which one can lose, find or have a crisis of, has as its components, at least, the various social roles or positions one inhabits, together with some conception of how these fit or fail to fit together; as such it includes the rules and reasons for various types of activity internal to the occupation of those positions and some strong evaluations which form the horizon of 'worth' within which having such an identity has some value or point.[34] The characterization is rough, but the idea familiar. Now in refusing such an identity, one loses both the grounds for particular actions appropriate to a social position and the horizon of meaning which has formed the ground of those various positions coming together to form a 'self'. In order to form a new collective identity, then, one must surrender: (i) one's given social identity in terms of its contents; (ii) the conception of the social as such as is required by the having of those (old) identities; and (iii) one's claim to autonomy. A collective identity can be possessed only through the recognition of others; but an other's recognition is, as Hegel showed, what I can never will.[35] Risk, then, presupposes the recognition of non-autonomy; one's radical dependency on the other, under conditions where the very having of a self or position is what is at issue, is what defines the activity of collective identity formation as one of risk. What makes the risk involved in radical acts of collective identity formation absolute is their character of being ontologically interrogative; by putting one's social identity at risk one equally and necessarily puts at risk the nature and limits of the social as such, or, what is the same, the given comprehension of the line dividing *physis* and *nomos*, nature and society/history. For that division, through which any given social world is constituted as social, is always a consequence of a mode of collective self-gathering and collective self-understanding, not a premise; it is instituted as a condition.[36]

Praxis is revolutionary risk; the kind of risk necessary for revolutionary activity, where a new "system of truth" is to be instituted, is what separates that activity from any done under the governance of the metaphysics of presence. Risk is neither active nor passive; to risk is to put oneself at risk. To be at risk here is not to be 'one' (with oneself) at all; one is neither one (the object of history) nor the other (the subject of history). Nor in this sort of risk is it clear that one is risking one's social life and not one's natural life, or that one can risk the one without the other; for risk is antecedent to that division, prior to but not the ground of it. Risk is always the risk of determinate meaning; its space is a non-space, its time a non-time [37]; it is an opening to some 'other' space and time, some other scene of meaning. Further, risk cannot itself be willed or produced 'at will'; the space in which one can put oneself at risk cannot be self-induced nor is it naturally, necessarily or generally available. Risk requires others also willing to risk their social identities. Risk is the praxial recognition of excess; it is serious difference.[38]

Despite the almost undeniable insistence of risk as the figure of an unmasterable excess, conditioning negativity and overcoming, as underwriting, as it were, the seriousness of negativity in dialectic, Derrida chooses, through his pointed defense of Bataille's reading of Hegel, to mark out that moment in Hegel's text, amongst the most vividly ruptural in philosophy, as the repression of absence by presence, as the moment *par excellence* where the hegemony of presence insinuates itself, cancelling, through the "restricted economy" of dialectical overcoming, the possibility of any alterity resistant to its movement. Roughly, and quickly, Derrida follows Bataille's analysis of the dialectic of desire, the dialectic of lordship and bondage, where lord and servant come to recognize as a result of their risk of life in battle with one another, that natural death would be the cancelling of all meaning; therefore, life, natural life is necessary for self-consciousness. Once made, this recognition entails that recognition of autonomy, recognition of oneself as a self-consciousness, cannot be had in the medium of nature, but requires another medium and another concept of life. Hegel denominates this new medium of intersubjectivity "spirit" (*Geist*); it is a domain of social forms which becomes the arena within which self-consciousness has its (spiritual) life. Biological life is superseded by spiritual life; the latter is the truth of the former. Death, natural death, is thus cancelled and recuperated; it comes to signify abstract negativity; it comes to function as a moment in the dialectic where self-consciousness is first formed and learns the terrain in which its destiny is to be decided. Derrida/Bataille charge Hegel with covering over the real excessiveness, the absolute, unrecoverable negativity of death. Let me quote Derrida at length.

> What is laughable (in Hegel's system) is the submission to the self-evidence of meaning, to the force of this imperative: that there must be meaning, that nothing must be definitely lost in death or, further, that death should receive the signification of "abstract negativity", that a work must always be possible which, because it defers enjoyment, confers meaning, seriousness, and truth upon the "putting at stake". This submission is the essence and element of philosophy, of Hegelian ontologics. Absolute comicalness is the anguish experienced when confronted by the expenditure of lost funds, by the absolute sacrifice of meaning: a sacrifice without return and without reserves. The notion of *Aufhebung* ... is laughable in that it signifies the busying of a discourse losing its breath as it reappropriates all negativity for itself, as it works the

"putting at stake" into an investment, as it amortizes absolute expenditure; and as it gives meaning to death, thereby simultaneously blinding itself to the baselessness of the non-meaning from which the basis of meaning is drawn, and in which this basis of meaning is drawn, and in which this basis of meaning is exhausted. ... Laughter alone exceeds dialectics and the dialectician: it bursts out only on the basis of an absolute renunciation of meaning, an absolute risking of death, what Hegel calls abstract negativity. A negativity that never takes place, that never presents itself, because in doing so it would start to work again.[39]

The Derrida/Bataille deconstruction of Hegel identifies the moment of death, destruction and sacrifice, all that is risked in the risk of life, as the blindspot, the moment of excess around which the representation of meaning is organized but which cannot itself be included in the system.[40]

One must be clear, and generous, to Derrida here. In claiming that Hegelian dialectic blinds itself to the excessiveness of death he is pointing to the way in which what is other than language and meaning fails to get recognized in its alterity. Far from claiming that everything is language or textuality or meaning or writing, as his critics aver, Derrida is attempting to demonstrate how the tradition has reduced, through the fatalities of its discourse, what is not meaning to meaning. Deconstruction's motive is the reconnoitering in texts of their extra-textuality, and hence of an exit to the 'world' beyond meaning.

All the more remarkable, then, is Derrida's refusal, his pronounced displacements of the discourse of dialectic by another, strategic lexicon: risk is displaced into play, fear into laughter, and the seriousness of the negative into absolute comicalness. How are these shifts to be diagnosed? What separates praxis from deconstruction? One could, of course, simply do away with the question by pointing to, say, Derrida's preference for Nietzschean gaiety or for certain poets; but this would say too little, leaving those preferences unexplained and unexamined. And while such an examination would be to the point, here we need something else: a circumspect questioning of the deconstruction of dialectic itself.

Derrida/Bataille observe the risk of life from the angle of vision of what transpires from it, which is doubly problematic. Granted, in retrospect, death has come to signify, to mean something for meaning in general; in prospect, however, this is never so, since in advance there would be no risk if its terminus were knowable, calculable, a probability, a good bet. In prospect, risk is necessary, not rational; for, rationally, within meaning, life is necessary for self-consciousness. Further, however, the dividend paid on risk cannot be indefinitely reinvested; we cannot, that is to say, work without risk, as if the risk, once made and accomplished, would be tacitly there for meaning ever afterwards. Without the absolute fear of death, spiritual and natural death, work, transformative activity, is "only an empty self-centered attitude; for its form of negativity is not negativity per se ... ".[41] What Hegel signals by this claim is that as the work of negativity, dialectic must re-submit itself to the risk of life; it must continually risk the possibility of non-meaning. Activity without risk merely repeats given forms; trans-formative activity can throw given forms into question, can refuse forms whose givenness makes them a "second nature", a new immediacy, only through, again, making the risk of life. For Hegelian dialectic, then, the risk of life is not a superseded moment of the dialectic, but the form, the de-forming form, of dialectic itself. Dialectic is risk.[42]

Two contrasts may help us here turn this insight into dialectic, into a comprehension of deconstruction. First, in contrast to absolute fear, the result of risk which dissolves all that is natural in the self, hence the self as a congealed result of former work, may be posed laughter. Laughter, Derrida says in defense of Bataille against Sartre, "is not negative because its burst does not maintain itself, is neither linked up to itself nor summarized in a discourse; it laughs at the *Aufhebung*".[43] Laughter, as it is used here, is non-recoverable, a sheer force, a bloodless violence; laughter, the concept of laughter, is employed to mark excess, alterity as such. But why the 'as such'? Why the search for a mark of extra-textuality? Or even: why the insistent regularity of deconstructive practice? Does this not reduce what is covered over, repressed by the discourses of presence to a uniformity, an anonymity, a generality, as if the metaphysics of presence as such, which Derrida knows is not an 'as such', were the problem? But whose problem? Refusing particularity, Derrida refuses history, refuses, that is, to let philosophy go, to let meaning and the loss of meaning revert to the concrete historical spaces, where their occurrences might matter. Seriousness tokens historical particularity and is parasitic on it.[44] Contrast now praxis with catachresis. Derrida describes his practice of catachrestic writing in *Glas* as follows:

> Hence in *Glas* one finds classical philosophical analysis juxtaposed with quasi-literary passages, each challenging, perverting and exposing the impurities and contradictions in its neighbor; and at some point the philosophical and literary trajectories cross each other and give rise to something else, some other site.[45]

Catachrestic writing is to function here by the setting of two metaphysically opposed forms of discourse, literary fiction and philosophy, into relation with the hope that their interaction will produce some other site. Why this strategy, this form of catachrestic writing? Because the violence of the writing will not be the violence of a self-conscious subject, not an intentional violence, but a violence of language on itself. Self-consciousness (Derrida), then, would be catalytic in the process of transformation here, but not constitutive, not dominating and controlling. The philosophic subject, having staked out the metaphysics of presence as requiring a separation/purification of discourses - the discourse of truth (philosophy) and the discourse of non-truth or fiction (literature) - intends that their being strategically set alongside one another, will engender an interaction which will reveal the illusory character of their presumed purity and autonomy, and, eventually, cancel (overcome, transform) their duality. In a strategic gesture, Derrida renounces both transcendental subjectivity and the autonomy of truth from fiction. Fully to comprehend the details of Derrida's text, however, for the purposes to hand, a more remote line of questioning should suffice.

First, it is important to recall that dialectical Marxism, as opposed to so-called scientific Marxism, agrees with Derrida that, as received and reproduced, the discourses of philosophy (truth) and literature (fiction) instigate a factitious duality. What makes that duality factitious, however, is not only the always inadequate textual means through which it is produced, but also what conditions that production and flows from it: the repression of use-value by exchange-value, the re-education of political reason to instrumental reason, *etc.*[46] Hence, an unknowing, violent and playful, overcoming of that duality presupposes a generality which by-passes what could give the programme point.[47] Conversely, praxis requires a 'knowing' strategy, one which interrogates both the discourses of truth and fiction, and their institutional inscription; its agents are those for whom these questions have come to matter, not as such, but because they can be seen to be implicated in the historically specific character of their miseries.

Secondly, then, praxis and risk are not abstract; they require that subjects expose themselves, in their particularity, in what has given them an identity and worldly position, to what exceeds both that particularity and their control, namely, those others on whom they (will) depend, whose alterity must be acknowledged without domination; and more, without knowing what acknowledging will mean or involve here. Because he wishes to avoid the dangers of transcendental subjectivity, Derrida must avoid taking up a position, being exposed; he cannot risk being present. Pure self-negation, the refusal of self-consciousness, which leaves language to itself to work a transformation, leaves what distorts it unknown; while praxis negates articulated figures of the self as subject without assuming that its negations can be absolute. In one sense Derrida and Bataille are correct, dialectics does inscribe a restricted economy, its form is the "passage from one prohibition to another ... , history is the truth of the prohibition"[48]; but this is because non-meaning is not general; nor can restricted economy be tagged with the label of history as "economy", since economic forms prohibit, legislate and have juridical form via operations whose force is anchored in distortion: fetishism and reification, say. Dialectical Marxism addresses the specificity of those forces of distorting presence.

Self-consciousness cannot be refused, only transformed. Refusing the dialectical analysis of self-consciousness cannot but force Derrida into the extreme of empty, absolute negation since dialectical analysis itself operates a transformation on the concept of self-consciousness as it functions (transcendentally) within modern formations of present-ness.[49] Inadvertently, Derrida acknowledges this when, at the close of the 'Ends of Man', he asks who are we whose end the ends of man designate?[50] Lukács, too, made the question of end and beginning turn on who we are. Such a we is systematically elusive; it cannot, that is, be gathered or specified by a system, for we are not who we are, and the transformation through which we will become different will be the work of others.

NOTES

1.   Georg Lukács, *History and Class Consciousness*, translated by Rodney Livingstone, London, Merlin Press, 1971, pp. 83-222. All page references in the text of this essay are to this edition of Lukács' work.

2.   The bracketing of 'modern' is there to halt any easy totalising of the Western philosophical tradition - to halt and to question the unity that is signified by that designation.

3.   For a pre-Derrida attempt see Lucien Goldmann, *Lukács and Heidegger*, translated by William Q. Boelhower, London, Routledge & Kegan Paul, 1977.

4.   For some more details, see my *The Philosophy of the Novel: Lukács, Marxism and the Dialectics of Form*, Minneapolis, University of Minnesota Press, 1984, pp. 5-10. Hereafter this work will be referred to as *PN*. The present essay seeks to supplement a little the argument of my book. Lukács' theory of reification generalizes Marx' theory of commodity fetishism, in part through adding to it the distinctly Weberian conception of rationalization.

5.   What occurs to society as a whole, also occurs to individuals, entailing the so-called sciences of man - psychology, linguistics, *et al.*

6.   For more, see *PN*, pp.15-22.

7.   Lukács' account does not intend a reduction of these phenomena; he accepts the relative autonomy of various forms of discourse. What his analysis assumes is that, in the case of moral discourse say, the attempt to save the phenomena of morality is constrained by the alterations which have occurred in the structural forms of social life.

8.   Not *Being and Time*, but the rather more perspicuous account of *The Basic Problems of Phenomenology*, translated by Albert Hofstadter, Bloomington, Indiana University Press, 1982, p. 294.

9.   *Ibid.* p. 309; see also pp. 310-312.

10.   *The Questions Concerning Technology*, translated by William Lovitt, New York, Harper Colophon Books, 1977, p. 27.

11.   Jacques Derrida, *Writing and Difference,* translated by Alan Bass, Chicago, The University of Chicago Press, 1978, p. 67. My thought here, which I believe originated with my colleague Robert Bernasconi, is that the practice of deconstruction serves the purposes of preventing the Heideggerian programme from congealing, through its transmission, into another metaphysical system. Hereafter this work will be referred to as *WD*.

12.   'Letter on Humanism', in *Basic Writings*, ed. David Farell Krell, New York, Harper and Row, 1977, p. 193.

13.   For a brief summary of the critique of humanism see David Hoy, 'Jacques Derrida', in Quentin Skinner (ed.), *The Return of Grand Theory in the Human Sciences*, Cambridge, Cambridge University Press, 1985, pp. 47-49.

14.   Which is not to say that Derrida intends this as a critique of Heidegger. Indeed, Derrida does not write critiques; all serious texts will have the same duplex character.

15.   *Margins of Philosophy,* translated by Alan Bass, Brighton, Sussex, The Harvester Press, 1982, pp. 132-3. Hereafter, *MP*.

16.   *Loc.cit.*

17.   This is not altogether unlike the unfortunate Marxist distinction between pre-history and history.

18.   This is accepted as the goal of Heidegger's programme by Thomas Sheehan, 'Heidegger's Philosophy of Mind', in *Contemporary Philosophy. A New Survey.* vol. 4, London, Martinus Nijhoff Publishers, 1982, pp.313-4.

19.   So in *Identity and Difference,* translated by Joan Stambaugh, New York, Harper and Row, 1969, p. 68, Heidegger says: "The only thing that now matters for our task is an insight into a possibility of thinking of the difference as a perdurance so as to clarify to what extent the onto-theological constitution of metaphysics has its essential origin in the perdurance that begins the history of metaphysics, governs all of its epochs, and yet remains concealed as perdurance, and thus forgotten in an oblivion which even escapes itself."

20.   *MP*, p. 33. For a different handling of this point see John Sallis, 'Heidegger/Derrida - Presence', *The Journal of Philosophy* 81(1984), pp. 599-601.

21.   Reification, as Lukács uses it, combines the Marxist account of economic domination with a quasi-Weberian account of the consequences of that domination for the rest of social practice. My working assumption is that somewhere in this Marx/Weber combination is an analysis which has the structure of an account of a formation of presentness, without, of course, committing myself to the idea that there is a disclosive process; and hence without committing myself to a Heideggerian conception of being.

22.   "Essence" here marks out a terrain of questions and determinations, and thus does not cancel the previously insisted upon indeterminacy of history.

23.   See *PN*, pp. 1-5, 14-16, 270.

24.   See Gillian Rose, *Dialectic of Nihilism,* Oxford, Basil Blackwell, 1984. Her reading of Derrida has, belatedly, influenced my own.

25.   In saying this I am attempting to absolve Lukács of the charge of holding a philosophy of the subject of the sort which vitiates

at least some of Marx' thought. On this, see Seyla Benhaib, 'The
Marxian Method of Critique, Normative Presuppositions', *Praxis
International* 4, 1984, pp. 294-297.

26.   The notion of the meaning of history at work here comes,
of course, from Merleau-Ponty, *Adventures of the Dialectic*, translated
by Joseph Bien, London, Heinemann, 1974, pp. 44-5. However, a
similar view regarding the early Marx has been forwarded by György
Markus, 'Human Essence and History', *International Journal of Sociology* 4, 1975, p.105, "History is neither 'meaningful' nor
'meaningless' independent of the conscious human activities which
make it meaningful; history becomes meaningful to the degree that men
become capable of assigning historical perspective, historical meaning,
to their own actions ..." History can be rendered meaningful, but this
rendering is neither a positing nor a discovering.

27.   And while there are some negative necessary conditions for
socialism, there are not and will not be anything like a complete set of
conditions defining socialism short of the socialism we produce. The
reasons for this are discussed below.

28.   "... the 'transcendental' precondition of the possibility of
critical theory is the existence, the empirical-'lived' reality of radical
needs which in their content 'transcend' the present and are directed
towards a new organization of society and new forms of life. The actuality of these historical, or 'conditioned' needs, experienced at least in
the form of a mute dissatisfaction and anxiety, finds in the theory both
its explanation and interpretation." György Markus, 'Practical-Social
Rationality in Marx, A Dialectical Critique - Part 2', *Dialectical
Anthropology* 4, 1979, p. 22. Although apparently of Lukácsian
pedigree, the question of who the bearer of revolution is to be is, in
fact, misguided from within the perspective of the philosophy of praxis.
Without experience of a certain sort, what has come to be called the
experience of radical needs, analysis has no claim to our attention;
without analysis, explanation and interpretation, social misery remains
private and subjective. Theory's giving voice to radical needs involves
the inscription of a project, but not the determination of the contents of
that project; those are formed through praxial activity.

29.   Or, action is the passive forgetting of the question of being.

30.   *PN*, pp. 32-3.

31.   *Positions*, translated by A. Bass, Chicago, University of
Chicago Press, 1981, p. 24.

32.   Richard Kearney, *Dialogues with Contemporary
Continental Thinkers*, Manchester, Manchester University Press, 1984,
p. 123. It is worth noting here that this conception of Derrida simply
picks up a motif in Heidegger and Gadamer, namely, the focusing on
forms of activity whose meanings transcend their antecedents. Hence

their interest in artistic, creative activity and legal hermeneutics. I have discussed this in my 'Aesthetic Alienation, Truth at the End of Art', forthcoming.

33.   The price to be paid for such a rigorous immanence is high. As a recent writer on the question has stated it, "... there is certainly no reason why the course of actual history should not reach a point where it is transformed into a permanent stasis, where the affirmation of the social order is not so much the result of an ideological suppression of subjectivity, but the final transformation of subjectivity into something else altogether." Robert Pippin, 'Marcuse on Hegel and Historicity', *Philosophical Forum* XVI, 1985, p. 200.

34.   For amplification see, for openers, Martin Hollis, *Models of Man*, Cambridge, Cambridge University Press, 198?, Chs. 5-7; William E. Connolly, 'Appearance and Reality in Politics', *Political Theory* 7(1979); and Charles Taylor, 'What is Human Agency', now in his *Human Agency and Language*, Cambridge, Cambridge University Press, 1985, Ch.1.

35.   *Phenomenology of Spirit*, translated by A.V. Miller, Oxford, Clarendon Press, 1977, pp. 113-119.

36.   See Cornelius Castoriadis, *L'Institution imaginaire de la société*, Paris, Éditions du Seuil, 1975, Part II.

37.   See Walter Benjamin, 'Theses on the Philosophy of History', in his *Illuminations*, translated by Harry Zohn, New York, Schocken Books, 1969.

38.   See *WD*, p. 263.

39.   *WD,* pp. 256-7.

40.   *Ibid.* p. 259.

41.   Hegel, *op. cit.* p. 119.

42.   This is often evident in Hegel, as in the discussions of Antigone and "the terror". However, it does tend to get suppressed in the phenomenological mode of presentation, which leaves transformation as a blank between natural and philosophical conscious-ness. To me, at least, it makes sense to view the *Phenomenology* as a whole as a vast *memento mori*, as, that is, a philosophic death's head.

43.   *WD*, p. 335.

44.   But see, *e.g.*, *WD*, p. 256 for an even more metaphysical conception of laughter than this paragraph allows.

45.   Kearney, *op. cit.* p. 122.

46.   See *PN*, Chs.3 and 5, *passim*.

47.   See Gillian Rose, *op.cit.* pp. 162-165.

48.   *WD*, p. 275.

49.   For this see my 'From Self-Consciousness to Community, Act and Recognition in the Master-Slave Relationship', in Z.A. Pelczynski (ed.), *The State and Civil Society*, Cambridge, Cambridge

University Press, 1984.
   50.   *MP*, p. 136.

PART III

LUKÁCS ON HEGEL

T.I. OJZERMAN

Lukács' Hegel Interpretation

In the literary heritage of Georg Lukács, the interpretation of the history of philosophy plays a great, if not dominant, role. This is explicable, at least in part, by the complex path that he took to arrive at Marxism, at dialectical and historical materialism. During his intellectually formative period, he came under the influence of the idealist philosophy which was then dominant in Germany. The Great October Revolution, and the subsequent events in 1918 in Hungary, drew Lukács into the ranks of the Communist Party.

However, in those days Lukács was not a convinced adherent of the scientific worldview of Marxist philosophy. His well-known work, *History and Class Consciousness* (1923), is evidence of the fact that his worldview then was Marxism mixed with non-Marxist elements - some drawn from the philosophy of Hegel and some drawn from other idealist doctrines. Lukács later judged the basic theses of this book to be erroneous and foreign to Marxism. Appearing before the Moscow session in 1934 that celebrated the 25th anniversary of Lenin's *Materialism and Empirio-Criticism*, Lukács declared: "My struggle against the theory of reflection and against the Marx-Engels understanding of the dialectic in nature was a typical form of 'idealism from below' ..."[1] Lukács was brought to Marxist-Leninist philosophy, with its creative accomplishments, by his historic reconceptualization of the historical experience of the revolutionary transformation in the USSR, of the history of capitalism, and of the liberating movement of the proletariat. This research was carried out by this eminent Hungarian philosopher in close conjunction with the analysis of the basic tendencies in the development of modern European philosophy. Philosophic doctrines were taken by Lukács as the self-consciousness of the era in which they were formulated. "The history of philosophy, like the history of art and literature", wrote Lukács, "contrary to the views of bourgeois historians, is not the simple history of philosophic ideas or personalities. Philosophic problems and the means of solving them emerge via the development of the forces of production, through social development and the development of the class war. The precise outline of any philosophy cannot be illuminated except by study of these motive forces. The attempt to pose and solve problems of philosophic connections from the perspective of a so-called immanent development inevitably leads to an idealistic distortion of the important relations even when the historian has the necessary knowledge, the

197

T. Rockmore (ed.), Lukács Today, 197–220.

subjective good will, and the intent to be objective."[2] This materialist
understanding of the development of philosophy and of human
intellectual history in general became for Lukács the theoretical basis for
a correct understanding of Marxist philosophy as the revolutionary-
critical outcome of the entire previous philosophic development of
mankind.

While characterizing the eminently progressive significance of
Marxism, V.I. Lenin wrote:

> The history of philosophy and the history of social science show
> with perfect clarity that there is nothing resembling 'sectarianism' in
> Marxism, in the sense of its being a hidebound, petrified doctrine, a
> doctrine which arose *away from* the highroad of the development of
> world civilisation. On the contrary, the genius of Marx consists
> precisely in his having furnished answers to questions already
> raised by the foremost minds of mankind.[3]

This fundamental historical-philosophic declaration by Lenin undoubtedly inspired Lukács in his works devoted to explaining the progress of
philosophic knowledge that was crowned by the establishment of the
scientifically philosophic, dialectical-materialist worldview.

Karl Marx and Friedrich Engels accomplished the transition from
metaphysical and mechanistic materialism to a totalizing, dialectical-
materialist understanding. The revolutionary-critical, materialist re-
working of the idealist dialectic of Hegel - organically connected with
the dialectical reformation of previous materialism - was of decisive
significance for the great revolutionary turnaround in philosophy, the
results of which are dialectical and historical materialism.

The participants in the Second International - as is well-known -
under-estimated, and even denied, the significance of the Hegelian
dialectic in the historical process of the emergence of Marxism. They
generally saw dialectic as a conceptual method for representing real
processes, substituting itself for concrete, empirical research. The
materialist transformation of the Hegelian dialectic was seen by these
activists as an essentially utopian endeavor. The Leninist characterization of the dialectic as the *soul of Marxism* as well as his definition
of the dialectic as the *algebra of revolution* were, without a doubt,
directly aimed against opportunistic interpretations of the theory of
development.

Georg Lukács - who, already in his early works, opposed the
opportunistic denigration and distortion of the dialectic - took as his
most important task in relation to the history of philosophy the
investigation of the genesis of the Hegelian dialectic, of its theoretical
and ideological content, and of its historical links with bourgeois

revolutionary thought. The most basic and - one can say without exaggeration - innovative study of these problems is to be found in the fundamental work by Lukács, *The Young Hegel*, written by this Hungarian philosopher in the 1930s, while he was living in the USSR. The historical process of the emergence of Hegel's dialectical idealism is dealt with in this book as a reflection of the era of bourgeois revolution in Western Europe.

Lukács opens his book with a clear formulation of his theoretical and ideological tasks. He stresses that up to this time study of the early works of Hegel had been done by bourgeois philosophers, who ignore or directly deny, their revolutionary content and their clear connection with the era of the revolutionary annihilation of feudal social relations. The studies by Dilthey and Häring on the young Hegel reduce the genesis of his philosophy to the analysis of the theological problems that are described as central to the early works of Hegel.[4] Günther Nohl, a student of Dilthey, published many of the still unknown early works of Hegel under the title *The Theological Works of the Young Hegel*.[5] These early works of Hegel are only apparently theological. Their actual content is in conflict with Christian theology. This truth is convincingly demonstrated in Lukács' book which defeats the theologically conservative interpretation of the works of the young Hegel, the conceptual content of which can be clarified only in the context of the French Revolution and the social-political problems of that era.

For a general characterization of Lukács' monograph *The Young Hegel,* we must take note of two further circumstances. In 1932 the Institute of Marxism-Leninism of the Central Committee of the CPSU published the Paris manuscripts of Marx, with the title *Economic-Philosophic Manuscripts of 1844*. A parallel publication occurred in the same year in Germany. In the preface to this German edition Landshut and Mayer wrote that these manuscripts are the "sole document in which Marx' intellect appears in its full force".[6] Opposing these early works of Marx to his mature works - *Capital* in the first place - anti-Marxist commentators asserted that the hitherto economic grounding of socialism must be replaced by an anthropological and ethical one. Distorting the genuine content of the manuscripts, Landshut and Mayer wrote about the necessity of revising all of the subsequent development of Marx' doctrine. In particular, they suggested that the theory of class conflict was to be replaced by the doctrine concerning the alienation of human essence. Accordingly, Landshut and Mayer deny the proposition of the *Communist Manifesto* saying that class war is the moving force in the history of civilization; and they want to generalize the contents of the *1844 Manuscripts* as "All prior history is the history of human self-alienation." [7]

Using isolated formulae from Marx' manuscripts and ignoring their basic materialistic and Communist content, these authors try to repair the neo-Kantian notions of classless "epic socialism" by means of abstract judgments on the nature of man in general. It is to these sorts of judgments that the whole of the *1844 Manuscripts* is reduced. Landshut and Mayer were seconded in their essentially anti-Marxist interpretation of the *1844 Manuscripts* by Marcuse and de Man, who published articles on the subject in 1932. Marcuse attributed to Marx the assertion that economic social relations oppose human nature and have an essentially alienating character. De Man tried to show that Marx was an adherent of the idealistic *Lebensphilosophie*, whose materialist conception of history applies only to capitalism. Historical materialism is thus reduced to a theory of bourgeois society, and its extension to the whole of human history ... is its bourgeois interpretation.[8] We do not have the space here to go into the whole discussion on the young Marx, that continues to the present, and to which we have already devoted a special study.[9] We brought up the matter here only to point out that Lukács was the first Marxist to meet bourgeois distortions of the *1844 Manuscripts* with a correct and systematically developed Marxist appreciation. It is true that Lukács' *The Young Hegel* could not deal with the whole richness of these manuscripts by Marx. But such important segments of the *1844 Manuscripts* as those on alienation and critical examination of Hegel's *Phenomenology of Spirit* are subjected by Lukács to basic and profound analysis. What is more, we could say that the Marxian positions on alienation and the philosophy of Hegel are the *Leitmotifs* of Lukács' whole investigation. It is in his work that the problem of alienation first receives a systematic Marxist-Leninist analysis. It is, therefore, not difficult to see that Lukács' results here are important, going beyond the limits of his single work.

The second circumstance that deserves mention is the fact that in his analysis of Hegelian philosophy Lukács was able to make use of the *Philosophic Notebooks* of Lenin, which had just recently been published and the importance of which for Marxist history of philosophy would be difficult to exaggerate. This work by Lenin comes forward against a simplistic appreciation of German classical philosophy. Lenin mentions, in particular, serious errors in Marxist works on the philosophy of Kant. Summing up the results of his careful, and even masterful, analysis of the most important works of Hegel, Lenin notes that dialectical idealism is closer to dialectical materialism than to the old, metaphysical materialism.

Georg Lukács was the first Marxist to apply these important statements of Lenin in the systematic investigation of Hegel's philosophy, primarily in the analysis of the process of emergence of dialectical idealism.

In his *Philosophic Notebooks* Lenin places particular emphasis on the importance of a materialist interpretation of Hegel's dialectic for an understanding of Marx' most important work, his *Capital*. "It is impossible fully to understand Marx' *Capital* and its first chapter in particular, without working through and understanding the *whole* of Hegel's logic."[10] Invoking this statement by Lenin, Lukács connects it with Marx' well-known statement from the *1844 Manuscripts*, according to which, in his economic views, Hegel reaches the level of English classical political economy. The most important accomplishment of the latter, of course, is the labor theory of value, demonstrating the determining role of living labor (and, thus, proletarian labor) in the formation of capitalist wealth.

In his *1844 Manuscripts* Marx showed that, using the classical economic understanding of value as the embodiment of living labor and philosophically generalizing this position, Hegel came close to the materialist understanding of the role of labor in social development and in the establishment of the human individual as a member of society. Marx wrote:

> The greatness of Hegel's *Phenomenology* and its final result - a dialectic of negativity as the moving and generating principle - lies ultimately in the fact that Hegel regards human self-generation as a process, and objectification as alienation, as self-alienation and supersession of this alienation, and in the fact that he grasps the essence of *labor* and understands objective man, true and actual man, as the result of *his own labor*.[11]

Reflecting on these statements by Lenin and Marx, Lukács comes to a very important conclusion relative to the connections between Hegel's philosophic and economic views, stressing, thereby, the historically progressive significance of this philosopher's economic views for the formation of the dialectical method. In this way, Lukács does not limit himself to an examination of the philosophic sources of the Hegelian dialectic. He attributes serious significance to the non-philosophic, social sources - in particular, English political economy, although the latter is known not to have any historical understanding of social life. The dialectic of Hegel, Lukács shows, is not solely a result of philosophic development. An important source of this dialectic was a theoretical reflection on the era of bourgeois revolution and its complex ideological reflection.

The theoretical sources of Marxism - German classical philosophy, English bourgeois political economy, French utopian socialism - are usually viewed independently, as autonomous lines of thought. This view has, of course, a certain justification, in that these currents are really distinguished by their theoretical independence and do not necessarily correlate one with the other. However, such an isolated consideration of these theoretical sources of Marxism is decidedly one-sided; and it does not help explain how they came together in the revolutionary-critical synthesis realized by Marx and Engels. Marx did not limit himself to indicating the links between Hegel's *Phenomenology* and classical English political economy. We find also in Marx an analysis of the critique of bourgeois economic thought in the works of a series of utopian socialists. It is also important to note that the founders of Marxism greatly appreciated German classical philosophy from the viewpoint of the history of socialist ideas. Engels stressed that scientific socialism owes "... its origination not only to Saint-Simon, Fourier and Owen, but also to Kant, Fichte and Hegel".[12]

In this way, it becomes clear that the theoretical sources of Marxism - despite their autonomy from one another - have certain traits in common, which were indubitably generated by the era of bourgeois revolutions, and by the contradictions involved in the historical emergence and imposition of the capitalist mode of production. Noting this fact leads to the necessity of a variegated, multi-stage, even complex, approach to studying the formation of Hegel's dialectical idealism. Its theoretical sources cannot be found in a single, solely philosophic, doctrine. No matter how great the role of Kant, Fichte and Schelling in the historical process of the development of dialectical idealism, one cannot correctly understand the Hegelian dialectic without taking into account the economic views of the philosopher, as well as an analysis of his relationship to the capitalist development of France, England and Germany. And his relationship - although contradictory - was not that of an apologist.

It was Lukács who used such statements by Marx, Engels and Lenin - that, unfortunately, had not been taken seriously enough by Marxist researchers - to reformulate with great clarity the question as to the genesis of the Hegelian dialectic in the context of his combined philosophic, economic and social-political views. What is more, Lukács brought to the fore precisely the social-political views of the philosopher, especially his relationship to the French Revolution of 1789 and the subsequent capitalist development of Europe. The methodological significance of such an approach to a problem in the history of philosophy is very important, especially when its principles are actualized in concrete research - as happens in the case of Lukács. The development of philosophic ideas is not an autonomous process, flowing from the previous state of philosophic knowledge. Relations of rank among philosophic doctrines are conditioned by objective circumstances, and not by the logical linkage of ideas. How Fichte interprets Kant and how Hegel relates to the doctrines of Fichte and Schelling cannot be explained solely out of philosophy. Philosophic development is organically bound up with the development of non-philosophic knowledge, with historical experience, and with social practice. The materialist conception of history explains philosophy, and all other forms of social consciousness and knowledge, on the basis of social being, and of the development of material production - the forces and relations of production. The sequence of ideas and logical links among philosophers' doctrines are an idealist illusion which Hegel tries to ground via his panlogical ontology. However, the real emergence of the idealist dialectic in its most developed, Hegelian form can be satisfactorily explained only through philosophic-sociological analysis which does not simply compare ideas with each other but which links these ideas with historically determined, social-economic, objective reality. Such a reality was the French Revolution and subsequent bourgeois development which is wisely reflected on by Hegel in trying to understand this giant stride in human development.

Karl Marx characterized Kant's teaching as the German theory of the French Revolution. This characterization - which shows the weak, as well as the strong, aspects of Kantianism - can be applied, in our mind, to the whole of classical German Idealism - to the philosophy of Hegel and its dialectic in particular. Even in his declining years, when he was inclined to conservative political views, Hegel spoke with youthful enthusiasm about this great bourgeois revolution: "... this was a magnificent sunrise. All thinking beings were enthused about the era. At the same time, there was an enthusiastic and touching feeling; the world was filled with enthusiasm, as if only now did the divinity come into the world."[13] We cite these words not just as an example of the Hegelian relationship to the most prominent event of that era but as a *reminiscence* of the thinker about all that was experienced by him and his fellow-students, Schelling and Hölderlin, during the years of revolution.

The French Revolution was at the center, Lukács stresses, of the intellectual interests of the young Hegel. The importance of this revolution for the formation of his worldview was all the greater in that he was the "sole German thinker who seriously studied the *industrial revolution* in England".[14] The organic link between the revolutionary transformation in the development of the forces of production, with the affirmation in England (as a result of the successful bourgeois revolution) of the capitalist mode of production, could not, of course, escape the attention of Hegel, who had studied political economy and was fully aware of the economic consequences of the annihilation of feudal relations.

With the greatest perceptiveness, Karl Marx defined during the revolution of 1848 the historic significance of the English and French revolutions - the profound social-economic revolutions that Western Europe had undergone during a half-century. The revolutions of 1648 and 1789 were not *English* and *French* revolutions; they were *European* revolutions. They were not the victory of a *certain* class over the *old political structure*; they proclaimed the *political structure of a new European society*. The bourgeoisie was victorious in them; but the *victory of the bourgeoisie* meant the victory of a new social structure, of bourgeois property over feudal property, of nation over province, of competition over guilds and fragmenting of property, of dominance by the possessor of land over [those] subordinated to the possession of land, of enlightenment over superstition, of family over clan, of entrepreneurial skill over serfdom, of bourgeois right over medieval privilege. "These revolutions expressed more clearly the needs of that whole world, than the needs of those parts of the world - England and France - where they took place."[15]

We are far from attributing to Hegel the same materialist conception of history and the same penetration into the essence of the great bourgeois revolutions. We can only say (and the basis for this is found in the works of Hegel himself) that in his philosophy he senses, experiences, and hints at many aspects of these world-historical events. Herein lies, as Lukács correctly indicates, the deeper roots of the Hegelian dialectic; and this is the only possible explanation of its revolutionary character. The weaker aspects of the Hegelian method reflect the economic and political backwardness of Germany. As far as the revolutionary essence of the dialectic is concerned, it reflects revolutionary social development. Natural science - which was then beginning to display dialectical ideas which inspired the young Schelling - played, of course, a definite role in the process of the elaboration of the Hegelian dialectic. But, its most important aspect (and this has to be emphasized) is conditioned by the revolutionary reconstruction of social relations. This is what Herzen meant when he defined the Hegelian dialectic as the *algebra of revolution*.

The essence of revolution lies in the negation of the *status quo* and of the dominant reactionary social structures. Already in his student days in Tübingen, and more particularly during his work in Berne, Hegel resolutely came out against the ruling feudal ideology, which he called "positive religion". By this term he meant clericalism - centuries of domination by the Christian Church over the economic structure and the political institutions of feudal society.

Hegel is not at all an opponent of religion in general; he considered its content to be the spiritual life of the people. From these idealistic positions, he counterposes popular religion - which he defines as free religious feeling - to the institutionalized, alienated, dogmatic superstition, imposed from above. In a letter to Schelling of April 16, 1795, Hegel categorically declared: "Religion and politics always worked *together*. Religion propagated in a despotic manner has no respect for humanity and is incapable of any good or of being something with the help of its own forces."[16] This conviction marked the whole Berne period of the intellectual development of Hegel. It is in "positive religion" that Hegel, the idealist, sees the source of all the social evil generated by feudalism. Hegel linked the overthrow of this "positivity", foreign to the people, with the carrying out of the whole set of bourgeois-democratic transformations. The dominant religion was opposed to philosophy; not to philosophy in general, but to the doctrine developed by Kant. Fichte meant for Hegel a new and much higher stage in the development of idealism; in Schelling, too, one finds a pursuit of the spiritual liberation of the people. Joining this philosophic movement, Hegel sees its power in the effort to "elevate the dignity of man, to recognize his ability to be free - an ability that puts him on a level with all that is spiritual. It seems to me that there is no better sign of the times than that humanity is represented as worthy of such respect. This is a guarantee of the disappearance of the halo over the heads of earthly rulers and gods. Philosophers reveal this dignity and the people learn to sense it ...". This is how Hegel wrote to Schelling.[17]

In this way, the philosophic revolution in Germany happened in a manner analogous in its ideological content to that philosophic revolution that happened prior to 1789. However, the German philosophic revolution distinguished itself from its French counterpart not only in its greater moderation but also in its legal form of expression. The philosophic revolution in Germany - especially at the stage it reaches in Hegelian philosophy - is already master of the historical experience of post-revolutionary capitalist development. In any case, Hegel does not harbor the illusions about bourgeois society that inspired the French Enlightenment. He identified neither the capitalist present, nor its predictable future, with the notorious reign of reason. But, like his French predecessors, Hegel was firmly convinced that social reconstruction, according to the principles of reason, was both possible and necessary. In this approach of practical wisdom to historical development are contained the deep roots of the Hegelian dialectic, the elaboration of which - as Lukács shows - significantly involved reflection on the economic development of capitalism.

Of course, this practical wisdom concerning capitalist development could not yet occur in the Berne period. In those years, when Hegel was refusing "positive religion" and feudal ideological structure, he found his social ideal in the past - in particular, in a rebirth of ancient religion and the ancient republics as adequate expressions, in his eyes, of freedom. Georg Lukács correctly notes in this connection that

> for the young Hegel the positive religion of Christianity represents
> a defense of despotism and oppression, while the non-positive,
> ancient religions were religions of freedom and human dignity.
> Their renewal was, according to Hegel, the 'revolutionary goal, the
> attainment of which stands before humanity today'.[18]

Antiquity becomes in Hegel's eyes a utopian image of the republican
future of mankind. The French revolution is interpreted as a return to
the ancient republican spirit. It is indicative that Hegel counterposes to
Christ a Socrates presented as a concrete expression of the superiority
of the ancient mode of life over the society that, according to Hegel,
was generated by Christianity. Jesus Christ came to individual people,
and was not interested at all in society, or social structures. He
preached perfection within the limits of the human individual, while
Socrates talked about how to improve the state, social institutions, and
society. Analyzing the Berne period in the development of Hegel,
Lukács writes:

> Here is expressed with all clarity how the intolerance and lack of
> acceptance on the part of the young Hegel of positive religion and
> of Christianity has as a profound source a revolutionary
> enthusiasm.[19]

Thus, in the Berne period - the most important document of which
is Hegel's *Positivity of the Christian Religion* - the worldview of the
future founder of dialectical idealism is marked by an abstract negation
of feudal "positivity" and by an equally abstract representation of the
type of social structure that would make possible the development of the
freedom, self-development, and dignity of people. Such a negation -
no matter how radical it is - does not have the content that could come to
it only from what really exists. Only in his subsequent, Frankfurt,
period will Hegel sense the inadequacy of the abstract negation of what
exists. But, already in the Berne period - as Lukács shows - is
emerging a new approach to social reality. Reflecting on the causes of
the transition from the "free" religion of the ancient polis to the
anti-liberationist "positivity" of Christianity, Hegel comes to the
conclusion that what changes are the people and the whole character of
their activity. From this, according to Lukács, comes the more general
conviction that the "objectivity and independence of objects from human
reason can be conceived as the product of the development of this
selfsame reason, *i.e.*, as a product of this reason".[20] If we take into
account that what is involved here are social realities, then it is clear that

Hegel - as Lukács again shows - comes in an idealist context to the recognition that people make their own history - they are both actors and authors of their own historical drama. Of course, this approach cannot be brought to a conclusion in an idealist philosophy which is open to supernatural and supra-human sources. Such a posing of the question of the subjective and objective impedes an understanding that the social relations that dominate people - which Hegel reduces to "positive religion" and to the dominance of clericalism - result as historical consequences of the activities of people; these are their alienated and externalized forms. These ideas were further developed in the Frankfurt period.

Now "positivity" begins to appear in the reflections of Hegel not as something just to be rejected but as something complex and contradictory, that one cannot simply reject. Positivity, from this perspective, has to be seen as historically necessary but also as historically transitory. While in the Berne period all of world history after the downfall of antiquity was seen as a decline, in the Frankfurt period Hegel moves to a conception that is more complex; progress is contradictory; antiquity belongs to man's past; but a new and better future will arise through the development of contraditions that are present in positivity.

During this period, Hegel is studying the development of bourgeois society in England and France. Capitalist reality is treated by him as positive but not able simply to be rejected, as within its confines people are accomplishing their goals and their essence. In contrast to ancient society, capitalism is marked by a great increase in opposition between the haves and have-nots. But, even this contradiction is not to be seen as purely negative; it is undoubtedly a progressive alienation of human essence, but even the alienation is a form of development and of progress.

In Frankfurt, Hegel's relationship to "positive religion", *i.e.* to Christianity, changes. He now tries to differentiate within this positivity that which is historically transitory and that which maintains its meaning as the spiritual content of society. In this context, he begins to shift the concepts of positive negation and supersession which, to a certain degree, were already opposed to abstract negation. He radically changes his assessment of Christianity. Hegel now sees in it the antithesis to the mindless covetousness of a society based on private property. He interprets Christianity as the mighty force of love, thanks to which the road to social perfection is opened up. Lukács quite correctly notes that it is in the Frankfurt period that Hegel breaks with his radicalism and starts toward reconciliation with reality, with Christianity, and with capitalism. But, this is not an apology for existing reality, since the philosopher sees the social evil it is generating. He moves to the historicist position and tries to find a path toward the resolution of the contradictions that are present to capitalist society and its religion.

The paradoxical character of the conceptual development of Hegel in this period lies in the fact that, despite his recoil from radicalism, it is at this time that he begins dialectically to reflect on the social-historical process. Lukács explains this peculiarity in the development of dialectical idealism by the fact that Hegel, in contrast to the romantics, attained the progressive character of capitalism, and saw the social cataclysms generated by it as historically transitory contradictions of social development. However, as a bourgeois thinker, Hegel - despite his quite realistic assessment of capitalist reality - cannot conceive that the fight against the evils generated by capitalism must be the moving force of social progress. What he says about the need for religion and for what he calls Christian love, which he passionately rejected in his Berne writings, testify not only to unpurged elements of idealism, but also to the political and ideological frailty of the German bourgeoisie.

The emergence of Hegel's dialectic in the Frankfurt period, as Lukács convincingly shows, appears in the Hegelian polemic with Kant's ethics. Hegel sees the basic flaw of the latter in the absolute opposition between is and ought, between reason and feeling, and between morality and legality. The categorical imperative splits man into two irreconcilable parts, while in actuality he is one. Human life and conduct cannot be reconciled with an abstract, universal, extra-historical principle; devotion to duty does not exclude justifiable human feeling or a positive attitude toward human sensuality. "Hegel", writes Lukács, "rejects the Kantian ethic mainly because Kant does not have in view the whole, living person; on the contrary, Kant excludes real life from ethics, subjects it to something foreign to life, and thereby turns morality into something dead and positive in comparison to this living man."[21] From the perspective of Hegel, Kant simply absolutizes duty and ignores its historical variability, and tries to deduce isolated moral norms out of a supra-historical principle. Human obligations and moral acts are variegated and the relations among them are contradictory. Kant ignores these contradictions and thereby loses sight of the social content of morality. Hegel, on the other hand, attributes primary importance to the study of the content of norms, duties, and human relations - between the individual and society.

Kant's categorical imperative excludes from moral consciousness and the moral conduct of individuals even the slightest contradiction. Hegel, however, tries to study the contradictions of moral consciousness. For example, he shows that virtue (not virtue in general but a real virtue) is fully compatible with its opposite, vice. To the variety of human relations correspond a variety of virtues, inconceivable without a variety of collisions. Virtues cannot be explained by the categorical imperative, since each of them is relative and, consequently, is conditioned by certain circumstances, needs, conditions, *etc*. Each virtue is limited and cannot pretend to pre-eminence. Absolutization of a virtue would imply negation of the other virtues and thereby turn it into a vice. Moral activity is undoubtedly free activity but the latter is never, contrary to Kant, subject to moral necessity. Moral consciousness is rational, but its rationality contains contradictions that Kant did not want to see. Kant tried to deal with historical events from the viewpoint of morality, while Hegel held that history occurs independently of moral consciousness.

Lukács writes:

> The opposition between Kant and Hegel in the domain of methodology consists, speaking briefly, in the fact that Kant abandons the unresearched social content of morality, accepting it without historical critique, and tries to derive moral demands from the formal criteria of the notion of duty, *i.e.* out of the imperative itself; while for Hegel, each moral demand forms only an element of the living, constantly moving, social whole.[22]

Hegel's historicism and realism come into clear view in this polemic with Kant. These traits of the Hegelian vision of social reality are the fruits of a scrupulous study of European history, in particular of the economic and political history of bourgeois society. This leads to the conclusion that the Hegelian reconciliation with reality includes within it a dialectical understanding of the latter. However, this is, of course, an *idealist* dialectic, where the conservative aspect necessarily predominates. Engels has written that in the dialectic - the rationally understood - materialist dialectic,

> there is also a conservative side: every given stage of the development of knowledge and of social relations is justified by it for its time and its circumstances, but nothing more. The conservatism of this mode of understanding is relative; its revolutionary character is absolute - this is the only absolute, acceptable dialectical philosophy.[23]

This Engelsian statement makes it easy to understand the paradoxical union of the Hegelian withdrawal from political radicalism with the establishment of a dialectical worldview and method within the confines of objective idealism.

While noticing the same paradox, we cannot completely agree with Lukács when he repeatedly stresses as one of the basic theses of his research that the formation of the Hegelian dialectic is indissolubly bound up with the formation of Hegel's conservative social-political convictions. For example, in describing the importance of the Frankfurt period in the emergence of Hegel's dialectical idealism, Lukács writes:

> ...the further he [Hegel, *T.O.*] retreated from the revolutionary ideals of his youth, the more resolutely he 'harmonized' with the prevailing bourgeois society, the less his thought transcended these limits, then the more strongly and consciously the dialectic is felt in him.[24]

In contrast to Lukács, we suggest that the retreat from the abstract negation of positivity and the idealization of the ancient style of life (this is the idealization that, in short, ignored the slavery that was basic to ancient society) were not a transition to a position of social-political conservatism. Nor was there conservatism in Hegel's recognition of the reality of bourgeois society, which had just come to be at that time and represented not only the present but also the future of nineteenth-century Germany. The philosophy of Hegel was the ideology of the bourgeois revolution. Its conservative and even reactionary traits express, on the one hand, the fundamental limitedness of any bourgeois ideology and, on the other, the economic and political backwardness of Germany. It seems that the dialectic of Hegel must also reflect the conservative and even reactionary traits of the Hegelian worldview. But it is not they that define and stimulate the formation of the dialectic that forms the progressive, and even revolutionary, side of the philosopher's doctrine.

The Jena period in the intellectual biography of Hegel is marked by the perfecting of dialectical idealism. This period - with the publication of the *Phenomenology of Spirit* - draws special attention from Lukács. He also analyzes the *Realphilosophie* which often takes up the economic and social problems that fill the Hegelian *Phenomenology*. This period is frequently analyzed in contemporary, especially Soviet, writings on the history of philosophy[25], and we mention it here only to the extent that it is relevant to our current task.

In the Frankfurt period, Hegel came to the conclusion that religion (Christianity, interpreted as the religion of love and the most powerful force for human emancipation) is the historically constituted path for the overcoming of the social conflicts of "civil society" with its concomitant alienation of man, of his social essence and formation of his personhood. In the Jena period, as Lukács shows, Hegel re-examined this conclusion, and came to a new conclusion on the relationship of philosophy and religion, one that was very important for his whole worldview. Henceforward, religion is no longer treated as the highest form of consciousness, the adequate expression of the absolute. The absolute finds its authentic expression only in reason, dialectically overcoming the limited sensual representation typical of religion. Espousing objective idealism in his polemic with Fichte, Hegel interprets reason as a dialectically developing essence not just of mankind but of all being in general. The principle of the identity of being and thought, established in the *Phenomenology of Spirit*, is a dialectical conception of the unity of identity and non-identity, of the subjective and the objective, and of the individual and the social that is new in differing not only from the Fichtean and Schellingian versions but also from the idealist version, in general.

The central category of the *Phenomenology of Spirit*, Lukács shows, is that of alienation. Although this concept is present to a certain degree in pre-Hegelian thought, only in Hegel is it tightly bound up with economic views, with the analysis of labor activity and of its role in man becoming a member of society, and with the study of the development of capitalism. As we said at the outset, this fact was first noted by Marx, who wrote in the *1844 Manuscripts*:

> Hegel took the position of contemporary political economy. He considered *labor* as *essence*, as the self-confirming essence of man; he saw only the positive side of labor, not the negative... Hegel recognized only one type of labor - namely *abstract-spiritual labor*.[26]

Lukács' contribution lies in his being the first Marxist to use this most important statement to analyze the *Phenomenology of Spirit* and the works that preceded it in the Jena period.

The concept of alienation serves Hegel as a central element in the construction of his system of objective idealism. Objects that were initially characterized in the *Phenomenology* ... as opposed to individual sense knowledge appear in the sequel as reified, alienated forms of understanding, the basis of which is supposed to be formed by the impersonal, absolute reason - by substance becoming subject. In Hegel's system - in particular in the *Science of Logic* and the *Philosophy of Nature* - nature figures as the alienated being of the "absolute idea". However, Lukács shows that the Hegelian conception of alienation cannot be reduced to a speculative-idealist construction of objective reality. The rational kernel of this conception is Hegel's attempt to explain, with the help of the concept of "alienation", class-antagonistic social relations. The clearest proof of this is the small section of the *Phenomenology*... which is called 'Lordship and Bondage'. The content of this section is always part of popular presentations of Hegelian philosophy. One should not forget that it was precisely Lukács who first revealed its social essence in the 1930s. This is not at all clear, despite the unambiguous title.

In her *Path of Hegel to The Science of Logic*, N.V. Motrošilova - not without originality - notes that Hegel "did not at all have in mind to analyze lordship and bondage as real social phenomena, as a more or less defined historical phenomenon".[27] Lordship and bondage (Hegel uses *Knechtschaft* and not *Sklaverei*) means not only slavery, but also any situation of "menial" labor or servitude. Since the *Phenomenology...* is for Hegel the history of spirit, it has to deal with its divisions and its different hypostases. While Hobbes asserted that in the state of nature man was a wolf for man, Hegel's version has it that the personalized forms of self-consciousness are formed through confrontation. Personal self-consciousness requires recognition, and affirms itself only by subjecting to itself another self-consciousness, its other in the other person, its *alter ego*. In the *Philosophic Propadeutic*, where Hegel presented the content of the *Phenomenology...* in popular form, he imagines the emergence of servitude and social inequality in the following form:

> When each of two opposed self-consciousnesses in relation to and for another self-consciousness demonstrates and asserts itself as something absolute in-itself, then the self-consciousness that freely chooses *life* becomes *subservient* and thereby shows that he cannot by himself draw what he needs for autonomy from his present being.[28]

If we abstract from the phenomenological account of self-consciousness, then it seems that the concrete cause of servitude is explained by Hegel in the spirit of Aristotle, however, at the highest level of essential distinction, and that the *Phenomenology of Spirit* fundamentally excludes the presupposition of an unchanging self-consciousness, of an unchanging human nature. This work of Hegel is also noteworthy in that it provides a map of the development of self-consciousness, where an important factor in this developmental emergence is labor - even though it is work interpreted (as we saw above) only as spiritual activity, *i.e.* the "labor" of self-consciousness, of thought: it is a philosophic activity.

The Hegelian *Phenomenology* also characterizes servile self-consciousness as developing and enriching itself, as a consequence of its internal contradictions. This self-consciousness naturally comes into conflict with its fundamental and substantial essence, which is freedom. It is especially important that this conflict appears and develops through labor.

The slave works for the master, feeds him, and sees to his every need. The master cannot exist without the slave; he cannot feed or care for himself. As a consequence, the master fully depends on the slave while the latter, through his labor, guarantees his own existence. Do not the master and slave, under these circumstances, change places? Does the master not become the slave of his slave? Does the slave not become the master of his master? The contradiction is clear, yet the master stays master and the slave remains slave. Hegel's conclusion from the analysis of this contradiction is perfectly unambiguous: lordly self-consciousness is only apparently lordly. "Therefore, the *truth* of self-consciousness", declares Hegel,

> is *servile consciousness*. It is true that this latter first appears as *outside* itself and not as the truth of self-consciousness. But, just as lordship shows that its essence is the contrary of what it wants to be, so also servitude in its actualization turns out to be rather the opposite of what it immediately is... .[29]

No special perspicacity is needed to realize that the Hegelian notion of "lordship and bondage" - with all of its idealistic speculative character and its separation from historically actual social-economic conditions (that Motrošilova was able to stress) - is clearly anti-feudal and has a bourgeois-revolutionary cast to it. This is what is emphatically stressed by Lukács. Analyzing the dialectic of lordship and bondage in his own 'Political Economy of the Jena Period', Lukács notes that the

> great path of the development of consciousness in the *Phenomenology* runs through the consciousness of the slave, not of the master. It is in the dialectic of labor that arises, according to Hegel, the real self-consciousness, the phenomenological form of the dissolution of antiquity. The 'forms of consciousness', in which this dissolution is embodied - Stoicism, scepticism and unhappy consciousness (emergent Christianity) - arise in the presentation of Hegel precisely out of the phenomenological dialectic of servile consciousness.[30]

Lukács thus shows concerning all the speculative constructions of the *Phenomenology* that Hegel does not fully liberate himself from the real historical conditions, in which Christianity arose as a religion of slaves, while Stoicism, alongside the other currents of Hellenistic philosophy, served as its theoretical source. Of course, the speculative distancing of the Hegelian analysis from the real, mainly economic, conditions does not obscure these elements. However, such a

distancing (without too much stress on paradoxicality) contains a
certain, historically progressive, social intention. It is no accident that
Hegel uses the word "*Knecht*" which indicates not so much a slave as a
feudal serf. That he does not talk directly of serfdom indicates, to our
mind, his circumspection. Nevertheless, there can be no doubt that
Hegel's critical analysis of the master-slave relationship, despite the
references to antiquity, is aimed most directly against the feudal form of
the oppression of man, which existed in Germany in Hegel's time
(especially in Prussia) in the form of feudal privileges.

There is yet one more, not unimportant, particularity of the
Hegelian analysis of the oppression and exploitation of man by man. As
an ideologist of the bourgeois revolution, Hegel found himself under
the sway of bourgeois-democratic illusions. He was convinced that the
liquidation of feudal privileges would guarantee to all members of
society - in accord with their capacities, education, professional skill,
etc. - the conditions for successful operation at any "level", by which
Hegel did not mean the class-antagonistic structure of feudal social
classes, but the social groups which result from the social division of
labor. Freedom of conscience, on the one hand, and removal of
extra-economic constraints, on the other, were imagined by Hegel as
the conditions for the removal of obstacles in the way of free
development of all members of society. Lukács writes:

> Hegel, as a result, tenaciously held to the view that society is
> divided into estates, but that individuals belong to these estates not
> by descent but according to individual talents. We can say that the
> Hegelian 'universal estate' is much closer to the Napoleonic soldier
> and gentry than to the gentry of the semi-feudal states.[31]

Bourgeois-democratic illusions are an idealization of capitalism.
They were inevitable, and to a certain extent historically progressive
during the emergence and dominance of this social formation. Hegel -
who had a better idea than the Enlightenment thinkers of the eighteenth
century of the actual economic structure of bourgeois society - added to
these illusions (without which one is not a bourgeois thinker) a more or
less clear understanding that the new society was not the realization of
the Enlightenment's reign of reason. In the *Realphilosophie* Hegel
asserts that in bourgeois society the individual exists as an alienated
individual. The concept of "positivity" is replaced in the
Phenomenology by the concept of alienation. Lukács notes that this is
not just a terminological substitution of one term for another. This is
the move from the critique of feudalism to a critical stance toward the
new bourgeois society.[32] This critical stance includes - as Lukács
correctly notes - a tragic contradiction, to the extent that Hegel treats

bourgeois society as the highest stage of social development. He could not, of course, while in those historical conditions of the affirmation of bourgeois society, see the possibility - let alone the objective necessity - of a new social structure that would put a definite end to human alienation. Therefore, for Hegel, alienation can be overcome only in thought. It is this position that shows the idealism and bourgeois limits of this philosopher, but also the elements of the very careful critical evaluation of capitalist society that one finds in Hegel.

These contradictions of the Hegelian relationship to bourgeois society make it possible correctly to understand the *reconciliation with reality* which Hegel elevates to the highest principle of philosophy, since reality is treated as rational. There is no doubt that one finds in this reconciliation - a circumstantial analysis of which is provided by Lukács - elements of that servility that Marx criticized in his analysis of the Hegelian philosophy of right. Marx wrote of Hegel in 1843 that "he deserves blame not because he presents the essence of the contemporary state as it is, but because he takes what is to be the *essence of the state*".[33] Marx, however, was far from denying, or even diminishing, the importance of the philosophy of right of Hegel and its critical relationship to contemporary reality. He saw in this doctrine "... a critical analysis of the contemporary state and of the reality bound up with it, and the strongest critique of all hitherto existing forms of German political and legal consciousness ..."[34] These statements by Marx are a sufficient characterization of the *contradictory character* of the Hegelian principle of reconciliation with reality. Engels subsequently touched on this contradictory character in analyzing the famous Hegelian thesis that "the real is rational and the rational is real".[35] The class limitations of Hegel find expression in this thesis and in the principle of reconciliation in general - as has been sufficiently pointed out in Marxist works. The contribution of Lukács is to have dealt with the positive side, illuminating the internally contained dialectical aspect: namely, the orientation in the direction of a *progressively developing* social reality. Such a "reconciliation" not only does not include a critical relationship to the social *status quo*, but even presupposes the latter.

V.I. Lenin brilliantly exposed the contradictions of the Hegelian principle of reconciliation with reality which, according to its dialectical version, also includes opposed tendencies, which clearly emerge in neo-Hegelianism.

The belief of Hegel in human reason and its rights and the basic thesis of Hegelian philosophy that is, that in the world there is a constant process of change and development, led those students of the Berlin philosopher who did not want to make their peace with reality to the thought that the fight against existing injustice and the realm of evil is based in the universal law of eternal development.[36]

In the light of this Leninist characterization of the revolutionary aspect of Hegel's doctrine, Lukács' interpretation becomes intelligible and is seen to contribute to an advancement toward the understanding of the Hegelian principle of reconciliation.

We recall the neo-Hegelians as thinkers who - even if inconsistently - interpreted the Hegelian principle of reconciliation in the spirit of a fight against all that impeded development. Such an understanding of this principle was even more typical of the Russian revolutionary democrats - in particular of N.G. Chernyshevsky, the "great Russian Hegelian and materialist", according to Lenin's famous characterization.[37] The historical optimism of Chernyshevsky was intimately bound up with a dialectical understanding of development and the corresponding assessment of each of its historically transitory stages. Chernyshevsky wrote:

> ... the eternal change of form, the eternal rejection of forms, generated by a known content by a striving as a result of the reinforcement of the striving, the highest development of the same content - whoever has understood this great, eternal, universal law and who has learned to apply it to every phenomenon, Oh how peacefully he will increase his opportunities by which others are confused.[38]

To conclude, it might do well to note the very important methodological statement of Lenin, cited by Lukács in the introduction to *The Young Hegel*. Lenin wrote in the *Philosophic Notebooks*:

> Plekhanov criticized Kantianism (and agnosticism in general) more from a vulgar-materialist than from a dialectical-materialist viewpoint since he only *rejects* his judgments *a limine* but does not correct them (as Hegel corrects Kant), digging deeper, generalizing, extending them, and showing the *links* and *transitions* of each and every concept.

Further down the same page, generalising this concrete remark, Lenin concludes: "Marxists criticized (in the early twentieth century) Kantians and Humeans more in a Feuerbachian (and Buchnerian) fashion than in a Hegelian one."[39]

It is not possible to over-estimate the value of this critical remark by Lenin (made, it should be said, in the course of a careful study of the works of Hegel) for Marxist-Leninist historians of philosophy. It is directed against simplistic critiques of idealism and agnosticism, against forgetting the obvious fact that the errors of the great philosophers (great errors) contain great anticipations, hints toward great truths and great discoveries. One cannot but agree with Lukács when he uses the above quotations from Lenin and stresses that they do not apply just to the philosophy of Kant. "It is clear", he writes, "that these important remarks of Lenin also apply completely to the methodology of the historical and critical judgments of Hegelian philosophy."[40] Within the confines of the present article we have been able to examine only some - but the most important - theses of Lukács' *The Young Hegel*. We have not taken into account other works by the Hungarian Marxist philosopher, where the dialectical-materialist examination of Hegelian philosophy occupies a place of no less importance. What we have examined allows us nevertheless to say that it is perfectly clear that Lukács' study of Hegelian philosophy has served to enrich the Marxist-Leninist methodology of the history of philosophy, which is the scientific theory of the historical-philosophic process.

The Young Hegel, like many other works of Lukács, was a militant and polemical investigation. It was oriented against the bourgeois - especially irrationalist - and idealist-theological interpretation of the genesis of dialectical idealism and of Hegelian philosophy as a whole. More than thirty years old, this work of Lukács has not lost its polemical punch. Contemporary bourgeois researchers into Hegel just keep repeating the arguments of their predecessors, since they are all standing on the same ideological platform.

Georg Lukács' *The Young Hegel* has stood the test of time. This is evidence of the continuing importance of every really Marxist researcher.

Translated from the Russian
by Thomas J. Blakeley
(Boston College)

NOTES

1. Cf. G. Lukács, 'Značenie "Materializma i empiriokriticizma" dlja bol'ševizacii kommunističeskich partij' (The Significance of *Materialism and Empirio-Criticism* for the Bolshevization of Communist Parties), *Pod znamenem marksizma* 1934, 4, str. 147.

2. G. Lukács, *Die Zerstörung der Vernunft,* Berlin, 1955. S.5.

3. V.I. Lenin, *Soč.*, t.19, str. 3 (*Selected Works*, Vol.1, p.41).

4. W. Dilthey, *Jugendgeschichte Hegels*, Berlin, 1905. Th. Häring, *Hegel. Sein Wollen und sein Werk: Eine chronologische Entwicklungsgeschichte der Gedanken und der Sprache Hegels*, Leipzig, 1929.

5. G. Nohl, *Hegels theologische Frühschriften*, Tübingen, 1907.

6. S. Landshut, J.P. Mayer, 'Die Bedeutung der Frühschriften von Marx für eine neue Verständnis', in *Karl Marx. Der historische Materialismus*, Bd.1, S.XXVIII, Leipzig, 1932.

7. *Ibid.* S.XXXIII.

8. H. Marcuse, 'Neue Quellen zur Grundlegung des historischen Materialismus', *Die Gesellschaft* (Berlin) 1932, 8; H. de Man, 'Neu entdeckte Marx', *Der Kampf* 1932, 5 and 6.

9. Cf. T.I. Ojzerman, *Formirovanie filosofii marksizma* (Formation of the Philosophy of Marxism), M., 1974, c.1, gl.3.

10. Lenin, *Soč.* t. 29, str. 162.

11. K. Marks, F. Engel's, *Iz rannych proizvedenij* (From the Early Works), M. 1956. str.127. Introducing this quotation, Lukács stresses: "Marx shows here the great degree to which Hegelian philosophy presents itself as a movement of thought, analogous to classical English political economy. But, while in the latter the concrete problems of bourgeois society appear in their economic form, in Hegel they occur only as the abstract (idealist) reflection of the most general principles. However, on the other hand, Hegel is the only thinker who attains the dialectical character of this movement and is able to move forward thence to elaboration of a general dialectic." (Lukács, *Der junge Hegel*, Berlin, 1954. S.26)

12. K. Marks, F. Engel's, *Soč.* t.19, str. 323.

13. G. Hegel, *Filosofija istorii* (Philosophy of History), *Soč.* M., n.d., t. 8, str. 414.

14. Lukács, *op.cit.* S. 25.

15. Marks, Engel's, *Soč.* t.6, str. 115.

16. G. Gegel', *Raboty rannych let* (Works of the Early Years)

M., 1974. t. 2, str. 224.
   17.   *Loc.cit.*
   18.   Lukács, *op.cit.* S. 47-48.
   19.   *Ibid.* S. 100.
   20.   *Loc.cit.*
   21.   *Op.cit.* S. 191.
   22.   *Loc.cit.*
   23.   Marks, Engel's, *Soč.* t. 21, str. 276.
   24.   Lukács, *op.cit.* S. 281.
   25.   Cf. K. Bakradze, *Sistema i metod filosofija Gegelja* (The System and Method of the Philosophy of Hegel), Tbilisi, 1958. Ju.N. Davydov, 'Fenomenologija ducha i ee mesto v istorii filosofskoj mysli' (The *Phenomenology of Spirit* and its Place in the History of Philosophy), (preface to the 4th volume of Hegel's collected works, Moscow, 1959). N.V. Motrošilova, *Put' Gegelja k "Nauke logiki"'* (Hegel's Path to The Science of Logic), M., 1984.
   26.   Marks, Engel's, *Iz rannich...* str. 627.
   27.   Motrošilova, *op.cit.* str. 164.
   28.   G. Gegel', 'Filosofskaja propedevtika' (Philosophic Propaedeutic), M., 1973. str.88 (in Vol.2 of *Raboty rannych let*).
   29.   G. Gegel', *Fenomenologija ducha, Soč.* t. IV, str. 104. This Hegelian thesis is to a great extent a logical prolongation of Fichte's thesis: "...everyone who considers himself ruler of another is himself a slave. Even when he is not actually such, he still has the soul of a slave ... He alone is free who wants all around him to be free ..." (I.G. Fichte, *O naznačenii učenogo* (Über das Wesen des Gelehrten, und seine Erscheinungen im Gebiete der Freiheit), M., 1935. str.79-80). What is expressed by Fichte with Jacobin straightforwardness, not trying to veil its idealist speculation, is formulated by Hegel rationally, strictly in a liberal spirit.
   30. Lukács, *op.cit.* S. 379. Coming back to this basic conclusion at another place in the book, Lukács even more pointedly reformulates Hegel's "very important thought" that the "ultimate development of self-consciousness is carried out through labor, *i.e.*, through the consciousness of the laboring slave and not that of the idle master." (*Ibid.* S. 546).
   31.   *Op.cit.* S. 365.
   32.   *Loc.cit.*
   33.   K. Marks, *K kritike gegelevskoj filosofii prava*, Marks, Engel's, *Soč.* M. 1955, t. 1, str. 291.
   34.   *Ibid.* str. 421.
   35.   Cf. Marks, Engel's, *Soč.* t. 21, str. 274.
   36.   Lenin, *Soč.* t. 2, str. 7.
   37.   *Ibid.* t. 18, str. 381.

38.   N.G. Černyševskij, *Poln. sobr. soč.* (Works), t. 29, str. 161.

39.   Lenin, *Soč.* t. 29, str. 161.

40.   Lukács, *op.cit.* S. 24.

TOM ROCKMORE

Lukács on Modern Philosophy

All philosophy is hermeneutical, at least in an irreducible, minimal sense. Whether or not a thinker chooses to interpret earlier views in the history of the tradition, to pursue philosophy at all is to presuppose an interpretation of the philosophical discipline. But, despite the importance of the hermeneutic element for the philosophical process itself, it is unclear how philosophers can best interpret the historical tradition. It is significant that, at this late date, we possess neither specific rules, nor even an accepted basic framework, governing the reception of preceding philosophy.

In calling attention to this problem, my intention is not to resolve it. Rather, the aim is to point out the importance of Lukács' approach to the history of philosophy. The Hungarian thinker, Georg Lukács, was arguably the most knowledgeable Marxist interpreter of the history of philosophy. Since Engels, Marxists have often roundly and routinely condemned a rich intellectual tradition which they knew poorly at best. On the contrary, Lukács possessed a solid knowledge of modern philosophy, an exceptional grasp of German Idealism, and a more than passing acquaintance with later European thought. This knowledge of modern philosophy is displayed in a long series of articles and books, whose polemical, often political, nature does not obscure their innovative, always learned, frequently insightful character.

The purpose of this paper is to examine the main features of Lukács' reading of modern philosophy. As both the structure of this period and Lukács' approach to it are complex, it will be useful to indicate some features of the discussion in advance. The discussion begins with an account of various attitudes towards the history of philosophy, then turns to a description of Lukács' reading of the modern philosophical tradition, and finally considers his interpretation of Hegel in greater detail. The attention to different approaches to the history of philosophy is meant to situate Lukács' Marxist perspective against a wider interpretative background. In the description of his perspective, it will be useful to differentiate his views on philosophy in general, on modern philosophy, on German Idealism, and on Hegel's thought. In the present context, Hegel's position is significant as a test case for Lukács' Marxist reading of the history of philosophy. Since Lukács is well-known for his interpretation of Marx in relation to classical German philosophy, and to forestall possible misunderstanding, let me note that I will have little to say specifically about Marx' position.

T. Rockmore (ed.), Lukács Today, 221–241.

As merely one approach to the history of philosophy, it will be useful to situate Lukács' Marxist perspective in the wider context of forms of interpretation. For present purposes, it is unnecessary to provide more than a schematic description of the history of the history of philosophy, a discipline which is at best imperfectly known.[1] It will be sufficient to distinguish some main attitudes towards past philosophy.

In Greek thought, an explicit theory of the history of philosophy is not yet present. Neither Plato nor Aristotle regards the history of philosophy as more than a collection of the views of previous thinkers, beginning with Thales. Plato occasionally mentions his predecessors' views, but he never studies them systematically. Aristotle is more interested than Plato in prior philosophy, since he often analyzes earlier views of a topic before stating his own position. But he does not appear to possess a specific theory of the relation of the history of philosophy to philosophy.

For the Greeks, the views of previous thinkers were an optional concern at most. This attitude changes rapidly in modern philosophy, where we encounter two other, diametrically opposed, perspectives. On the one hand, there is the claim that the history of philosophy is irrelevant to philosophy. This claim, which follows, for instance, from Kant's concern to differentiate between systematic and historical approaches to philosophy[2], motivates the desire, frequent in the modern philosophical tradition, to begin again from the beginning. The belief that philosophy must not be confused with its history is a constant theme in modern thought. On the other hand, there is the claim, due to Hegel, that philosophy and the history of philosophy are strictly inseparable.[3]

Hegel's insistence on the inseparability of philosophy and its history introduces several major changes in our understanding of the preceding tradition. First, it provides a way to grasp the history of philosophy as a unitary process, unfolding over time. According to Hegel, since its inception philosophy has always been concerned with the problem of knowledge, which he regards as the demonstration of the unity of subjectivity and objectivity. Second, and as a direct consequence, Hegel introduces teleology into the development of the philosophical tradition; later positions build upon their predecessors, which they cannot ignore. Third, Hegel argues for a relation between thought and its historical context. The direct result of this argument is to deny the belief, expressed often in the philosophical tradition since the Greeks, that philosophy, or thought in general, is independent of its surroundings.

This latter point is useful to distinguish between Marx and Marxism, whose views are often conflated. Marx never criticizes philosophy as such. Rather, he criticizes a form of philosophy, above all the positions of Hegel and the Young Hegelians. According to Marx, the inability of German philosophers to comprehend social reality is due to their failure to understand that the human subject is rooted in the social world. This leads to a methodological deficiency in that German thought seeks to descend from Heaven to earth whereas the correct approach is to ascend from earth to Heaven. Because of their distance from social reality, German thinkers cannot grasp it.[4]

Marxists often hold a different, more radical, view of philosophy. Whereas Marx rejects some kinds of philosophy, since Engels Marxists have frequently equated philosophy as such with ideology, which they distinguish from science. Only science can provide a true picture of the way things are. Philosophy in general is no more than the conceptually distorted reflection of the socially distorted context, which is the result of capitalism.[5]

The difference between the attitudes of Marx and Marxism to philosophy can be expressed in terms of Hegel's thesis about the relation of thought to its context. Whereas Marx suggests that some philosophy is deficient because it is too distant from the context it seeks to know, Marxists often regard all philosophy as distorted by an inability to distance itself from its social surroundings. In view of this difference, it is significant that Lukács' basic orientation to the history of philosophy is less Marxian than Marxist.

II

Lukács' reading of the history of philosophy is already prominent in his initial Marxist work, *History and Class Consciousness*, especially in the celebrated central essay. In later writings, Lukács demonstrated an increasingly deep acquaintance with the German Idealist tradition, especially Hegel's position, and wider knowledge of selected strands of more recent European thought.

Lukács' attitude towards the history of philosophy is similar to the Young Hegelian belief that the philosophical tradition comes to an end in Hegel's thought. The central feature of Lukács' interpretation of the history of philosophy, present throughout his entire Marxist period, is the unqualified acceptance of Marx' position as the truth of German Idealism, from which it differs not in degree but in kind.

Clearly, Lukács' reading of the philosophical tradition presupposes an understanding of Marx' relation to it. In Lukács' writings, we can distinguish two ways in which he understands this relation. In the initial stage, present in *History and Class Consciousness* only, Lukács is close to Engels' view, which he criticizes on other grounds. Here Lukács suggests that philosophy is ideology; and he further suggests that Marx' position - in particular the analysis of commodity structure - is science. Like Engels, Lukács at this point presupposes a clear distinction between philosophy and science, and further believes that Marx' position is not philosophy but science.

In subsequent writings, Lukács relativizes the Marxist dichotomy between philosophy and science; he silently moves away from this central thesis of Engels' approach at the same time as he publicly retracts earlier criticism of Engels' position. Lukács defends Engels' view of the exclusive dichotomy between idealism and materialism, although he no longer regards materialism as an extra-philosophic science. From this perspective, materialism is the theory which provides knowledge of society. Idealism cannot offer social knowledge, but it is an indispensable stage for the later emergence of Marx' materialism. Lukács further follows Engels' rejection of any possibility of an alternative to the idealism/materialism dichotomy, for instance in existentialism.[6] And he insists on the negative role of bourgeois thought in a detailed discussion of the relation of fascism in particular, and irrationalism in general, to later German Idealism.[7]

III

This description of Lukács' attitude towards philosophy is entirely general. To render it more specific, we need to determine how he differentiates between different philosophical periods. In his initial Marxist phase, Lukács draws these distinctions in terms of the problem of the reification of consciousness. It is well-known that Hegel regarded the entire history of philosophy as a series of dialectically interrelated attempts to resolve the central, on-going problem of the relation of thought and being. Lukács' view of reification is a form of the subject/object problem, which he transposes into a relation between social consciousness and society. The term "reification" is understood at this point as the effect of which the fetishism of commodities is the cause.[8]

We can begin with Lukács' understanding of the Greek tradition. Lukács is not unaware of ancient philosophy. In his final stage, he discusses Aristotle's view in the course of an attempt to develop a Marxist social ontology. But in his initial Marxist phase, he merely mentions ancient philosophy in passing, although he does so in a manner which reveals an un-Hegelian attitude towards the history of philosophy. As noted, Hegel stressed the overall unity of the philosophical tradition; on the contrary, Lukács insists on the absolute discontinuity of its ancient and modern portions.

This insistence is the result of a strict inference from his concept of reification, a phenomenon which he understands as correlated with the form of society in which it occurs. Lukács acknowledges the presence of forms of reification even in ancient Greece. But the qualitative difference which separates it from modern society means that modern philosophical concerns are strictly incomparable with those of earlier philosophy. Accordingly, he denies the underlying continuity of the philosophical tradition.

> But as the problems and solutions of the philosophy of the Ancients were embedded in a wholly different society, it is only natural that they should be qualitatively different from those of modern philosophy. Hence from the standpoint of any adequate interpretation, it is as idle to imagine that we can find in Plato a precursor of Kant (as does Natorp), as it is to undertake the task of erecting a philosophy on Aristotle (as does Thomas Aquinas).[9]

Although the claim for the discontinuity between the ancient and modern portions of the tradition is interesting, the picture of ancient philosophy is not clearly drawn. The opposite is the case for modern philosophy, especially German Idealism. Here the description is clear, and the stress is placed on continuity. One might expect that Lukács would approach German Idealism from the vantage point of modern philosophy; in fact he reverses this procedure in order to interpret all of modern philosophy from the perspective of German Idealism, in particular through Kant's position.

In his reliance on Kant, Lukács follows Hegel. It is not widely enough known that in the *Differenzschrift*, Hegel's initial philosophical publication, he stressed his belief that the contemporary philosophical task was to bring to a close the revolution initiated by the critical philosophy. And in the mature description of his system, in the *Encyclopedia of the Philosophical Sciences*, Hegel construed the entire metaphysical tradition in relation to Kant's view, that is as pre-critical, critical, and post-critical moments.[10] But since Lukács also owes allegiance to Marxism, the result is a strangely hybrid approach to modern philosophy, consisting of elements drawn from sources not often combined within a single theory.

The reliance on Marxism is easily understood in terms of Lukács' unswerving commitment to Bolshevism throughout his Marxist period. The interest in Kantian themes is less obvious, but can be grasped through Lukács' close contact, during his years in Heidelberg, with many leading neo-Kantians, especially with Emil Lask.[11] Although not often mentioned, Lask's influence on Lukács' neo-Kantian approach to modern philosophy is clear and deep.

In general, the neo-Kantians drew a distinction between fact and value, which is better known in contemporary circles as the 'is/ought' distinction. In his dissertation, which was quickly republished as a book, Lask applied this distinction to the interpretation of German Idealism.[12] He used it to distinguish Kant's analytic approach from Hegel's synthetic perspective. According to Lask, Fichte's thought, which mediates between Kant and Hegel, is vitiated by an incompatibility between form and content, or thought and its object. For the neo-Kantian Lask, the Fichtean object of experience is transformed into a kind of thing-in-itself, which cannot be known because of the asymmetry between form and content.

Lask's brilliant Fichte interpretation was influential on other writers. Richard Kroner[13], for instance, adapted it as the basis of his interpretation of Fichte and Schelling as merely transitional figures between Kant and Hegel. In his own reading of modern philosophy, Lukács generalizes Lask's neo-Kantian approach to Fichte's position to include all of bourgeois philosophy. On his view, bourgeois philosophy is intrinsically unable to grasp the nature of society in which it arises because of a tension between form and content. Quick to grasp the resources of a Kantian approach to modern philosophy, Lukács argues that Kantian themes are characteristic of modern philosophy from its beginning until Marx.

In Lukács' approach, we can distinguish a general claim about modern philosophy from a restricted claim about German Idealism. It is well-known that the Copernican Revolution, which is the basis of the critical philosophy, requires a view of the subject as active. More precisely, a necessary condition of the possibility of knowledge is to deny the independence of the object, which then becomes dependent on the knowing subject. According to Lukács, this view of the relation of subjectivity to objectivity is the solution to the single problem, which traverses the entire period of modern philosophy.

> In ways diverging from that of Vico who in many respects was not understood and who became influential only much later, the whole of modern philosophy has been preoccupied with this problem. From systematic doubt and the *cogito ergo sum* of Descartes, to Hobbes, Spinoza and Leibniz, there is a direct line of development whose central strand, rich in variations, is the idea that the object of cognition can be known by us for the reason that, and to the degree in which, it has been created by ourselves.[14]

According to Lukács, the modern concern with epistemology is further related to the demand for system. This demand gives rise to reflection on the conditions of systematicity and an awareness of the impossibility of total system. Briefly stated, the difficulty is the tension between the aim at universal system and the recognition of the facticity of the given. Lukács states his understanding of this tension in an important, frequently quoted passage, in which he differentiates classical German philosophy from its modern predecessors. The distinction between rationalism and German Idealism lies in their respective attitudes towards the problem of system. Although rationalism raises this demand, it ignores the effect on it of the given, which is only recognized later in German Idealism. Its acknowledgment of this 'antinomy' characterizes German Idealism.

> It is evident that the principle of systematization is not reconcilable with the recognition of any 'facticity', of a 'content' which in principle cannot be deduced from the principle of form and which, therefore, has simply to be accepted as actuality. The greatness, the paradox and the tragedy of classical German philosophy lies in the fact that - unlike Spinoza - it no longer dismisses every *donné*[e] as non-existent, causing it to vanish behind the monumental architecture of the rational forms produced by the understanding. Instead, while grasping and holding on to the irrational character of the actual contents of the concepts it strives to go beyond this, to overcome it and to erect a system.[15]

On the other hand, Lukács perceives a further flaw of German Idealism in the failure to understand that thought is ultimately rooted in the social context which it seeks to interpret.

> For we are not concerned to present a history of modern philosophy, not even in crude outline. We wish only to sketch the connection between the fundamental problems of this philosophy and the basis in existence from which these problems spring and to which they strive to return by the road of the understanding.[16]

If thought is in some undetermined sense parasitic on the wider social context from which it emerges, then an abstract vision can never be satisfactory. For abstract thought is inadequate to grasp the nature of the social context. This inadequacy is reflected in the antinomic character of classical German thought. The only way to emerge from this conceptual blind alley is through a fundamental theory of society itself. Thus for Lukács the inherently problematic structure of modern German philosophy leads to Marx' position:

> For at this stage in the history of mankind there is no problem that does not ultimately lead back to that question [*i.e.* the analysis of commodities - *T.R.*] and there is no solution that could not be found in the solution to the riddle of commodity-structure .... That is to say, the problem of commodities must not be considered in

isolation, or even regarded as the central problem in economics, but as the central structural problem of capitalist society in all its aspects.[17]

It follows that for Lukács, philosophy is not the science of sciences in a Platonic sense; and it is not independent of the social context. Rather, philosophy concerns real social problems, but on a conceptual level where they cannot be resolved. Accordingly, the real social problems, which philosophy takes up, must be solved on an extra-philosophic plane.

IV

In the discussion so far, I have tried to provide a faithful account of Lukács' approach to philosophy, especially German Idealism. I have emphasized how he combines Marxist and Kantian themes in order to argue that so-called bourgeois philosophy is inadequate to comprehend bourgeois society. In the remainder of this paper, I would like to test Lukács' view of bourgeois philosophy through his reading of Hegel's position.

As for philosophy in general, Lukács' study of Hegel is never an end in itself; it is always related to his own form of Marxism. Lukács' interpretation of Hegel's thought is interesting in itself, for the light it throws on Hegel's position, and as a specifically Marxist reading of absolute idealism. From the latter perspective, Lukács' Hegel discussion is doubly distinguished: as one of the first Marxist accounts of the Hegelian background to Marx' thought, and as the first full-length, Marxist study of Hegel's thought.

Lukács was certainly not the first Marxist to call attention to the significance of Hegel for Marx' position. This significance was noted by Engels; and it was later restated by Lenin. Lukács was further not the only Marxist to revive the earlier approach to Marx through Hegel's view. Another prominent Marxist writer who participated in this revival was Karl Korsch.[18] But at least among Marxists, Lukács' Hegel reading was distinguished by the depth of his knowledge of absolute idealism and of the surrounding German philosophical tradition.

Lukács' attention to Hegel in *History and Class Consciousness* inaugurated a new phase of the discussion through his concern to elucidate the precise relation between Marx' thought and idealism. In practice, this concern has been both useful and detrimental. Its obvious value lies in directing attention to Marx' relation to the German philosophical tradition, with special attention to Hegel. But the utility of that approach, which casts light on the genesis of Marx' thought, is limited by the unfortunate tendency, to which it also leads, to limit the discussion merely to that problem. If, as Engels suggests[19], the proximal origin of Marx' thought is in Hegel's *Philosophy of Right*, it does not follow that he did not also draw on other positions.

Attention to Hegel is not a prominent feature of Lukács' pre-Marxist period. In the lengthy Marxist period, which begins with the famous conversion to Bolshevism in December 1918, Hegel becomes a permanent feature of Lukács' discussion. I propose now to describe the main phases of Lukács' Hegel discussion, which we can correlate with three main works: *History and Class Consciousness*, *The Young Hegel*, and *Zur Ontologie des gesellschaftlichen Seins*. The view of Hegel which emerges from inspection of these three books is not the same in all respects, since Lukács' perspective evolves over time. But there is throughout a constant concern to demonstrate an antinomy between system and method in Hegel's thought. It is this steady emphasis on the manner in which Hegel's position is vitiated by an intrinsic tension between form and content which makes it an excellent test of Lukács' view of the inadequacy of bourgeois thought.

In his early Marxist writings, Lukács approaches Hegel's position within the framework of his post-Hegelian, neo-Kantian reading of modern thought. From this perspective, Hegel's thought appears as an effort to overcome the intrinsic tension between rationality and irrationality present in the central concept of the thing-in-itself. His great achievement is to discover a dialectical view of history, in which Kant's rigid opposition is relativized through the historical process. This alone establishes Hegel's philosophy as the high-point of German thought. But in the effort to discover the unity of rational form and irrational content, Hegel is driven beyond history to mythology. A correct approach to this antinomy requires a systematic analysis of the irrational contents of experience as the reified product of modern industrial society. For a solution of the central problem of classical German philosophy is possible only if we acknowledge that the commodity is the universal category of social being.

Like the interpretation of modern thought, at this point the interpretation of Hegel's position is extremely broad. Although Lukács has already acquired a deep knowledge of Hegel's thought, the discussion lacks the detailed reference to different texts, which it will later exhibit. But Lukács has already accepted the standard Marxist dichotomy between idealism and materialism as a distinction in kind. In later writings, he never questions this distinction, which he consistently presupposes as the basis of his claim for the inadequacy of bourgeois thought.

Another feature of Lukács' early Hegel interpretation is his emphasis on the subject/object problem as centrally important and as solved by Marx. The origin of the latter claim is in Engels' view of the distinction between idealism and materialism as the watershed problem of all philosophy.[20]   At this stage, the introductory nature of Engels' philosophical discussion is clearly acknowledged by Lukács, for instance in comments on Engels' attempt to refute the thing-in-itself through reference to experiment and industry. In his later writings, Lukács publicly takes back his criticism of Engels, although he silently renounces the latter's simplistic approach to all philosophy in terms of the so-called watershed problem.

In virtue of his belief that Marx' position is the truth of Hegel's, Lukács' interpretation of absolute idealism is foreshortened. For he never considers Hegel's thought as other than the most important source of Marx'. In a sense, Lukács' Marxist interpretation of Hegel resembles Hegel's own reading of his great contemporaries, Fichte and Schelling. Although he continued to regard them as the only other contemporary philosophers worthy of the name - after an initial fascination with Fichte - Hegel increasingly presented their positions as mere stepping stones on the way to his own, devoid of intrinsic interest.

V

As noted, Lukács' initial approach to Hegel and classical German philosophy aims to demonstrate that Marx, on the plane of political economy, resolves the central problem of bourgeois thought. The basis of this assertion is the traditional Marxist distinction between philosophy and political economy. From this perspective, Marx' position must be devoid of philosophical elements - otherwise it would be philosophy. But the belated publication of several of Marx' early writings, including the *Paris Manuscripts*, made it increasingly difficult to maintain a distinction in kind between philosophy and political economy; and it further made it unimportant to hold that German bourgeois thought was ignorant of economic themes.

Like Lukács' other works from his Stalinist period, notably his studies of existentialism and irrationalism, his monograph on Hegel is characterized by an unpleasant form of Marxist orthodoxy. This zealous orthodoxy is present even in the new edition for the German Democratic Republic, completed in January 1954, that is, after Stalin's death. Examples include: the abandonment of all criticism of Engels, whose insights are continually praised; a stress on Feuerbach, whom Lukács controversially describes as the indispensable link between Hegel and Marx, and as a thinker on Hegel's level; the assertion, later echoed by Mészáros[21], that Lenin was aware of the content of the *Paris Manuscripts* although he did not read them; and the praise, not only of Marx and Engels, but of Lenin and even Stalin as great critics of Hegel.

Despite its politically orthodox flavor, as an approach to the history of philosophy this book is more satisfactory than *History and Class*

Consciousness. In part, this is due to Lukács' correction of some earlier errors, including the celebrated conflation of alienation and objectification under the heading of "reification"; this conflation is now mistakenly attributed to Hegel. There are also basic changes in Lukács' approach to philosophy, which enable him to take more seriously its claim to truth. In particular, Lukács now seems to renounce the traditional Marxist interpretation of philosophy as ideology in favor of Hegel's view that a position is limited by the historical moment in which it occurs. He applies this idea to the interpretation of Hegel's thought, which he here regards as composed of philosophic and economic components.

In spite of his violent critique of bourgeois thought, it is no accident that Lukács' Hegel study has been well received within the non-Marxist Hegel discussion.[22] This study is an example of the best kind of Hegel research: informed, patient, aware of conflicting points of view, and concerned to place Hegel in the historical context. Lukács here indicates a mastery of the early texts, their historical and conceptual background, and their prior discussion in the secondary literature. His inquiry falls naturally into four parts, corresponding to Hegel's residence in Berne, Frankfurt, and Jena, followed by a careful analysis of the break with Schelling and the structure of the *Phenomenology of Spirit.*

Lukács describes his study of Hegel as part of the attempt to develop a Marxist history of classical German philosophy. This task requires a demonstration of the relation between philosophy and the great socio-cultural events of the period, especially the French Revolution. Lukács' thesis is that, as the only German thinker who made a serious effort to come to grips with the Industrial Revolution in England, Hegel's view of dialectic is based on a grasp of political economy. Despite the limits of his idealist perspective, his position is continuous with the birth of dialectical materialism, in particular through the discovery of the dialectic of economic life. More precisely, Lukács intends his discussion as an illustration of Marx' well-known remark in the *Paris Manuscripts*, which he cites:

> The greatness of Hegel's *Phenomenology* is then ... that Hegel views the self-creation of man as a process ... and therefore that he grasps the nature of labor and understands objective man, true, because real man as the product of his own labor.[23]

According to Lukács, "Marx shows here the extent to which Hegelian philosophy forms an analogue of English classical economics."[24] This interpretation, centered on the role of economics in Hegel's thought, is helpful in revealing a then unstudied aspect of the position. Lukács' pioneering contribution to the understanding of this side of Hegel's thought has received explicit acknowledgement in the specialized Hegel discussion.[25] But this approach is also restrictive in that it tends to take the part for the whole. Marx' appropriation of Hegelian insights in the formation of his own perspective is evident in an illegitimate transition - in fact a *non-sequitur* - between the idea of the self-production of man as a process and the idea of real man as the product of his own labor. Certainly, Hegel does not equate these two ideas, although their equation forms the basis of Lukács' Hegel interpretation of Hegel's thought in this book.

As it is not possible to follow the analysis in detail here, I shall restrict this account to mention of several main themes. Against Rosenkranz, Hegel's biographer, Lukács maintains that Hegel adopts the standpoint of modern political economy. Hegel's theory of history leads to the concrete realm of human praxis, which he correctly regards as a dynamic complex of contradictions. The limitation of Hegel's economic thought, which Lukács obscurely relates to its idealist character, is two-fold: the failure to deduce class structure from economics, and the related failure to analyze the relation of state and government in terms of class conflict.

There is no question that Lukács' discussion throws considerable light on a significant, but little known, dimension of Hegel's thought. But it should be noted in passing that the limitation of the discussion to the early writings enables Lukács to avoid a test of his thesis that Hegel's grasp of economics is restricted by its idealist character, for instance, through study of the *Philosophy of Right*.

Insistence on the significance of Hegel's knowledge of economics for his position leads to a re-examination of his view of religion. Lukács' treatment of this delicate topic, important for an understanding of Hegel's position, is judicious and fair, especially by comparison with commentators who strive to draw Hegel wholly towards or wholly away from religion. Lukács rejects the attempts by Häring and Lasson, no doubt influenced by Hegel's proud claim to be a Lutheran[26], to assimilate absolute idealism to Protestantism. According to Lukács, Hegel's initially critical attitude towards religion in Berne was replaced by a favorable attitude in Frankfurt, which then became ambiguous in Jena. He quotes Heine's well-known remark on actuality and rationality, whose authenticity has recently been confirmed[27], in order to suggest that contemporary radical intellectuals regarded Hegel as a progressive thinker at least. He further suggests that Hegel remained ambiguous on the question of religion because he was unwilling to concede that otherworldliness is its essence. This point correlates well with his observation about Hegel's later unwillingness to seek a social solution outside contemporary society after the latter had ceased to believe in the reconstitution of the Greek social context.

One of the most interesting features of the book is the discussion of

Hegel's view of alienation. Lukács' analysis depends on a distinction between positivity (*Positivität*) and alienation (*Entäusserung*). In Hegel's early writings, "positivity" refers to a suspension of the moral autonomy of the subject, for instance, in the difference between social freedom and dead subjectivity. In Jena, he gradually introduced a fundamental distinction between positivity, which he now understood as "a quality of social formations, objects, things" and alienation construed as "a specific mode of human activity as a result of which specific social institutions come into being and acquire the objective nature peculiar to them".[28] As concerns the *Phenomenology*, Lukács distinguishes three stages of the Hegelian concept, in relation to work, fetishism, and thinghood, or objectivity.

The function of this part of the discussion in Lukács' larger argument is clear. It enables him to locate the antecedent of Marx' concept of alienation in Hegel's thought; and it further enables him to attribute his own conflation of alienation and objectification to Hegel's idealism. Accordingly, Marx' criticism of Hegel's concept of alienation in the *Phenomenology* becomes a key step in the transition from idealism to materialism.

Despite the interest of his discussion, Lukács' analysis of Hegel's view of alienation does not achieve its goal; it does not demonstrate the superiority of Marx' concept. Clearly, Hegel and Marx employ this term - although Marx uses others as well, such as *Entfremdung* - for different ends. In a word, the difference between Marx and Hegel is not that the former solves the latter's problems through a change in method; Marx' concern is not for precisely the same set of problems, but for another set of problems from a different perspective.

VI

Lukács' account of the theme of political economy is a mature, knowledgeable study of this aspect of Hegel's early thought. Although the overall thesis of this work - that Marx is the truth of Hegel - is unchanged, and despite the restriction to a single theme, the study offers a fuller and more satisfying treatment of Hegel's position than did *History and Class Consciousness*. The third, final phase of Lukács' Hegel study is provided by 'Hegels falsche und echte Ontologie'.[29] This is a lengthy chapter in the huge, unfinished treatise, which Lukács intended as the crown of his lifework.

It is beyond the scope of this discussion to characterize the latter work further than as a Marxist ontology based on what is valid in Hegel's view of this domain. In *The Young Hegel*, Lukács was concerned with Hegel's early writings. In the final phase of his Hegel interpretation, the focus shifts back to the position as a whole, mainly in the *Encyclopedia of the Philosophical Sciences* and the *Science of Logic*, in a discussion which is richer than *History and Class Consciousness*, but more schematic than *The Young Hegel*. At this point, an interesting development is the appearance of some criticism of Marxism, for instance, concerning the excesses of Stalinism and the shallow character of Engels' remarks on categorial transition. But, in other respects, Lukács now accepts the classical Marxist approach, including the need to base a dialectical view of society on a dialectic of nature. This point, which derives from Engels' concern, in his final period, to develop a dialectic of nature, is important for Lukács' interpretation of Hegel in this work.

Once more, Lukács maintains that Hegel's position contains an intrinsic antinomy between method and system. Interestingly, he makes little direct reference either to economics or to alienation. The result is to abandon two themes central to his previous Hegel inter-pretation: the stress on political economy in Hegel's writings, and its relation to the problem of reification. Rather, at this point he argues for a tension in Hegel's thought, which results from the presence in it side by side of two different ontological perspectives.

In *The Young Hegel*, Lukács suggested that Hegel's position con-tains both dialectic and mere speculation. He now develops this point through Hegel's relation to previous thinkers. According to Lukács, where Hegel's ontology is most dependent on earlier positions, in particular critical philosophy, it is mainly false; where it strikes out in new directions, it provides insights which, like Aristotle's, are enormously useful at present.

Unfortunately, Lukács died before he was able to complete this book. In view of its unfinished nature, it cannot be expected to be fully coherent or even devoid of repetition. The discussion is unequally divided into two parts: a longer account of 'Hegels Dialektik "mitten im Dünger der Widersprüche"'[30], an expression borrowed from Marx; and a shorter account of 'Hegels dialektische Ontologie und die Reflexions-bestimmungen'.[31] In general terms, the theme of the initial part is the identification of contradictions following from the coexistence in Hegel's position of two different ontologies; in the latter part, Lukács provides an account of that form of Hegelian ontology which he regards as viable.

In the first part, Lukács maintains that the antinomic character of Hegel's ontology must be understood through the dual perspective of Enlightenment thought and the French Revolution. The Enlightenment stressed reason as the final principle of nature and society; and it further insisted that an ontology of social being can be constructed only on the basis of an ontology of nature. Hegel's intent is to develop a single ontology englobing nature and history, in which the former grounds the latter; this can be seen from the fact that his dialectic of history arises directly out of nature. His dialectic makes two presuppositions: (1) history has an immanent teleology, which is irreducible to individual action; (2) and from this methodological perspective, the coming together (*Zusammenfallen*) of fulfilled idea and historical present is grounded in logic.

Despite Hegel's monistic aim, inspection reveals two disparate ontological perspectives within his position. On the one hand, there is the logic of dialectical contradiction. This is the source of Hegel's theory of history, which results from his reinterpretation of the Heraclitean view of change under the heading of the concept of immanent contradiction. On the other hand, there is the concept of spirit, which is Hegel's attempt to adapt the Enlightenment concept of nature.

The principal antinomies in Hegel's position result from the incompatibility of his two ontological views. A cardinal example is the identical subject/object, familiar from Lukács' initial Marxist phase, which he now describes as a mere philosophical myth, leading to an undervaluation of nature. Beyond Hegel, Lukács clearly has in mind his own effort to uncover this identity in Marx' thought. But it is not clear why this result is unattainable. Lukács appears merely to assert this unattainability since, as a follower of Marx, he rejects the view that social contradictions can be reconciled within the framework of advanced industrial society. Other examples Lukács cites, which follow from Hegel's concern to base his view of society on an ontology of nature, include: a tension between his idea of work (although he provides a correct analysis of the relation of natural causality and teleology) and the idea of work in English political economy; and the incoherent appeal to work to relate chemism and mechanism. In sum, although Hegel grounds ontology in logic, he also supposedly 'privileges' thought before reality, which imparts a religious tinge to his position.

Lukács' insistence on the tension in Hegel's thought between its logical and experiential dimension is an important point. This is a recurrent problem, which arises as well in the views of Kant and Fichte. This is not the place to discuss this problem in detail. Suffice it to say that this difficulty is the inescapable consequence of any attempt to evolve a categorial schema for the interpretation of experience on a wholly apriori basis. The only way to avoid this difficulty within a categorial perspective is to make it only relatively apriori in respect to experience. In that way, the categorial framework arises from experience, is useful to interpret it, and ultimately depends upon it.

Since the consequences of Lukács' objection are important, it is unfortunate that he does not pursue his criticism. Rather, in the second part he makes a different argument. Here he maintains that the opposition in Hegel's position between two incompatible ontological perspectives can be overcome if a dialectical logic arises directly out of experience. According to Lukács, the appropriately dialectical logic is available in the concept of reflection (*Reflexionsbestimmungen*), which he regards as Hegel's central methodological discovery. This concept is useful on a number of levels, including: (1) to relate reason and understanding in order to surpass Kant and Fichte; (2) to relate the concepts of *Schein*, *Erscheinung*, and *Wesen*; (3) to enable us to grasp immediacy and mediacy as specifically social forms of ontological phenomena; (4) and to comprehend the dialectical view of work as a process of interaction, through which Hegel surpasses the Aristotelian, teleological understanding of the same phenomena.

According to Lukács, the theory of reflection is doubly useful: to found what Marx understood as the interaction of society and nature, and to found a dialectical ontology of social being.

VII

In the discussion so far, I have limited myself to a general account of Lukács' Marxist-inspired reading of the history of philosophy, with special attention to his interpretation of Hegel. I have stressed that for Lukács what the Marxists call the bourgeois German philosophical tradition is unable to resolve the problem of knowledge posed by the social context, which is solved by Marx on methodologically different grounds. At this point, I would like to make some general remarks towards an assessment of Lukács' approach to the history of philosophy.

I believe that the insistence on method accounts both for the strengths and weaknesses of Lukács' approach. Now, in itself, the attention to method is not novel. Since Descartes and at least until Husserl, a long, distinguished list of modern thinkers has maintained that the decisive step in philosophy is to discover a method which can open the path to knowledge which is otherwise closed. The originality of Lukács' discussion lies in the application of a neo-Kantian perspective, derived proximally from Lask, to interpret modern philosophy and to prove the Marxist claim of Marx' superiority.

Lukács' emphasis on method as the decisive element enables him to make three contributions. First, he is able to present a unitary reading of the entire modern tradition from a single perspective. Second, he can understand Marx' position against the background of the German idealist tradition, which he does not merely dismiss. The importance of Lukács' historically oriented reading of Marx' thought is widely recognized. It is significant that Kolakowski, who is highly critical of Lukács, also regards him as the first interpreter to understand Marx' position through the stress on the Hegelian interplay of subject and object in Marx' thought. Third, the vantage point of method makes it possible for Lukács to go beyond mere assertion to argue for the superiority of Marx' approach through detailed analysis.

Lukács' intent is clear. His suggestion is that the contradictions of social being can be comprehended through a logic of reflection, which is incompatible with the concept of an identical subject/object. The wider point is that Hegel's teleological theory of work provides the basis for an adequate theory of reflection. According to Lukács, the theory of reflection is doubly useful: to found what Marx understood as the interaction of society and nature, interplay of subject and object.[32] Third, the vantage point of method makes it possible for Lukács to go beyond mere assertion to argue for the superiority of Marx' approach through detailed analysis.

My criticism concerns the effect of Lukács' political commitment on his interpretation of the history of philosophy. Although he is not the only writer to have a political commitment, the latter cannot be allowed to interfere with the approach to the texts. In Lukács' case, his commitment to the superiority of Marx' position over all others, on political grounds, means that his interpretation of the history of philosophy is not aposteriori, but apriori. Instead of 'fitting' his analysis to the text, he is obliged to 'fit' the text to his predetermined view of it. In the Kantian perspective Lukács adopts, there is an intrinsic tension between the apriori form of what he knows must be true, and the aposteriori content, independent of his political commitment, through whose analysis he performs his demonstration.

This point will bear restatement in general form. As noted, Lukács' concern is to show that Marx' position is the truth of modern philosophy, in particular of Hegel's. In order to prove his claim, he interprets all of modern philosophy, including Hegel's position, through Marx' view, which he then presents as the positive outcome of the philosophical tradition. This way of loading the conceptual dice may be politically reassuring, but it does not demonstrate Lukács' reading of Marx' thought. In language familiar from *The German Ideology*, we can say that Lukács only appears to ascend from earth to Heaven. In fact, the logic of his argument demonstrates that he descends from Heaven to earth, that is, from Marx to modern philosophy, German Idealism, and Hegel, before ascending again to that place from whence he came.

Several examples will show that Lukács forces the textual evidence to fit a preconceived schema. The description of modern philosophy *in toto* as a series of variations on the central theme "that the object of cognition can be known by us for the reason that, and to the degree in which, it has been created by ourselves"[33] is seriously misleading. No prominent representative of either rationalism or German Idealism holds that the object of knowledge is created by ourselves. Beginning with Descartes, rationalists typically maintained that the problem of knowledge concerns an independent object; starting with Kant, German

Idealists typically argued that the subject produces its object as a necessary condition of knowledge.

A second example is Lukács' demonstration, central to his reading of the history of philosophy, of the superiority of materialism over idealism for a grasp of the social context. He does not test this claim against the relevant portions of Hegel's writings, as noted, or of other German Idealists. But he must test his claim against the texts, if it is to be accepted on grounds other than simple faith. Lukács further assumes, at least initially, that the aims of Hegel and Marx are relevantly similar, so that one can succeed where the other has failed. Yet in his later renunciation of an identical subject/object as an idealist fancy, Lukács implies that Marx and Hegel have different aims, which renders their views strictly incomparable.

A third example concerns the relevance of an approach to modern philosophy as such through the problem of method. Such an approach is arguably most pertinent for the rationalists in general and for Kant. But it is questionable concerning empiricism. And it is specifically inadequate for the views of Hegel and Marx, both of whom refuse the isolation of form from content. Hegel's critique of the critical philosophy commits him to a synthesis of form and content which precludes their separation.[34] Marx' insistence on practice (*Praxis*) as the standard of truth means that he cannot defend an apriori method.[35] More generally, neither Hegel nor Marx has a specifiable method; it follows that an approach to either view or an attempt to characterize their differences from this perspective cannot succeed.

This last remark points towards a tentative conclusion. I have stressed Lukács' concern to establish that Marx' position is the truth of the entire philosophical tradition, above all of German Idealism, through consideration of the problem of method. The reductionism inherent in this approach distorts his interpretation of modern philosophy in at least two ways. For Lukács cannot recognize the intrinsic worth of bourgeois philosophy other than as a source of Marx' position which, accordingly, differs from it not in degree, but in kind; and he extends to the entire modern philosophical tradition a theme which is arguably central to a part only.

I believe that Lukács' political commitment often blunts the acuity of his insight into the history of philosophy. He is most insightful when he ignores the intrinsic logic of his strategy to disclose new dimensions of previous thought, such as: the concept of reification in Marx' view, the change in the idea of alienation from Hegel to Marx, or the extent of Hegel's acquaintance with political economy. He is least insightful when he makes sweeping claims; for instance, for the unlimited value of Marx' position, or the complete inability of bourgeois thought to know social reality.

Lukács' insistence on the significance of the relation of form to content for the problem of knowledge applies to his own reading of the history of philosophy. His reading suffers from a methodological flaw, which inhibits his comprehension of the philosophical tradition. This flaw lies in his consistent tendency to place the form of the interpretation before the content. For as concerns the history of philosophy, and knowledge in general, it is always correct to adapt the content to the form, or the theory to its content; and it is never correct to proceed conversely.

NOTES

1.   On this point, see Lucien Braun, *Histoire des histoires de la philosophie*, Paris, Ophrys, 1973.

2.   See, *e.g.*, *Critique of Pure Reason*, B 864, where Kant distinguishes between *cognitio ex datis* and *cognitio ex principiis*.

3.   This theme, which is a constant in Hegel's thought, first appears in the account of the 'Historical View of Philosophical Systems', at the beginning of the *Differenzschrift*, his initial philosophical publication.

4.   This is the view developed in *The German Ideology*, Part 1, Section A.

5.   For this view, see F. Engels, *Ludwig Feuerbach and the Outcome of Classical German Philosophy*.

6.   See his *Existentialisme ou Marxisme?* Paris, Nagel, 1961.

7.   See his *Die Zerstörung der Vernunft*, Neuwied/Berlin, Luchterhand, 1974, 3 vols.

8.   For this view, see the central essay of *History and Class Consciousness*, 'Reification and the Consciousness of the Proletariat'. For Marx' concept of fetishism, see *Capital*, I, Chapter 1, Part 4.

9.   *History and Class Consciousness*, Rodney Livingstone, trans., Cambridge, Mass., The MIT Press, 1972, p. 111.

10.   On this point, see the important discussion of the 'Attitudes of Thought to Objectivity'.

11.   For Lukács' account of the significance of Lask, see his 'Emil Lask. Ein Nachruf', in *Kant-Studien*, vol. 22 (1918), pp. 349-370. For a study of the relation between Lukács and Lask, see Hartmut Rosshoff, *Emil Lask als Lehrer von Georg Lukács. Zur Form ihres Gegenstandsbegriffs*, Bonn, Bouvier, 1975.

12.   See *Fichtes Idealismus und die Geschichte*, in Emil Lask, *Gesammelte Schriften*, Tübingen, Mohr, 1923, vol. 1.

13.   See his *Von Kant bis Hegel*, Tübingen, Mohr, 1921 and 1924, 2 vols.

14.   *History and Class Consciousness*, p. 112.

15.   *Ibid.* p. 117.

16.   *Ibid.* p. 112.

17.   *Ibid.* p. 83.

18.   See his *Marxismus und Philosophie*, Frankfurt, Europäische Verlaganstalt, 1966.

19.   See F. Engels, *Marx-Engels Werke*, Berlin, Dietz, 1956-1968, vol. 16, p. 362.

20.   See *Ludwig Feuerbach*, Chapter 2: 'Idealism and

Materialism'.

21.   See I. Mészáros, *Marx's Theory of Alienation*, London, Merlin, 1970, p. 93.

22.   See, *e.g.*, Jean Hyppolite, *Studies on Marx and Hegel*, trans. John O'Neill, New York, Harper, 1973, Chapter 4: 'Alienation and Objectification: Commentary on G. Lukács' *The Young Hegel*'.

23.   G. Lukács, *The Young Hegel.* Studies in the Relations between Dialectics and Economics, Rodney Livingstone, trans., Cambridge, Mass., The MIT Press, 1976, p. xxvii.

24.   *Loc. cit.*

25.   See, *e.g.*, H.S. Harris, *Hegel's Development I: Towards the Sunlight*, Oxford, Oxford at the Clarendon Press, 1972.

26.   See G.W.F. Hegel. *Werke in zwanzig Bänden*, Frankfurt, Suhrkamp, 1971, vol. 18, p. 94.

27.   See Shlomo Avineri, 'The Discovery of Hegel's Early Lectures on the *Philosophy of Right*', in *The Owl of Minerva*, vol. 16 no. 2 (Spring 1985), p. 202.

28.   Lukács, *The Young Hegel*, p. 314. Lukács' emphases.

29.   *Zur Ontologie des gesellschaftlichen Seins*, 'Hegels falsche und echte Ontologie', Neuwied/Berlin, Luchterhand, 1971.

30.   *Ibid.* pp. 5-70.

31.   *Ibid.* pp. 71-127.

32.   See Leszek Kolakowski, *Main Currents of Marxism*, P.S. Falla, trans., Oxford, Oxford at the Clarendon Press, 1978, vol. 3, p. 297.

33.   *History and Class Consciousness*, p. 112.

34.   See, *e.g.*, *Enzyklopädie der philosophischen Wissenschaften*, paragraph #10, in *G.W.F. Hegel Werke,* vol. 8, pp. 53-54.

35.   On this point, see the second of the 'Theses on Feuerbach', in *The Marx-Engels Reader*, Robert C. Tucker (ed.), New York, Norton, 1978, p. 144.

PART IV

LUKÁCS' LATER THOUGHT

NICOLAS TERTULIAN

Lukács' *Ontology*

Georg Lukács died in June 1971 without having given his imprimatur for the complete publication of his last, great philosophical work, *Zur Ontologie des gesellschaftlichen Seins* (*On the Ontology of Social Being*).

We can ask ourselves if the voluminous manuscript of more than two thousand pages (including the *Prolegomena*, written in the year before his death) appears like a gigantic torso which still needed a basic revision and polishing; or if, on the contrary, we confront here a more or less completed work[1], a true *terminus ad quem* of an exceptionally long intellectual itinerary. In any case, study of the text which became Lukács' *opus posthumum*, his true philosophical testament, clearly indicates its importance apart from any hypotheses we can formulate on the ultimate intentions of its author with regard to it.

As concerns the genesis of the *Ontology*, more precisely the gestation process of the work and the deep reasons which led Lukács to undertake it, we can formulate a certain number of hypotheses in relation to indications present in his correspondence and in relation to the results of research undertaken in the Lukács Archives in Budapest. There is no doubt that the *Ontology* began against the background of the project of an *Ethics*. A letter sent by Lukács on May 10, 1960 to his friend Ernst Fischer enables us to specify the moment when he had finished the composition of the first part of his great *Aesthetics*.[2] I am still in the transitional period after a birth", Lukács wrote to Fisher,

> The aesthetic manuscript is ready and I need now to place myself within the atmosphere of ethics. That is not an easy task, since the entire nervous system needs to be directed to perceive and to associate otherwise than it has been accustomed in recent years. I am afraid this rearrangement will take at least a few weeks, if not months. Only then can the really fruitful thought begin. Accordingly, this transition will be accomplished.

Concerning the lengthy period of work accorded by Lukács to the preparation of the *Ethics*, beginning in the spring of 1960, we have clues in a certain number of notes, which are available in the Lukács Archives under the generic title 'Kleine Notizen zur Ethik'.[3] In this heap of tiny pages, several times we can find indications concerning the basic idea which progressively took shape in Lukács' mind during his

T. Rockmore (ed.), Lukács Today, 243–273.
© *1988 by D. Reidel Publishing Company.*

work on the *Ethics,* and which led him to modify his initial plan and to write, in the first place, a voluminous *Ontology of Social Being*[4]: "No ethics without ontology", "... the impossibility of positing an ethics without also positing a world-situation (*Weltzustand*)". In working on his *Ethics,* Lukács was led to the conclusion that it was not possible to work out a theory of moral action without a complete perspective on the essential components of social life, hence, without sketching an ontology of social being. The letters sent at the end of 1964 and the beginning of 1965 indicate his decision to transform what was initially destined to be only an introduction to his *Ethics* into a major, autonomous work.

The change in orientation with respect to the initial project is not really a surprise. Lukács was surely aware that if he wanted really to abolish the rigid dualism between moral praxis and the other forms of praxis (beginning with those of daily life), between the noumenal world and the phenomenal world (in the terminology of the *Critique of Practical Reason*), it was necessary to redefine the fundamental categories of social life. It seemed to him indispensable to question the finalistic or deterministic prejudices of traditional Marxism on this topic. The particular character of moral action could not be identified otherwise than through its rootedness in other types of praxis. If he wanted to avoid the pitfall of moralism (whose basis seemed to him to be the transcendentalism of Kantian morality), as well as that due to the *Realpolitik* (which means capitulation before the social *status quo*), it was necessary to highlight the interconnection between moral and other kinds of values, by questioning the functioning of social life as a whole. Accordingly, he devoted himself to the project of an *Ontology of Social Being.*

But the project of an *Ethics* remained present until the end. In finishing the second main chapter of the theoretical part of the *Ontology,* on 'Reproduction', Lukács, in a letter of April 23, 1966 to Frank Benseler, expressed his confidence in the positive final result of his work, and added, in the guise of a conclusion: "I am going to rejoice a lot, because in this way the road towards the *Ethics* will be liberated."[5]

Several years later, in a letter he sent in January 1969 to Adam Schaff, he stated his intention to provide definitive form to the manuscript of the *Ontology* and to turn to the writing of the *Ethics.*[6] He was able to write only the *Prolegomena* to the *Ontology of Social Being* during 1970, since illness and, almost immediately thereafter, death (in June 1971), kept him from realizing his project so long under consideration.

Lukács' initiative, in establishing the basis for an ontology of social being, a theoretical operation that the philosopher considered necessary for the elaboration of an *Ethics*, is neither an enterprise as solitary nor as unusual as the title of his work might lead us to believe. Georg Simmel, the first intellectual mentor of the young Lukács, had already, in his *Sociology*, posed the decisive question which haunted the thought of the *Ontology*'s author: How is society possible? In the Thirties, Alfred Schutz, the well-known disciple of Husserl, had published an important work dedicated to the meaningful construction of the social world, *Der sinnhafte Aufbau der sozialen Welt*. And the much more recent writings of Jürgen Habermas, after his contributions to a "reconstruction of historical materialism", up until his research on communicative action, also belong to the same direction. But it seems to us that the originality of Lukács' final philosophical synthesis ought to be sought for elsewhere, in another historical perspective.

Before we indicate the place that this work occupies in Lukács' intellectual biography, we are tempted to identify one of its deepest sources, if not its most important source, in an extremely powerful movement of thought, which today we can say literally transformed the German and international philosophical scene beginning in the 1920's. The resurrection of ontology as a basic philosophical discipline after decades of neo-Kantian thought is, in effect, linked to two great names, for which the future reserved, clearly, very different audiences, but which has each marked with his seal contemporary philosophical thought: Nicolai Hartmann and Martin Heidegger. In this way, those who know the philosophical trajectory of the Hungarian thinker were surprised to discover the profound intellectual solidarity which links the thought of the last Lukács to the ontological philosophy of Nicolai Hartmann.

Lukács encountered the ontological thought of Nicolai Hartmann rather late in his own philosophical itinerary; nevertheless, we can affirm that this encounter played a decisive role in his turn towards ontology. It seems that it was under the influence of his former East-German correspondent, the philosopher Wolfgang Harich, that he decided to study Hartmann's work more closely. Neither *The Destruction of Reason* nor the other philosophical writings published by the author before the 1960s referred to N. Hartmann's ontological writings. In becoming aware of Hartmann's *Ontologie*[7] and the later writings[8], Lukács had the revelation of a method and a style of thought which, up to a certain point, agreed with his own philosophical objectives: a rigorously founded system of the categories of being was precisely what he needed in order to provide a solid philosophical basis for his project of elaborating a theory of social life as an entirety and an ethics.

Some readers will be surprised by this convergence between the thought of an engaged Marxist, deeply anchored in the idea of the historicity of being and of its categories, a form of thought marked by the great social and philosophical crises of the century, and that of a philosopher belonging to the pure tradition of the German university, much nearer by its ambitions to the *philosophia perennis*, even animated by an explicit distrust of "historicism". But we must believe that this distrust was above all directed to the form of thought begun by Dilthey, against which Lukács also adopted a strongly critical attitude, despite the seduction that it was able to exercise on him during his youth. However, Lukács found himself on familiar ground in Hartmann's ontological philosophy: the magisterial criticism developed by Hartmann against teleology in all its forms, including the thought of Aristotle and of Hegel, was fruitfully utilized by Lukács to question the teleological interpretation of history advanced by those who claimed allegiance to Marx.

Of course, the crucial philosophical problem concerning the proper relation between teleology and causality was present in Lukács much earlier than his awareness of Hartmann's analyses with which he was to find himself in agreement (although he criticized Hartmann in a fundamental manner for neglecting the decisive role of work in the articulation of this relation): it is enough to refer to the important chapter devoted in the book *The Young Hegel* to the problem of work in Hegel.

The lively interest by Hartmann for Hegel's *Logic* and for the inexhaustible richness of the Hegelian analyses devoted to the categories, as well as his faithfulness to a certain fruitful attitude in Spinoza's thought, could only find a very favorable echo in Lukács - not to mention the exemplary value of the philosophical itinerary traversed by Hartmann, who was able to detach himself completely from the neo-Kantian Marburg School and from Husserlian phenomenology, in providing a radical critique of idealist philosophy. As concerns the precocious interest manifested by Hartmann for Hegel's *Logic* and for the fashion in which he consummated his radical break with transcendental idealism and effected his turn towards ontology, we find extremely interesting indications in the correspondence with Heinz Heimsoeth.[9]

It is correct that the extraordinary effort displayed by Nicolai Hartmann throughout a *corpus* of great richness, to displace the center of the philosophical problematic from epistemology towards ontology, to interrogate above all the *ratio essendi* of things, by subordinating to it the *ratio cognoscendi*, and to reactualize accordingly the great metaphysical tradition which stretches from Aristotle through medieval ontology until Kant and Hegel's *Logic*, did not seem to have the results and effect intended by its author. If we judge by the silence, weightier and weightier, which surrounded Hartmann's *corpus* in the decades following his death in 1950, we can even believe that his effort to re-establish ontology with its full rights resulted in failure.

The pre-eminence of existentialism and of neopositivism on the contemporary philosophical scene furnish the required proof. Martin Heidegger's situation is, certainly, entirely different, since the influence and audience of his thought did not cease to grow. But we must admit that after the famous *Kehre* (after the conversion in the period following *Being and Time*), after the author had himself renounced the concept of "fundamental ontology", which he held to be still too deeply rooted in the metaphysical tradition of philosophy, and certainly after he had undertaken in numerous texts the "deconstruction" (or, more precisely, the destruction) of this ontological tradition, we began to forget how much the resurrection of ontology in contemporary philosophy is linked to the decisive impulse of the thought of the first Heidegger: the deep affinities which link it on this level, despite their great differences, even their oppositions, with Nicolai Hartmann's thought, seem to us to be evident. It is certainly now, thanks to the publication within the series of complete writings of the course of lectures from the period of 1924-1930, *Prolegomena zur Geschichte des Zeitbegriffs* (lectures given in Marburg in 1925), *Die Grundprobleme der Phänomenologie* (course from 1927, also in Marburg), *Metaphysische Anfangsgründe der Logik* (course from 1927 in Marburg), without forgetting the more recent *Die Grundbegriffe der Metaphysik. Welt, Endlichkeit, Einsamkeit* (course from 1929-1930 in Freiburg), that the weight of this eminently ontological aspect of Heidegger's thought can be appropriately measured.

Four decades after the appearance of Nicolai Hartmann's fundamental study, *Wie ist Kritische Ontologie überhaupt möglich?* in 1923, and after the publication of *Being and Time* in 1927 by Heidegger, Lukács again takes up, in his *On the Ontology of Social Being* (which he began to write in 1964), with different intellectual instruments, the program of these two thinkers, that is, to reconstruct ontology as the fundamental discipline of philosophical reflexion. If it were a question of situating the ideal geometrical site for Lukács' ontology with respect to those of his two predecessors, we could say, in an extremely compressed and approximative formula, that he undertook to elaborate an "analytic of being there" (but Heideggerian *Dasein* was understood this time in the spirit of Marx, by definition as social being), with categories and concepts much nearer to Nicolai Hartmann's realist ontology: by forcing things a little, we could say that it is a question, in Lukács' *Ontology*, of validating an ideal *tertium datur* between two antagonists, Hartmann and Heidegger, while underlining energetically the infinitely closer relation linking him to the former.

The Heidegger-Lukács *rapprochment*, on the other hand, should not seem too risky if we recall the repeated speculation concerning the resemblances between the problematic of the critique of reification in the work of Lukács' youth, *History and Class Consciousness*, which appeared in 1923, and the Heideggerian analysis of the tension between inauthentic existence and the authentic existence of being-there, developed in *Being and Time*. If his attitude respecting Heidegger remains very critical in the *Ontology* (essentially he restates, on the strictly philosophical level, the criticisms formulated in his book *The Destruction of Reason*), we should not, in effect, forget that as an ontology of social being, Lukács' work takes form, in its most interesting part, as a philosophy of the subject, through attributing a more important place to the analysis of what we can call the phenomenological levels of subjectivity: acts of objectification, of exteriorization, of reification and of alienation or of the dealienation of the subject. This problematic inevitably recalls the Heideggerian analyses of the ontological structure of *Dasein*, specific to the period of *Being and Time* (although the fundamental differences separating their respective philosophical positions are evident), while in Nicolai Hartmann's work, if we are not mistaken, the concepts of reification and of alienation appear very rarely as such. The sources of these Lukácsian concepts are evidently in the writings of Hegel and of Marx (Lukács devoted the final section of his important book on *The Young Hegel* to Hegel's concept of alienation), and not in Heidegger. But in passing we can recall the concepts of *Versachlichung* (thingification) and of *Vergegenständlichung des Geistes* (objectification of the mind) in the *Philosophie des Geldes* by Georg Simmel (a book which strongly influenced the first Lukács) and that of *Verdinglichung* in the study by Husserl entitled 'Philosophie als strenge Wissenschaft' (which appeared in the journal *Logos* in 1910-1911, the same year as Lukács' essay on the 'Metaphysics of Tragedy'), two authors who strongly influenced the young Heidegger.

At the end of his life, Lukács was persuaded that it was in his *Ontology* that he had furnished the essential and definitive form of his thought[10] (even if, as we have noted, he was not entirely satisfied with his manuscript). He was used to saying that it was the privilege of several philosophical geniuses such as Aristotle or Marx to have clarified early on, at twenty years of age, the essential part of their original thought; for the others, for ordinary mortals, it could happen, as was the case, as he said not without humorous intent, that this could occur only towards the age of eighty that they could succeed in clarifying the essential part of their philosophy. In effect, Lukács' intellectual itinerary exhibits so many transformations and spectacular conversions from the neo-Kantianism and the *Lebensphilosophie* of his first youthful writings (besides Georg Simmel and Max Weber, he counted among his professors and friends Emil Lask, the least orthodox of the neo-Kantians of the Sudwestdeutsche Schüle, who strongly influenced Heidegger), in passing by the strongly Hegelianized Marxism of his book *History and Class Consciousness*, until the rigorous Marxism of his mature period (a period which begins at the start of the 1930s), so we can ask ourselves under what angle we need to scrutinize his social ontology in order to see in it the final moment of a laborious process. There were also apparently extra-philosophic reasons to want to read this ontology.

The intellectual destiny of Lukács was so strongly marked by his participation, during more than fifty years, in the Communist movement (he became a member of the Hungarian Communist Party in December 1918 and remained one until the end of his life, with the exception of a suspension of eleven years, after the events of October 1956, when he was Minister of Culture in the government of Imre Nagy), so we could hope to find in the philosophical discourse of his last *magnum opus* an enlightening response to a hotly debated question. As the conclusion of a long pathway, the *Ontology* should enable us to decide finally if Lukács' thought had effectively undergone, after the abandonment of certain views in his book, for a long time the most famous one, *History and Class Consciousness*, and after his long passage through the Stalinist epoch, a corruption of its fiber, a philosophical evolution, equivalent to a veritable act of *sacrifizio dell'intelletto* (to take up again the expression of his aggressive adversary Theodor W. Adorno, although it was already a little bit the thesis, in a much more nuanced form, of Maurice Merleau-Ponty in *Adventures of the Dialectic*); or, on the contrary, if his thought had ripened in the good sense, in being capable, through the *Ontology*, of furnishing a really universal theory of the categories of existence, capable of immunizing consciousness against all forms of alienation by political power: in a word, if he reached the end, notably thanks to the formulation of a concept well articulated in the real *humanitas* of *homo humanus*, what Lukács calls the *Gattungsmässigkeit-für-sich* (the human species-for-itself), the *point d'orgue* of his *Ontology*, which should be taken in effect from above, in dissipating the distrust which has so long surrounded it. We can, in this sense, deplore the fact that one of his most recent adversaries, Leszek Kołakowski, in his voluminous *Main Currents of Marxism*, in three volumes, has not seen necessary to take into account the *Ontology* in order to test the central thesis expressed in his strongly hostile chapter devoted to Lukács: 'Lukács or Reason in the Service of Dogma'. It is true that the full text of the work was not, and has only recently become, available in its original German version[11]; nor is there an English or French translation; with the exception of the three chapters published separately in three small volumes by Luchterhand,

of which two have also been translated into English; for a long time we
disposed only of the Italian translation in three volumes, besides the
translations into Hungarian and into Romanian, of which the latter is
only a partial translation.

In Lukács' papers, there is a revealing indication concerning his
own intellectual biography, an indication which can help us better to
understand the place of the *Ontology* in his evolution. In referring, in a
letter to his editor, Frank Benseler, to a parallel between the intellectual
itinerary of Ernst Bloch and his own, with an explicit reference to the
different significance of the Marxist conversion for each of them,
Lukács wrote[12]:

> During my entire youth, there existed in me a profound conflict,
> never able to be resolved, between the aspiration towards
> philosophical generalization in the sense of the great philosophies
> of antiquity, and the tendencies to pure scientificity. If you
> compare the passages of my old book[13] on the drama and the style
> of *The Soul and Its Forms* (the two books were written in the same
> period) you can become clearly aware of this conflict.

And in speaking of his adhesion to Marxism, he adds: "For me it
represented the solution to the central interior conflict of my youthful
period, for Bloch much less, since at the time of the *Spirit of Utopia*[14],
he could simply incorporate Marx into his apocalyptic fantasy."
Lukács' letter is dated November 21, 1961; it accordingly belongs to a
stage when the relations between the two old friends were undergoing a
certain deterioration, characterized by more and more accentuated
philosophical differences, visible also in Lukács' Preface to his *Theory
of the Novel*, written shortly after the same period.

The significance of the interior conflict from his *Jugendzeit*, of
which Lukács speaks, ought not to be underestimated, since it in effect
can provide us with the hermeneutical key needed to understand his
philosophical trajectory until his final works. The coexistence within
him, in the beginning, of two different natures - that of the sociologist
of literature, imbued by a desire for positivity and methodological rigor
(his concerns in this sense derive from concepts due to Marx and
Simmel, or rather of a Marx "filtered through Simmel") and that of a
metaphysician of tragedy or of a mystic moralist, which his absolute
thirst led to search in the paroxysm of pure interiority for a secure
foundation for a life freed from all inessentials - is in effect visible if we
juxtapose the fragments entitled 'Zur Soziologie des modernen Dramas'
(the whole book, in its definitive form, was published in 1911) and the
essay 'Metaphysics of Tragedy', or the dialogue on 'The Poverty of
Mind', (writings which date from the same period). Between the two

philosophical "souls" which were at war within him, one turned towards the empirical and the other toward pure transcendence, it is perhaps the second one which at the time was dominant, as witness the ardor with which the young Lukács sought successively in the "intelligible self" of Kant (with which he identified the tragic self), in the *Abgeschiedenheit* (the solitude) or the "poverty of mind" of Meister Eckhart, or in the figures like Dostoevsky's Prince Myshkin or Kierkegaard's Abraham, a form of expression for his aspiration towards the meta-psychological or the transempirical. The refusal of psychologism or of empirical determinism of the soul (visible above all in the dialogue on the 'Poverty of the Mind' published in 1912) and the fervor with which he tried to secure the stable point of his tragic self, a superlative expression of the essence of life, in a zone situated not only above "natural" life, but also above culture (in this sense he wrote[15] to Leopold Ziegler in mid-July 1911 that the tragic could not be for him a "concept of the philosophy of history"), enable us to foresee, through their radicalism, certain views which Heidegger's fundamental ontology will later develop: the distrust by Heidegger of psychologism and the desire to define the "fundamental articulations of Being" (*die Grund-artikulationen des Seins*), beyond any cultural or empirical consid-erations, justify such a *rapprochement*. The common matrix can per-haps be found again in Georg Simmel's thought, since in his essay on 'Kant and Goethe' he tried to circumscribe a space for "supra-empirical relations" (through the fusion of Goethe's "vitalism" and Kant's transcendental idealism) and he was the first to speak of the "tragedy of culture" as an irreducible conflict between authentic life and cultural objectivation.

But Lukács never ceased being traversed by the dualism of a relativistic sociological vision of cultural values and of an acute awareness of their ability to transcend the space and time of their genesis: this hiatus was not resolved by the thought of the young Lukács. The particular sensitivity manifested rather early in regard to the Hegelian distinction between objective mind and absolute spirit - the former materializes in social institutions (the law, mores, the State, *etc.*), whereas the latter is incarnated in the higher forms of consciousness: art, religion, philosophy - belongs to the same context. How can one be able to satisfy the demands of "absolute spirit" (those of pure morality, for example, of the"soul" - *der Seele* - or of the "second ethics" in the terminology of the young Lukács) without leaving the hard ground of real history? The problem never ceased to haunt the author of the essay 'Tactics and Ethics', published in 1919. We can note here that the reflections on the Hegelian duality objective spirit/absolute spirit, with the dilemmas to which it gives rise for the young Lukács (for example, the choice between the first ethics - the duties with regard to institutions, the State, *etc.* - and the second ethics - the pure imperatives of the soul) are present as well in the youthful writings (in the manuscript of the book on Dostoevsky) or in the review of Croce's book *Teoria e storia della storiografia*, which dates from 1915, as in the last part of the book *The Young Hegel* (where Lukács defends the demands incarnated by absolute spirit against the relativism of vulgar sociology) or in different places in the *Ontology*: for instance in the final chapter, where the author emphasizes the significance of the movement of sects and of heresies against the established Church, in underlining that they incarnate the aspirations of the human species-for-itself (*Gattungsmässigkeit-in-sich*) - the Lukácsian variant of the Hegelian "absolute spirit" - against the values of the social *status quo* which the Church institutionalizes as manifestation of the aspirations of the human species-for-itself of the "objective spirit" of the epoch of which it would be the bearer. We can now better understand the meaning of the passage quoted above from a letter to Frank Benseler. The affirmation that the thought of Marx offered him a solution to the duality of the tendencies which he mentioned becomes intelligible, especially in terms of the project of the *Ontology*: the structure of the work shows us, in effect, that Lukács begins from the analysis of the most elementary forms of social activity (beginning with work) and tries progressively to reconstruct the genesis of the principal social complexes (economics, politics, law, mores, *etc.*), by climbing the ladder towards superior forms of conscious activity (art, philosophy, the great moral acts).

It is accordingly thanks to a method which we can call ontological-genetical, by proceeding from below towards above, with the aim of successively specifying the articulations and the intermediary links between the elementary forms of social life (object of empirical sociology, hence of a more or less rigorous science) and superior objectivations (traditionally the object of philosophical reflexion), that Lukács hoped to overcome the hiatus to which he alluded in his letter. If he desired to distance himself from Bloch, it is because Bloch, preoccupied by the same problem, stressed, in the last chapter of his *Spirit of Utopia*, the reattachment to Marxian economic analysis of the values traditionally incorporated by religious transcendence.[16] In denouncing the unilaterality of economism, Bloch was able to write that "Marxism [has been brought - *N.T.*] into the neighborhood of a critique of pure reason for which no critique of practical reason would yet have been written." Now, the attempt by Lukács, in the *Ontology*, will precisely be to provide a bridge between the categories of pure reason and those of practical reason (to keep the Kantian terminology) through a purely immanent method, by providing a series of genetic mediations between the two levels, up until the higher forms of intersubjectivity, without any concession to religious transcendence. It is this which profoundly separates it from Bloch's thought: in a passage of the *Ontology* he will later explicitly reject the Blochean idea of the phenomenological autonomy of the soul, set out in *The Spirit of Utopia*, by seeing there an unacceptable concession to idealism.[17]

This might be the place to say something about the relations between Lukács and Bloch. These relations, which extended over an exceptionally long period, more than sixty years, included both highs and lows, in following a rather complicated trajectory.[18] If we note here only the aspects concerning the end of their careers, we can say that Bloch welcomed with surprise and with a real interest Lukács' initiative in writing an *Ontology*, all the while expressing a deep discontent with the attention accorded by Lukács to the work of Nicolai Hartmann. On this point, he became aware of Lukács' intentions only through rumors, because the text of Lukács' work was still not accessible in its entirety at the time.[19] Bloch did not at all value the writings of Nicolai Hartmann in which he saw only the epigonic continuation of the ancient static ontology, preferring rather to dip into the work of the other Hartmann, Eduard von Hartmann, whose Schellingian inspiration in the theory of the categories was much closer to his own cosmogonal fantasies.

We can even ask ourselves if the decision by Bloch to write *Experimentum mundi*, a work which is largely an exposition of the categories of being (the book was written between 1972 and 1974; it was therefore begun a year after the death of Lukács), was not stimulated by the undertaking of his old friend to write the *Ontology of Social Being*: there is in the *Experimentum mundi* a direct, positive reference to Lukács' *Ontology* and to this way of approaching the theory of the categories in an objective (ontological) manner and not only reflexively (as the idealist tradition would want), without forgetting the fact that the other last great work by Bloch, *Das Materialismusproblem* of 1972 is precisely dedicated to his "friend from my youth, Georg Lukács".

A comparison of the two works of ontological character written by the two thinkers at the end of their lives would however be of the sort to show that, despite all that linked them together in their common fidelity to Marx' thought and his socio-political intentions, profound philosophical differences subsisted between them until the end. The autobiographical notes drawn up by Lukács several months before his death, which had the title 'Gelebtes Denken', in fact referred explicitly to these divergences, whose origins went back already to the period of their youth, especially in mentioning Bloch's conception of nature.

The Blochean idea of a possible isomorphism between man and nature, through which would occur a felicitous encounter (if not a fusion) between the human subject and the "subject of nature", through a radical metamorphosis of nature itself, was profoundly contradictory to Lukács' basic anti-teleologism. Indeed, the very idea of a *Natursubjekt* would have seemed to Lukács to be a contradiction, since it would signify an illegitimate anthropomorphization of nature.

But we can go even farther in order to discover the matrix of these divergences: we can hardly see, for example, that Lukács would accept Bloch's idea that the categories of the world are the progressive objectifications (Bloch called them experiments) of a primordial will (the final substrate that Bloch calls, following Eduard von Hartmann, *das Thelische*, the equivalent to a "hunger for existence"), while for Lukács the categories of the prehuman world are only the progressive articulations of a purely causal substrate, deprived by definition of a teleological intent. The crypto-teleology of Bloch's ontology, which necessarily led to a utopic vision of a final happy apocalypse, until the end remained profoundly alien to Lukács' ontology.

The judgments on Bloch which Lukács advanced in his private correspondence, especially in the 1960s (in his letters to Frank Benseler, but also, for instance, in a letter to Professor Podach of Heidelberg)[20], in a period when Bloch also began to make public his reservations with respect to the overly narrow form of Lukács' Marxism, manifest a constant ambivalence. Lukács did not cease to question the extravagance and the precarious nature of Bloch's philosophical views, all the while expressing his admiration for the unshakable fidelity of his old friend with respect to his left-wing beliefs. This paradoxical mélange of a "left-wing ethics" and of a "right-wing theory of knowledge", in the words utilized by Lukács in 1962 in his Preface to the *Theory of the Novel* (where Bloch was explicitly targeted), never ceased to intrigue Lukács. Here, for example, is what he wrote to Frank Benseler on March 9, 1962, after having become aware of Bloch's opuscule *Philosophische Grundfragen I, Zur Ontologie des Noch-Nicht-Seins*[21], the first publication by Bloch after he left East Germany in order to settle in the West[22]: "It is an Italian salad with a fascinating decorative effect, composed of a subjectivism which pretends to be objective and a very poor and abstract objectivity. I had the pleasure of seeing that Bloch has still not abandoned his left-wing ethics." Several years later, in a letter sent November 21, 1965 to the same correspondent, Lukács formulated in an even sharper fashion the same idea, without any hesitation in indicating even the structural affinities between Bloch's philosophical romanticism and that of their great common adversaries, from Spengler to Heidegger[23]:

It is correct that you speak of romanticism. With his talent, Bloch should without doubt have been able effectively to compete with all the right-wing dreamers (*rechte Phantasten*), from Spengler to Heidegger. He stood, however, without flinching, always on the extreme left wing, even if the essence of his philosophy was much closer to those on the extreme right wing than to Marx. I have always admired from the ethical perspective this paradoxical constancy in Bloch's thought (*denkerisch paradoxe Ausharren Blochs*) and I have always seen there a phenomenon completely unique for our time.

Several letters sent the same year by Lukács to Benseler indicate his mistrust with regard to the conjunction between the "principle of hope" of Bloch and the religious needs of the epoch, as Bloch's work seemed to him to nourish the illusion of a "religious socialism"[24]: "You are entirely correct when you fear that the Blochean radicalism could engender a quietism."

In writing his *Ontology of Social Being* Lukács tried to answer a certain number of questions of an apparently purely speculative nature, but whose practical significance is immense: as the product of the teleological activity of individual subjects, does the history of society acquire a univocal sense, an imposed finality due to the sovereign action of subjects on social matter (of which the teleology of the Hegelian philosophy of history remains the superlative example)? Or, on the contrary, is it a product of the objective causal chain which is able to impose its effects beyond consciousness and the desire of individuals, so that the history of society develops according to a rigorous determinism which in the final analysis surpasses the finalistic activity of consciousness? In attempting to avoid the trap of teleology as well as that of determinism, and to rescue the interpretation of Marx' thought from what he considered to be two symmetrical deformations, Lukács was not able to complete his project without a radical interrogation concerning the categorial foundations of social life.

The autarchic existence of being with respect to consciousness - this is the basic thesis of realistic ontology, that of Nicolai Hartmann as well as that of Georg Lukács (who prefers, himself, to speak of materialist ontology). Nicolai Hartmann never ceases to insist in his writings, with inexhaustible energy and so firmly since it seems to him to shake a number of prejudices essential to a teleological ontology or traditional rationalism, on the sovereign indifference of the categories of being with respect to their cognitive apprehension. Lukács could have been struck by the astonishing similarity between the definition of the categories that we find in Marx: *Daseinsformen, Existenzbestimmungen* (= forms of being-there, determinations of existence) and the central thesis of Nicolai Hartmann on the categories as properties

intrinsic to being itself (the distinction between"categories of being" and
"categories of knowledge," despite their partial identity, returns like a
leitmotif in the works of Hartmann). Heidegger in turn, in his courses
from the period of *Being and Time*, speaks of the apprehension of the
"fundamental articulations of being" (*Grundartikulationen des Seins*) as
the aim of his fundamental ontology, but in an entirely different sense
than Hartmann or Lukács.

In following an ontological procedure, Lukács decided to set out a
theory of the levels of being, of the progressive stratification (inorganic
nature, biological nature, social being), with as the principal objective to
specify the categories constitutive of social being, in their irreducible
specificity. Ontology understood as a theory of the categories
(*Kategorienlehre*) - here there is a common trait between Hartmann and
Lukács. The center of gravity of his *Ontology* becomes an analysis of
work, considered as originary phenomenon and as the generative cell of
social life: work appears to him, of course, also as the key to
anthropogenesis.

Lukács accordingly locates at the base of social life "teleological
position" (*die teleologische Setzung*), the finalistic activity of the
subject: for the first time, thanks to work, consciousness abandons the
role of simple epiphenomenon in the objective causal series (which it
still conserves among the higher animals) in order to acquire a
dimension intrinsic to it, that of *antiphysis*, of a factor active and
constitutive of the real. Nature in itself (what Nicolai Hartmann calls
das *Ansichseiende*) is characterized, by definition, by teleological and
axiological neutrality. Through work, teleology, as the activity which
provides meaning to sense and values, erupts into the chain of the
objective causal series.

Teleological activity interrupts, or breaks with, the spontaneous
causality of nature in introducing into it entirely different relations,
inconceivable through the simple play of natural causality. The
distinction between spontaneous causality (that of nature-in-itself) and
instituted causality, thanks to teleological activity, here plays a capital
role. Lukács sees in finalistic activity, which erupts with the appearance of work, the ramified nucleus of social life, on all its levels,
from material action on nature (work in the precise sense) up to the
most complex forms of intersubjectivity, where it is a question of acting
on the consciousness of others.

Opposed to a simple passivity or pure automaticity, the concept of
"teleological position" seems rather near to that of the intentionality of
consciousness, taken over from the psychology of Brentano by the
phenomenology of Husserl and of Heidegger. But Nicolai Hartmann
and Lukács decline to disassociate in radical fashion the intentionality of
consciousness and causal objectivity, comprehension and explanation,

while recognizing all the while their qualitative heterogeneity. The originality of their position is to have stressed, with extreme energy, the narrow connection which exists between efficient finalistic activity of the subject and the respect for objective causal determinations. The emergence of teleological acts implies by definition the interpolation of an ideal moment in the objective causal series (the aim in the process of work); otherwise consciousness would effectively be only an epiphenomenon of the determinism of nature. But the ontological import of the final nexus (the result of the projected action) depends on the valorization of the intrinsic properties of the objects themselves - the *energeia* can only base itself on the *dynamis*.

Nicolai Hartmann furnished in his little book *Teleologisches Denken* (the complement to his *Philosophy of Nature*), a work which Lukács regarded highly, a subtle demonstration of the fact that the particularity of the finalistic activity of consciousness only appears when we abandon prejudices concerning a finalism or a rationality immanent in the world. Teleological activity, the privilege of the active subject, only represents a segment in the infinite becoming of the world. The ontological pre-eminence of the category of causality over that of finality seems to Hartmann self-evident: he undertook a spectacular operation to rehabilitate the ontological import of the category of causality in underlining the infinite productivity of the objective causal series with respect to the inherent finitude of teleological acts.

In situating an act of ideal nature at the base of social life, namely the "teleological position" (*die teleologische Setzung*, the finalistic activity of consciousness), which, however, is intimately associated with material determinations of objects (work is the paradigm of this intimate fusion of the ideal and the real), Lukács inevitably is able to make the "should-be" (*das Sollen*) and the value of categories constitutive of social being. The institution of a goal necessarily signifies the emergence of a should-be and by definition is accompanied by the appearance of a value. Nature, the empire of pure causality, knows neither one nor the other. But it is precisely the inexistence of an absolute sovereignty of consciousness (it is always rooted to begin with in a material *hic et nunc*) and the absence of a transcendent empire of values (this would be to admit the existence of objective teleology), which is able to open the way to a realistic explanation of the genesis of values. We do not think that we are wrong in affirming that it is the non-sovereignty of teleological activity, the fact that it is ceaselessly nourished by the resistances and obstacles opposed to it by the network of objective causality - in a word the relation of dialectical tension which forms between the teleology of human aims and the causal series of reality - which furnishes the true source of values. Nicolai Hartmann could in this sense, at a certain time, affirmatively state that it is "the failure of the instinctive reaction which is the precipitating factor of finalistic activity (*der Erwecker der Zwecktätigkeit*)".[25]

The principal aim of the ontological-genetical method developed by Lukács in his last work is to show how, in beginning from the elementary act of work, social life constitutes itself as a tissue of objectifications of greater and greater complexity, as interhuman relations better and better articulated, thanks precisely to the relation of dialectical tension between the teleological·activity of individual subjects and the network of objective causal determinations. The definition even of man - *ein antwortendes Wesen* (a being which answers) - illustrates well this direction of his thought. We find ourselves here in the zone of the actual confluence between the metaphysical ontology of Nicolai Hartmann and the ontology of social being sketched by Georg Lukács. In apparently paradoxical fashion, it is the autonomy of the infinite causal series of the real with respect to the inevitably finite character of the teleological activity of the subject, the fact that the finite consciousness (circumscribed) can never be entirely coextensive with infinite reality, which explains the incessant proliferation of teleological acts and the renewed multiplication of values. The productive nature of consciousness is stimulated by the resistance of the real and by the infinite character of its determinations: the objective causality, so criticized for its "mechanical" character or unilinearity, reveals itself, rather, as an inhibiting factor or inhibition, a stimulating terrain for the exercise of freedom.

Lukács considers the teleological acts of individuals as the *principium movens* of social life, thus stopping short of any determinist conception, of a mechanist or fatalist kind, of society. The assimilation of the functioning of the laws of society to that of the laws of nature, through the pure and simple identification of society to a "second nature", becomes ontologically impossible. But the focus of conceptual risk can be found in the analysis of the teleological act: by utilizing the ontological model of work, he makes the idea of the *alternative choice* into the essence of their act. Thanks to work, man has acquired *distance* with respect to the objective causal linkage, the distancing necessary in order to choose between several possible acts. The pre-eminence of the ideal moment, the representation *in mente* of the aim is obvious. In his book, *The Young Hegel*, Lukács criticizes Spinoza for having too quickly interpreted the *causa finalis* as simple variant (or continuation) of the efficient cause, through covering up its irreducible specificity. Hegel, on the contrary, is strongly praised for having, through the analysis of work developed in his Jena writings, brought out this particularity.[26]

Lukács detects in Spinoza an underestimation of the moment of the emergence of the *causa finalis*; the intransigent determinism of Spinoza pushes him to denounce the illusion of the autonomous emergence of the *causa finalis*. Now, Lukács, all the while acknowledging the beauty of Spinoza's reasoning, wants to bring out the particularity of the "teleological position" (*die teleologische Setzung*), irreducible to the pure linkage of efficient causes. The emergence of an aim signifies an interruption in spontaneous causality, an act which breaks the pure linkage of efficient causality: the moment of choice, of invention in the "teleological position" never can be reduced to a simple effect of an efficient cause. Hegel would have been the first to stress the qualitative novelty of this act, while, following Lukács, Hobbes and Spinoza would have underestimated its irreducibility. But it must be added that Lukács always manifested a great admiration for Spinoza's work, in acknowledging his great debt towards it (for example in the Preface to his *Aesthetics*).

The alternative decision, the essence of the teleological act, implies by definition deliberation, progressive experimentation, hesitation (eventually) between several possibilities: at the same time it takes form inevitably as a horizon of concrete circumstances which the subject finds before it and which he did not himself create. In making of the alternative decision the dynamic principle of social life and the constitutive moment of the act of freedom itself, Lukács contests *ab initio* rectilinear causality as the law of social development.

It is interesting to recall that in the pages devoted to the problem of freedom in the chapter on "Work" in his *Ontology*, Lukács rejects the famous Hegelian definition of freedom as the "truth of necessity", as well as its too faithful reproduction by Engels. He begins by admitting that each free act must base itself on adequate knowledge of the circumstances in which it takes place: he admits accordingly a correlation between freedom and necessity (in admitting in this sense that Engels is correct). But he finds the analyses of Hegel and of Engels too restrictive. He objects against Hegel to the excessive extension of the concept of necessity. The real does not only include the necessary relations between phenomena, but also the latent or virtual possibilities (of which the Aristotelian category of *dynamis* is the expression), as well as a mass of accidents. The apanage of the free act is to valorize all modal categories of the real, through exploring the latencies as well as the contingent phenomena (with respect to the fixed aim): Raphael knew how to draw an unprecedented profit from the form of the windows in the rooms where he painted his famous frescoes "The Parnassus" and the "Liberation of Saint Peter" (a disadvantageous accident was accordingly transformed into a value for the original organisation of the space). The affirmations of Hegel on freedom as the "truth of necessity" or as the expression of "true necessity" ("internal" necessity opposed to purely exterior or "blind" necessity) are tributaries of a too logical mind and certainly of a hidden finalism, which considers that the mission of each category (in fact, that of necessity) is only to prepare the ascension towards the higher category: a finalism of this kind, symmetrical with univocal determinism, is profoundly unacceptable, and Lukács opposes to it a more flexible and more nuanced representation of the free act.

The structure of social being is hence defined by fundamental ambivalence: no determination occurs in social life which is not founded on the teleological acts of individuals; however, the social process in its entirety does not have a teleological, but a strictly causal, character.

Individuals model reality in reordering the objective causal series as a function of their respective aims, but the effects of their actions surpass the initial intentions. The heterogeneity of objective causal series (which are *ex definitione* infinite) with respect to teleological acts (whose horizon, always by definition, is finite) can at first glance explain the existence of such disparities. Unforeseeable examples, even sometimes in contradiction with the intent, can be found in the field itself of interaction between man and nature: to illustrate the ontological autonomy of the unfolding of causes with respect to intentional acts, the possibility of certain contrary effects, even harmful, with respect to teleological positions, Lukács cites at a certain point, in the chapter on 'Work', the example of "the corrosion of iron". Sartre is also concerned, in the *Critique of Dialectical Reason*, with such phenomena, which he labels "counterfinalities". In the field of social life, envisaged from the point of view of intersocial relations in the narrow sense, the disparities between the intentions of individuals and the results of their actions take on a specific character: the actions of an individual or of a group of individuals interfere with those of another individual or of another group of individuals; this multiple interaction leads to a new reality, a final consequence, which necessarily surpasses the initial intentions and the individual desires.

The objectivity of such a result can be called *sui generis*, inasmuch as it is not the product of spontaneous causality as happens in nature, but a synthesis of numerous individual acts whose sum in reality constitutes itself autonomously, with a necessary character (notably in the sphere of economics). This is in fact the interpretation which Lukács gives to the celebrated Marxian thesis which affirms that "men make history, but not in conditions chosen by them ...".

The author of the *Ontology* affirms, in order to support his thesis, the three fundamental tendencies of the historical process, defined as follows: the reduction of the work time necessary for the reproduction of life, ever greater socialization of social life by the repression of nature and the progressive unification of various types of society in an integrated humanity, which would be affirmed as the necessary result of social development, in independence from the conscious intentions and aims intended by individuals.

Lukács strives to remain in permanent contact with two poles of social reality so defined, namely: on the one hand, the objectivity transcending individual intentions and, on the other, subjectivity - the constitutive factor of social life in its entirety. He reactualizes accordingly in this latter domain the Hegelian distinction between essence and phenomenon, while attributing to it new nuances. The system of objective relations into which individuals are drawn in the course of the process of production and self-reproduction and which in its final correlations could have been engendered independently of the intentions and aims of these individuals, represents the level of the essence; the plurality of individual reactions, the variety of social institutions created in the interior of this level of the essence and which are inseparably linked to it, represents the level of the phenomenon. On the level of the essence, a relative stability would be characteristic (Hegel had spoken of the "calm" of the essence), while the phenomenal world is diversified, in perpetual movement and inexhaustible in its swarming variety. Lukács considers for example that the appearance and the survival of surplus work (the fact, in other words, of producing more than is necessary for existence) follows from the level of the essence, while the variety of historical forms instanced by the phenomenon of *Mehrarbeit* would belong to the level of the phenomenon.

The question which we cannot avoid is the following: does the relative autarchy, the coercive power which Lukács attributes to the level of the essence in the stratification of social life, not bring us back to the old rigid determinism of "historical necessity", understood as a sort of *Deus absconditus* of social life, an implacable force, a force transcendent to intentions and to individual aims? Do we not here find a restoration of the "ontology of necessity" that the four authors of the text *Aufzeichnungen für Genossen Lukács zur Ontologie* (F. Feher, A. Heller, G. Markus, Mihaly Vajda) denounced as in flagrant contradiction - according to them - with the other ontology, which criticizes the "naturalism" of a certain Marxist "orthodoxy"?[27]

Lukács strives to defend himself (perhaps he foresaw the possible objections) against such an error, in stressing that in social life the world of the essence, unlike necessity in nature, constitutes itself equally as a result of the activity of individuals. Even if the constitutive correlations appear independently of their intentions and conscious aims, they are nevertheless indebted to their activity, inasmuch as individuals react, by definition, to the objective reality of which they are obliged to keep track, by looking to submit it to their transformative actions.[28]

But we should not forget that such independence with respect to conscious acts supposes even these as its ontological foundation, hence that social being on the level of its highest and purest objectivity can never possess the total independence from natural events with respect to its subjects.

However, Lukács has not entirely elucidated the dialectic of the relations between the level of necessity (or that of essence) and the individual or collective actions of the human subject. Since he speaks of "the final irresistible tendency" (*letzthinnige tendenzielle Unaufhaltsamkeit*) of the essence, we can correctly compare the essence to a profound subterranean current of historical life which advances implacably, despite the different currents at the surface and the eddies caused by individuals. The former cannot modify the form of the process, the phenomenal world of essence; the development of capitalism in Western Europe would be one of the implacable processes deriving from the essence, the different fashions of its manifestation in France and in England, for example in the agrarian domain, would illustrate the role of the alternative activity of individuals and, for this reason, would embrace the phenomenal world. How can we reconcile such a fashion of envisaging the problem with Lukács' tendency to "deabsolutize" historical necessity, by showing its circumstantial and relative character - as a function of the given conditions (it is what he calls, by utilizing a concept similar to N. Hartmann's, *Wenn-Dann-Notwendigkeit*, in other words "the necessity of the if-then"), in other terms, with the idea that the historical necessity itself (the essence) finds itself submitted to the impact of human actions?

History takes on in Lukács' *Ontology* the aspect of an extremely ambivalent process, sometimes malefic or paradoxical, in the course of which individuals make an effort to impose their will and to attain their ends, but see themselves, since in principle the result is different from their intentions, always constrained to take up again - in new conditions and on a higher level - their constituting efforts.

Lukács' *Ontology* results necessarily in a theory of subjectivity and its constitutive levels. In making of the always renewed tension between the finalizing activity of individuals and a social reality which inevitably surpasses them the motor of the historical process, he pursues in subjectivity itself the progressive effects of this process: the articulation of its different levels, up to the full affirmation of the true *humanitas* of *homo humanus*. It is here perhaps that the confrontation with Heidegger imposes itself most fully. The courses from the period of *Sein und Zeit* show, in effect, how much the problem of the being of consciousness, or what Heidegger liked to call "the subjectivity of the subject", was on the first level of his interests. A recent course published in the series of complete works, that entitled *The Fundamental Concepts of Metaphysics. World-Finitude-Solitude* (given in Freiburg in the Winter semester of 1929-1930 and dedicated to the memory of Eugen Fink), offers us the surprise of seeing Heidegger undertake a detailed comparative analysis of three levels of being: inorganic being, that is *weltlos* (a stone is taken as an example); organic being (with ample excursions into biological science); and human being, the only one invested with the ability to constitute a "world". Such an ontological analysis of a comparative type recalls as well the object of Nicolai Hartmann's reflections, and enables us to specify the divergences and the oppositions between the three philosophers. Lukács' method, in his analysis of the levels of subjectivity, remains genetic: he even criticizes Nicolai Hartmann for a certain blindness concerning the genetic point of view in the analysis of passages between the different levels of being, in deploring above all the absence of such a point of view in the analysis of the *Finalnexus*, of the "teleological position."

The dialectic between the pressure (or the constraint) of objective circumstances and the alternative choice, as an active response to this pressure, is at the center of Lukács' reflection on the genesis of teleological positions. He proposes to observe at the interior of each teleological position two distinct, although closely associated, moments: objectification and exteriorization. If the former expresses the action of modelling the objective causal series or the given situations in order to inscribe there the aim in view (each efficacious teleological act implies such an objectification), the latter marks the retroactive effect of this objectivating activity in the constitution of the subject. The most elementary acts of work imply, besides the objectivating activity (to forge a new object with respect to pure natural determinism), exteriorizations of the subject: skill, inventiveness, even a certain personal "style" imparted to the product, *etc*. But despite their narrow connections, these two acts: objectification and exteriorization, can develop themselves in different ways. The structural polarity of social being, the fact that the final consequence of individual acts necessarily surpasses their initial aims and that individual spontaneities find themselves thus ceaselessly confronted with unexpected situations, explains the possibility of this tension between objectification and exteriorization. Because of the imperatives of social reproduction (because of economic constraint, in the first place) individuals are pushed to acts of objectification (in the context of the division of labor for instance), to which do not necessarily correspond acts of true exteriorization (slavery is a limiting case); the expression of aptitudes and of individual qualities in this case is reduced to a minimum. On the other hand, the same process of objectification can be accompanied by a very diversified spectrum of acts of exteriorization (self-expression) which, when it does not attain an adequate objectivating expression, in the material nature of the structure of society, remains in the state of virtuality or latent subjectivity. Lukács offers us accordingly an image more supple and more finely articulated of the relations between the objective and subjective factors of social development than that to which we were accustomed.

The most original part of this phenomenology of subjectivity (or epigenesis of subjectivity), pursued across the inquiry into the history of social being, is furnished to us by the definition of alienation. The non-coincidence between objectification and exteriorization is pursued this time in the interior of the act of exteriorization itself, postulated as the possibility of a contradiction between the development of qualities (of capacities of the individual which can accumulate themselves in heterogeneous fashion) and their synthesis in the homogeneous unity of the personality. Lukács makes the self-affirmation of personality, which is understood as a synthesis of more or less heterogeneous qualities, the *terminus ad quem* of social development, its ultimate finality. The ontological place of alienation (the object of the last chapter of the *Ontology of Social Being*) is specified there where the multiplication of the qualities of the individual, the result of the relation of dialectical tension with his milieu, functions exclusively in order to assure its survival and its social reproduction (it hence has a pure existence-in-itself, since it is born of the game of the division of work and the struggle for self-preservation), in concealing what should have been its central finality: the auto-affirmation of particularity as autonomous individuality or as personality.

The center of gravity of Lukács' reflections is the tension between what he regards as the two fundamental levels of the human species: the human species-in-itself and the human species-for-itself (*Gattungs-mässigkeit-an-sich* and *für-sich*). Lukács pursues in the interiority of the subject the migration of the main social conflicts: the rendering subservient of the subject to the imperatives of social reproduction can be accompanied by a proliferation of the qualities and the aptitudes of the individual (it is the stage of the human species in itself, deprived still of the transcendence of the for-itself); but the telos of social life remains the surpassing of this more or less heteronymous stage of existence in order to reach the self-affirmation of the individual as a person, hence as an entity which conditions itself and fulfills itself freely (which thus raises itself to the stage of the human species-for-itself). In the tragedy of Sophocles, Ismene, through her spirit of self-compromise and the fervor with which she spreads to her sister the submission to existing law, that of Creon and of the reason of the state, incarnates the stage of the human species-in-itself (all *Realpolitik* leads to such a conservation of the existent), while Antigone, through the irreducibility of moral demands, which transcend all empirical calculations, by going as far as the annihilation of oneself, incarnates the irrepressible aspiration towards the human species-for-itself.

The Lukácsian distinction is fundamentally based on the development of Marx' famous thesis concerning the transition from the reign of necessity to the reign of freedom. But one here finds as well a central thread of his own youthful reflections. The "second ethics" of which he spoke in the manuscript on Dostoevsky and in his letters to Paul Ernst, opposed to the logic of the institutions of the state (the "first ethics"), always expressed this powerful aspiration towards a moral utopia, which led his friend Ernst Bloch to call him at the time a "genius of morality". In the notes for the book on Dostoevsky, there is a revealing proposition: "Dostoevsky and Dante: the second ethics an apriori of the epic stylization."[29] The ethical and the aesthetical were in effect always associated in intimate fashion by Lukács (without the specificity of the two spheres in any sense being diminished): he pursued in the interior movement, the most secret of works, the existence of moral substantiality (thereby finding, without knowing it, one of Croce's central theses: "*fondamento di ogni poesia è la coscienza morale*")[30]. This is the reason why not only has he always defended the point of view of Jesus against the realistic and cynical pragmatism of the Grand Inquisitor, in commenting on the celebrated scene from the novel the Brothers Karamazov by Dostoevsky, not only did he praise the figures of Jesus and Socrates in his *Ontologie* as paradigmatic expressions of the human species-for-itself, but he sees in literary personnages such as Electra, Antigone, Don Quixote or Hamlet so many incarnations of an interior moral incorruptibility, so many expressions of the human species become aware of its highest requirements.

Paul Claudel in a letter to André Gide, concerning the dialogue between the Grand Inquisitor and Christ, defended the point of view of the Church, in writing[31]:

Dostoevsky has however sensed the grandeur of the Church in his dialogue from the *Brothers Karamazov*, although he had the meanness to refuse faith to the Grand Inquisitor. He was absolutely correct against this false Christ who troubles for an ignorant and prideful speech the magnificent order of redemption. The Church means union. Whoever does not join with me divides. Whoever does not act as a member of the Church cannot act in its name, he is a pseudo-Christ and a divider.

Lukács very clearly rejected what he regarded as a closure in the *status quo* of the human species-in-itself incarnated by the existent Church. In upholding against Claudel the message of the Dostoevskian Jesus, he introduced his statement on the contestational vocation of sects and heresies, and profited from the occasion to provide vibrant praise of Simone Weil.[32] It should not be forgotten that the young Lukács had strongly nourished his thought in the writings of such unorthodox mystics as Meister Eckhart, Johann Tauler, Sebastian Franck, Valentin Weigel, or Saint Francis of Assisi: the *Ontologie* considers the sects as so many expressions of the aspiration towards the human species-for-itself, but which because of their intrinsic religiosity desires to burn the mediations linking the stage of the human species-in-itself and that of the human species-for-itself. It is thus that Simone Weil established a solution of continuity between authentic faith and devotion for a social cause: now, for Lukács, the essence precisely resides in the discovery of mediations linking the two stages of the evolution of the human species.

We can only be struck by a certain parallelism which exists between Sartre's approach in the *Critique of Dialectical Reason* and Lukács' project in his *Ontology of Social Being*. The two works were born from a common ambition: to put an end to the reductive schemata of a sclerotic Marxism and to rehabilitate the infinite complexity of the historical process. Lukács indicated in a letter of September 19, 1964 to Frank Benseler his intention, at a certain point, of writing an article on Sartre's *Critique*, but he added that he had given it up as he did not feel himself capable of doing so[33]: "The book is very much alright (*sehr anständig*), but extremely confused and boring." Three years earlier, he had written to the same correspondent on April 3, 1961[34]: "... I have read the first two hundred pages of Sartre's book, but without drawing any great lesson" (to his interlocutors, Lukács said that he had not continued his reading). We can say that Lukács was in error in abandoning the reading of Sartre's work: the similarity of the problematics between Sartre's and his own are evident. The dialectical tension between the teleological activities of individuals and a stratified social field on several levels, the result of relations between practical organisms and inorganic matter, is also the center of Sartre's *Critique*: the extremely nuanced distinctions between the field of the *practico-inert*, where individuals lead a serial existence, under the sign of the impotence and exteriority, and the group, where he affirms the totalization of individuals' aims in view of the realization of a common project (the group in fusion), between the constituting dialectic and the dialectic constituted (or dialectic of passivity, that of alienated praxis), between the collectives and the groups, inevitably cut across the analyses that Lukács will develop on the bipolar nature of the social being and on the transition of the human species-in-itself to the stage of the human species-for-itself. It is not possible here for us even to sketch a comparative analysis of the two works, nor to indicate the great differences which separate them both on the level of method and on that of the results obtained, and we will confine ourselves merely to indicating the interest of such a *rapprochement*.

The true antipode of the method developed by Lukács in his *Ontologie* is found in the thought of Martin Heidegger, although profound similarities of problematic appear here (as we have already noted). The more and more virulent criticism developed by Heidegger, beginning in his courses of the 1920's, against the hegemony of *logos* and of *ratio* in the interpretation of the world and his demand to come back to a more originary reflexion on the Being of this being has a certain parallelism with the critique of logocentrism and of exaggerated rationalism pursued by Nicolai Hartmann in his ontological research, a critique taken up again we have already noted, by Lukács. We must not forget that there is in this sense a distancing by these three thinkers, so different, even opposed between themselves, with respect to neo-Kantianism, positivism and neopositivism, and even with respect to Husserl's phenomenology (it is the thesis of Husserl on philosophy as "rigorous science" which provoked, in 1925, the recriminations of Heidegger, who began to disengage himself more and more from the thought of his master). The refusal of Nicolai Hartmann to accept the Aristotelian identification of the substantial form of phenomena with their logical essence, a refusal reiterated in the name of the conditioning of form by matter, is at the basis of his critique of finalism and of rationalism. Lukács roundly criticizes as well logicism, in the name of an ontological materialism, throughout his last work. It is no less significant to note that the Hegelian identification of ontology or of metaphysics with logic, more precisely the dissolution of ontology in this sense in a "science of logic", is questioned in 'turn by each of the three thinkers: Hartmann, Heidegger, and Lukács.

The critique of alienation (or, in a more restricted sphere of reification, of *Verdinglichung*) is another central theme that the views of Heidegger and Lukács have in common. Both present alienation as a process of radical occultation of what in their eyes constitutes the essence of human existence. (Heidegger often employs the word *Verdeckung*, occultation, to describe this process.) But here large differences appear, even a radical opposition, which separates the two philosophers. Faithful to his ontological-genetic method, Lukács sets out a dialectical conception of the genesis of human being, including reification and alienation, a conception based on the tension between teleology (the finalistic activity of the subject) and objective causality. Heidegger explicitly rejects dialectic (in his course from 1929 he postulates the impossibility of dialectically surpassing the finitude consubstantial to human existence[35]: "Endlichkeit macht die Dialektik unmöglich, erweist sie als Schein"), in privileging an apriori conception of human being and of its fundamental structures under the aegis of inauthenticity as well as of authenticity. The description in particularly striking terms of the different aspects of inauthentic existence, which is developed in the horizon of banal everydayness (*Alltäglichkeit*) under the sign of indecision and indecisiveness, is intimately linked by Heidegger to the critique of what he calls "the ontology of the subsistent being" (*Ontologie der Vorhandenheit*), of which the principle of causal explication is an essential component. This is the ontology which allegedly dominated Western metaphysical thought from Plato and Aristotle to Kant and Hegel: in desiring to pluck man from different forms of inauthentic existence and in aiming on the level of thought at a rupture with "vulgar intellect" and the surpassing of metaphysics", Heidegger appeals to a metamorphosis of human being (in his courses from the end of the 1920s he speaks of a *Verwandlung des Menschen*), through a return to his originary dimension. The distrust of the principle of causal explanation (or *das Erklären*, to which he opposes in decisive fashion comprehension, *das Verstehen*) finds in Heidegger pregnant expression, for instance in a part of his course on Hölderlin.[36]

Now, it is precisely the principle of causality, and the desire to found on the dialectical relation between teleology and causality a rational ontology of social being, which are the basis of Lukács' thought. He defends with no less energy than Heidegger the singular irreducibility of human existence with respect to other forms of existence. But the teleological act (*die teleologische Setzung*), the central notion of the Lukácsian *Ontologie* (which inevitably borders on the notions of intentionality, project, transcendence or temporality, familiar in the phenomenological or existentialist literature), does not arise for Lukács *ex nihilo*. It has a genesis, it develops in a context, that of work and of the multiple interactions between practical organisms and the ambient milieu, on the foundation of objective and subjective causal chains. Teleology and causality are inextricably linked. We can speak of an epigenesis of subjectivity in Lukács: its nature is *par excellence* dialectical, since the interrogations and the answers successively formulated by human being take shape under the impulsion of the resistance of the real and of possibilities or of existential latencies in the immanence of objective causal chains. The great *Aesthetics* in two volumes furnished a first example of such an archeological and epigenetic study of subjectivity. The *Ontology of Social Being* is the continuation and at the same time the foundation; the apologists of the young Lukács have still not furnished the least plausible argument for the willful decision to ignore these two works.

To illustrate the cleavage between the position of Heidegger and

that of Lukács we choose a last example in the zone which might appear
marginal or entirely eccentric: the philosophical interpretation of biological research. The readers of Heidegger can discover for the first
time, in reading his course from 1929 devoted to the three fundamental
concepts of metaphysics, world-finitude-solitude, clearly expressed, his
strongly negative attitude with respect to Darwinism. The fashion in
which Heidegger privileges biological research like that developed in
the work of Jakob v. Uexküll (who attributed to the organism a sort of
immanent power, quasi-musical, to articulate its milieu) and the refusal
of the theory of the "natural selection" of organisms, elaborated by
Darwin, seems to us to have a rather precise philosophical significance.
Heidegger's refusal, without embarrassing himself with any scientific
scruples, of the Darwinian theory of the evolution of the species, bases
itself, among other things, on the fact that Darwinism would seem to
support what Heidegger calls[37] "the economic approach to man": a
genetic theory of the formation of the qualities of organisms could only
be repudiated by a thinker who held in such little esteem the genetic
point of view, as well as that of dialectic. The approach to multiple
interactions between the organism and the ambient milieu is the basis of
the Darwinian theory, which anticipated, on the methodological plane,
mutatis mutandis, the ontological-genetic conception of the development
of the human species. It is hence entirely comprehensible that Nicolai
Hartmann and Lukács, in solid agreement on this point, have such a
deep interest in and profound agreement with Darwinian theory.

Through his contributions to the *Ontology of Social Being* Georg
Lukács pursued several objectives: to unveil, in all their ramifications,
the true philosophical bases of Marx' thought, to counter neopositivism
and structuralism, as well as ontologies founded on phenomenology
and *Existenzphilosophie*, and to develop a critique of historical reason,
inspired by the fundamental principle of the historicity of being and of
its categories. But the work wanted above all to be a vast introduction
to a future *Ethics*: the analyses that we have called the phenomenal
levels of subjectivity in the Lukácsian *Ontologie* come back ceaselessly
to this *Ethics*. We can say that Lukács has won his bet: the ontological-genetic method developed in his *opus posthumum*, as well as in
his *Aesthetics*, has shown itself fruitful in the analysis of social life and
its ever more complex objectifications, in conferring on the author an
important place on the scene of contemporary philosophy (even if it is
still marginal).

There remains the incontestable fact that these two works make
themselves known with difficulty: the *Ethics*, on the other hand, was
never written (Lukács was 85 years old when he wrote the *Prolegomena* to his *Ontologie*). But is the immediate audience or popularity
necessarily proof of the significance of a philosophical treatise?

Schopenhauer needed to wait nearly forty years before the *World as Will and Representation* acquired an audience. The non-finito character of the Lukácsian project also does not seem to us to be a decisive argument. The history of philosophy contains many examples of unfinished great projects: Were not the three *Critiques* of Immanuel Kant conceived as preparatory studies to a future metaphysics, which the author was never able to write? Sartre never wrote his ethics, nor did he see published the second volume of the *Critique of Dialectical Reason*.

Victrix causa diis placuit, sed victa Catoni (the cause of the victors pleases the gods, but that of the vanquished pleases Cato). Lukács, who, since his first reading, still as a child, of Homer's *Iliad* felt a profound sympathy for the cause of Hector, the vanquished, and not for that of Achilles, the victor, loved to cite in his later writings this maxim from Lucan: he had a great affinity for the Stoic ethics of Cato. Neither his *Ontology* nor his *Aesthetics* for the moment belongs to the victor's camp, in the contemporary philosophical discussion: but perhaps the enormous patience and the strength to fight against the current, Stoic virtues of which he made great use in writing his works will be finally repaid, and the anti-pragmatic ethics of Cato will reveal itself, yet once more, in the end, as worthwhile.

NOTES

1.   In a letter of August 5, 1970, he wrote to Frank Benseler, his editor in West Germany: "The work is going very slowly. I am rather dissatisfied with the manuscript." This letter, as well as others by Lukács cited below, are unpublished and were consulted by us in the Lukács Archives in Budapest.

2.   See his letter of May 10, 1960 to his friend, Ernst Fischer. We have quoted this letter in our article, 'Georg Lukács et la reconstruction de l'ontologie dans la philosophie contemporaine', in *Revue de métaphysique et de morale*, Octobre-Décembre 1978, pp. 498 ff. We have also quoted this letter at greater length in our article on Lukács' *Ontologie*, in *Lukács*, Guido Oldrini (ed.), Milan, 1979, pp. 287-288.

3.   'Kleine Notizen zur Ethik', 67. The first to refer to these notes are: E. Joós, in his *Lukács' Last Autocriticism: the Ontology*, Atlantic Highlands, NJ, Humanities Press, 1983, pp. 42 and 118; and György Mezei, in his 'Zum Spätwerk von Georg Lukács', in *Doxa* No. 4, 1985, pp. 38-40 and *passim*.

4.   See 'Kleine Notizen zur Ethik'.

5.   Letter of April 23, 1966 to Frank Benseler.

6.   See his letter of January 6, 1969 to Adam Schaff.

7.   See *Zur Grundlegung der Ontologie,* Berlin, de Gruyter, 1935.

8.   See, for example, *Möglichkeit und Wirklichkeit*, Berlin, de Gruyter, 1938; *Der Aufbau der realen Welt,* Berlin, de Gruyter, 1950; *Teleologisches Denken*, Berlin, de Gruyter, 1951.

9.   See *Nicolai Hartmann und Heinz Heimsoeth im Briefwechsel*, Frieda Hartmann u. Renate Heimsoeth (eds.), Bonn, Bouvier, 1978.

10.   At one of our last meetings, in March 1971, he said: "As a philosophical science, ontology is still young. I did not succeed in expressing my ideas as I did in the *Aesthetics...*"

11.   In the meantime, Luchterhand Verlag in West Germany has finally published the entire text of the *Ontologie*, including the *Prolegomena,* in two volumes: *Zur Ontologie des gesellschaftlichen Seins,* 1. Halbband, 1984, and 2. Halbband, 1986.

12.   Letter of November 21, 1961 to Frank Benseler.

13.   Lukács is referring here to his book *Entwicklungsgeschichte des modernen Dramas*, of which only parts appeared at the time, in the *Archiv für Sozialwissenschaft und Sozialpolitik*, Bd. XXXVIII, 1914.

14.   Bloch's book, which was first published in 1918.

15.   See the letter of mid-July 1911 to Leopold Ziegler in the

book *Georg Lukács Briefwechsel 1902-1917,* Hrsg. v. Eva Karadi und Eva Fekete, Stuttgart, Metzler, 1982, pp. 232-233.

16.   *L'esprit de l'utopie,* Paris, Gallimard, 1977, pp. 293-294.

17.   See Georg Lukács, *Zur Ontologie des gesellschaftlichen Seins,* 2. Halbband, S. 521.

18.   For a brief overview of this problem, see N. Tertulian, 'Ernst Bloch - György Lukács une amitié de 60 ans', *La quinzaine littéraire,* Paris, No. 455, January 16/31, 1986, pp. 21-22.

19.   On this point, see the text of a conversation with Ernst Bloch from September 24, 1971, 'Ernst Bloch kommentiert *Gelebtes Denken*' in *Ernst Bloch und Georg Lukács. Dokumente zum 100 Geburtstag,* MTA, Lukács Archivum, 1984, pp. 296-323, especially pp. 315-318.

20.   The letter of January 13, 1964 to Professor Podach was quoted in our *Georges Lukács. Étapes de sa pensée esthétique,* Paris, Le Sycamore, 1980, p. 292: "Was Bloch betrifft, war ich in meiner Jugend mit ihm gut befreundet. Er ist sicher ein geistvoller Mensch und ein guter Stilist. Aber für *Prinzip Hoffnung* kann ich kein Interesse aufbringen."

21.   Frankfurt, Suhrkamp, 1961.

22.   Letter of March 9, 1962 to Frank Benseler.

23.   Letter of November 21, 1961 to Frank Benseler.

24.   See his letter of August 6, 1965 to Frank Benseler.

25.   Nicolai Hartmann, *Teleologisches Denken,* Berlin, de Gruyter, 1951, p. 88.

26.   See Georg Lukács, *Der junge Hegel. Über die Beziehung von Dialektik und Ökonomie,* Zürich/Vienna, Europa, 1948, pp. 433-434.

27.   See F. Feher, A. Heller, G. Markus, M. Vajda, 'Notes on Lukács' *Ontology*', in *Lukács Reappraised,* Agnes Heller (ed.), NY, Columbia UP, 1983, pp. 137 ff.

28.   See Georg Lukács, *Zur Ontologie...* 2 Hb. S. 327.

29.   See Georg Lukács, *Dostojewski. Notizen und Entwürfe,* Budapest, Akad. Kiado, 1985, p. 39.

30.   Benedetto Croce, *Aesthetica in nuce,* Editori Laterza, 1985, p.18.

31.   See his letter to André Gide of July 30, 1908 in *Paul Claudel et André Gide, Correspondance, (1899-1926),* Paris, Gallimard, 1949, p.85.

32.   See Lukács, *Zur Ontologie...* 2. Hb. S. 626.

33.   See letter of September 19, 1964 to Frank Benseler.

34.   See letter of April 3, 1961 to Frank Benseler.

35.   Martin Heidegger, *Die Grundbegriffe der Metaphysik. Welt-Endlichkeit-Einsamkeit,* in *Heideggers Gesamtausgabe,* Frank-

furt, Klostermann, 1983, Band 29/30, p. 306.

36.　See Martin Heidegger, 'Hölderlins Hymnen ...', in *Gesamtausgabe,* Bd. 39, Frankfurt, Klostermann, 1980, pp. 246-247.

37.　See Martin Heidegger, *Die Grundbegriffe* ... p. 377.

INDEX